DATE			
JUL 29 1994			

© THE BAKER & TAYLOR CO.

THE THIRD DOOR

The
THIRD DOOR

The Autobiography of an American
Negro Woman

By ELLEN TARRY

NEGRO UNIVERSITIES PRESS
WESTPORT, CONNECTICUT

The Library of Congress cataloged this book as follows:

Tarry, Ellen, 1906–
        The third door; the autobiography of an American Negro
woman. Westport, Conn., Negro Universities Press [1971,
ᶜ1955]
        ix, 304 p. 23 cm.

        I. Title.

E185.97.T37A3   1971   813'.5'4   70–135613
ISBN 0-8371-5200-3   MARC

Library of Congress   71 [4]

Originally published in 1955 by David McKay Company, Inc.,
New York

Reprinted with the permission of David McKay Company, Inc.

Reprinted in 1971 by Negro Universities Press, A Division of
Greenwood Press, Inc., 51 Riverside Avenue, Westport, CT 06880

Library of Congress catalog card number 70-135613
ISBN 0-8371-5200-3

Printed in the United States of America

10 9 8 7 6 5 4 3 2

To Edna

IN ANSWER TO HER CALL

FOREWORD

I was born a Southern Negro.

It may seem strange to many readers that the insecurities and resentments which follow in the wake of segregation and discrimination were so late in becoming a part of my life. Perhaps I subconsciously rejected all outside indications of my "inferior" status, but I prefer to thank God for endowing me with a simple, trusting nature: a circumstance which has been at times my undoing, but more often a saving grace. I know it was this quality which was responsible for the happy childhood that allowed me to achieve a degree of maturity before I was scarred by racial prejudice. It was this same quality which subsequently cast the mold for the development of an adult equipped with the ability to see both sides of "the question."

A reporter once questioned Malvina Hoffman, the sculptress, upon her return to America from a globe-encircling trip. Miss Hoffman's reaction to man's ways the world over was summed up in words that meant: *Skins change, people don't.* The episodes and events recorded on the following pages exemplify this.

Many of these events have strengthened the writer's inherent belief that God is the ruler of all He has created. Never again need I ask to see Him to believe, for I have felt His presence when my need has been greatest. I have heard His voice through trouble-deafened ears. He has led me across angry waters and guided my feet through hostile lands. For me and for my people, He has thrown open doors long closed by hate-blinded men. And

vii

in His infinite mercy, He has shown me the long narrow road
that leads weary pilgrims home.

I have omitted the telling of certain events because their
inclusion might have infringed upon good taste and in no way
would they contribute to the total effect of this volume. Some of
these omissions were necessary to safeguard the welfare of innocent persons. This story is a part of the story of a young,
growing America, and told so that future generations may avoid
the mistakes of our time; so that they may know the price we
have paid for tomorrow. It is the hope of the author that this
book will sow happiness in place of discord, hope in place of
despair, and faith in our American future.

CONTENTS

THE THIRD DOOR

chapter 1

AFRICA BECKONS

If my family had lived in New York, Boston, or Philadelphia, a casual observer might have considered us an average American family. But Birmingham, Alabama, was our home, so we were not considered average—or American. Anthropologists would probably have said that my father was a mulatto and my mother an octoroon. I do not know what scientific name they might have used to describe my two sisters and me. I do know a lot of unscientific names that were used, but I was a young lady before I really understood them. Mama once laughingly said we were a "duke's mixture"; to me, that seemed closer to the truth than anything else.

Papa, who was a barber by trade, was born in Athens, Alabama, about 1868. He settled in Birmingham when the Magic City was still a tiny village close to the coal mines and steel mills that were pouring riches into the pockets of Northern industrialists. Mama migrated from the country, in this case, a small Gone-with-the-Wind community a few miles on the Alabama side of the Georgia-Alabama line.

Papa's customers were all white. Most of them were wealthy, too. And though Mama sewed for the wives of some of the men Papa shaved, they might never have met if a strong March wind had not blown her hat off one day when she was crossing a street in the Negro business district.

I have heard it told, over and over, how Papa got so excited when Mama lost her hat, and the red-gold hair that matched her

3

peaches-and-cream complexion came tumbling down. He vowed, then and there, to get an introduction. Mama had not been in Birmingham long, and though quite a few of the town's eligible young men of color were with Papa that day, Virgil was the only one who knew her. Virgil was a local undertaker and something of a ladies' man, and he did not want to part with any information concerning the "strange lady." But Papa got his introduction just the same.

In due time, Papa proposed and wrote my grandmother, Mama Ida, who was still down in Chambers County. A few days later, a white man stalked into Papa's barbershop with a big gun sticking out of each hip pocket and bellowed, "Which one of you barbers is Bob Tarry?"

Papa identified himself, as the other barbers looked on in trembling fear.

"I'm the sheriff from Chambers County," the man said. "I understand you want to marry Ida's girl, Eula. Can you take care of her?"

Papa must have satisfied the sheriff because they later became good friends. From then on, Papa barbered most of the whites who came to town from Mama's home.

Unfortunately, Mama never did like dogs. And when she met Papa he had twelve. Some were pedigreed, but most of them were stray mutts that took up with Papa because he fed them well and treated them kindly. All they had to do in return was to wait on the corner above our house until Papa passed on his way home from work. After supper, he took his canine cronies for a walk, and each night their wanderings ended at The Last Chance, the last saloon to close in our part of town.

A woman who lived near The Last Chance told me that they always knew when it was fifteen minutes before the midnight curfew because a hot breath of air came around the corner about that time. Somebody would be sure to say, "There comes Bob Tarry and his dogs. It's almost time for The Last Chance to close."

Mama and Papa were married in one of the biggest weddings

that had ever taken place at Reverend Buckner's church. I must
have heard a great deal about it, because I once told a new neighbor all about the wedding. I even described Mama's dress and the
dresses her bridesmaids wore. When the curious woman asked
how I knew all this, I told her I had to know, because I was sitting
on the front seat all during the ceremony.

Mama was furious when she heard what I had said. Papa
laughed.

"Maybe Ellen was on the front seat," he said, "because she was
was born nine months and five days later."

Our house, the house to which Papa carried his bride, was a
twin. Allena, Mama's girlhood chum, lived in the other house,
which looked just like ours. Allena and Mama could almost pass
for sisters, except that her hair was blond and Mama's was red.
From the time I was able to toddle, they put a broad plank between the two back porches. And it was across this plank to Allena
that I ran whenever a spanking seemed inevitable.

Mama and Allena had planted Virginia creepers around the
long south side of the porch. By the time I began taking notice
of such things, the vines had crept up and up until they covered
that side of the house. With flowers blooming in the yard and
the vines so shiny and green, it did not matter too much that the
houses never were painted. I always dreaded the cold weather
that came in December and lasted through March, because it took
the beauty away from our house and made it look like just what
it was—a shabby, unpainted frame cottage with green trim, and
with a front porch, parlor, hallway, two bedrooms, a dining room,
kitchen and a back porch, off which there was a water closet with
ample room for a big tin bathtub.

Since we had open fireplaces—in front of which I dreamed many
a beautiful dream—there was a large coal shed in the back yard.
Allena used one side and we used the other. The dogs used either
side they liked. Behind the shed stood a peach tree that furnished
Mama with an endless supply of switches. She must have stunted
that tree, for the peaches were never very good and it was not
half so tall as the cotton tree in Allena's side of the back yard.

The cotton tree was the favorite hangout for the boys in our neighborhood. I have a half-dozen leg scars to prove that I climbed to the top, too, even if I never managed a return trip without falling.

When Papa first brought Mama to his house, his mother, who was called "White Mama" because of her snowy white hair, and his sister, Nannie, lived with him. White Mama said she could die in peace whenever the Lord called her, because she knew her boy had at last found a good girl. After Papa married, Nannie spent most of her time hoping for me, and, after I came, taking care of me. So what our house lacked in prettiness on the outside was made up by the happiness inside.

Mama says the houses were well-kept, since that was the fashionable section of town for our people in those days. The houses on both sides of Sixth Avenue were frame. Several of the larger ones had plots of grass in front that we called lawns. The others were so close to the paved sidewalk that there was room only for a border of flowers, and two or three chairs when it was hot and stuffy in our valley. The breezes were locked in the trees on the mountainsides where the rich white folk lived.

Our neighbors were our friends—even the people who lived in the shotgun houses closest to Fourteenth Street. Mama was always whispering about "the bad houses on Fourteenth Street." But the people in those houses smiled at me from their front porches. And I was grown-up and living in New York before I understood what Mama meant and why there were always so many white men walking around that end of the street, jingling money in their pockets and whispering strange words. Up at our end, I had "Munny" (a childish version of "Mummy") Adams across the street, Allena to save me from whippings on one side, and Aunt Lizzie Thompson on the other.

Aunt Lizzie's house was really a huge double tenement and the Glenns lived in the other half. Tommie, Aunt Lizzie's husband, and George Glenn were barbers like Papa. So there was friendship all around us.

When I was four, Nannie moved to "the hill," as Enon Ridge was called, and White Mama went with her. Soon after moving,

White Mama ate a whole bagful of bananas one Saturday night and died of acute indigestion.

Ida Mae was born when I was five. I was not happy over having a sister. I did not want to share the joy of being "Bob Tarry's little girl."

I used to hear old women, who had nothing to do except sit on the front porch and talk, say Papa had a right to be so crazy about me because I "looked like he spit me out." Although I thought he was the most wonderful man in the world, every night when I said my prayers I asked God to let me wake up looking like my pretty blue-eyed mother with her red-gold hair. So it did not help for Ida Mae to be born looking so much like Mama, even though the fuzz on her head was not red but the color of corn silk.

I had been visiting Nannie when Ida Mae was born. She took me back to Sixth Avenue the next Sunday. Papa was on the front porch waiting. He had grown a mustache and it scratched when he kissed me. A nurse in a stiff white uniform came out and took me inside to see Mama and my sister. They had put the baby in my own little white bed, and I made a wild dash to pull her out.

As the nurse was dragging me out of the room, I looked back at Mama. She was sitting upright in her big bed, one fat braid thrown over her shoulder, with the most surprised expression on her face.

Nannie, who usually took my part in any battle, had disappeared. I waited tearfully while the angry nurse told Papa what I had done. He just smiled and said, "You're my *big* girl now. I'm depending on you to help take care of the little baby."

That made me feel special and important again. By the time people started stopping by after church, I had become Sister Ellen—and I still am.

I soon learned to take care of the baby, to wash diapers in an emergency, and to iron the rough-dried clothes.

People were always stopping at our house on their way to church or after services. We were encircled by seven Protestant churches. Also, the three big thrills in Papa's life, besides his family, were a good game of cards, a victory for the Birmingham Barons baseball team, and a pantry full of good things to eat and drink. I often wondered if Mama's good cooking did not have something to do with the stream of company that flowed in and out of our house on Sundays.

St. Paul's (Methodist), Sixteenth Street (Baptist), and the First Congregational were the churches nearest our house. I felt equally at home in all of them. Mama was a member of St. Paul's and it was there that I was christened when a baby. Papa was a Congregationalist, and though I got crushes on the single preachers at St. Paul's, "Brother Ragland" at Papa's church had whiskers and reminded me of Santa Claus. His quiet manner of saying, "Dearly Beloved, we are now gathered here . . ." soothed my restless spirit and made me feel loved and a part of all gathered there.

But I liked the Sixteenth Street Baptist Church best of all—because of the boys. I always preferred the company of boys because they could climb higher, run faster, and skate better than girls, and it was fun keeping up with them. And some of the best-looking boys in town went to Sixteenth Street Baptist. I also enjoyed the Bible drills they used to have at B.Y.P.U.

As far back as I can remember, every few months one of Papa's dogs would disappear. I was not very old before I discovered that Mama did not share my dislike for the dog-catcher. I realized next that she was actually glad to see him when he came to take one of the dogs away. By the time I understood that Mama herself usually sent for the dog-catcher, she had also promised me a switching if I breathed a word of it to Papa. She told me I would have to understand that she knew best, and that it was hard enough to feed the family without having a lot of hungry dogs around.

The last one to go was Bulger, an ugly brown mutt I loved. Papa and I missed Bulger, but hardly a month after he disappeared a beautiful white collie with brown spots came to our house. He just showed up one day and refused to leave—even for Mama. Papa knew a lot of dog names and when he said

"Laddie," the dog jumped up and down and licked Papa's hand. So Laddie he was—just as lovable as Bulger, much prettier, and the most wonderful companion any little girl could wish for.

A few months later, Laddie and I were on our way out to Nannie's. "Bubber" Moore, Nannie's son, was with us. I ran behind Laddie as he romped along, sniffing at hedges and scampering across lawns. I didn't notice the fire department car that had pulled up to the curb until a man leaned out of the window calling, "Laddie! Here, Laddie. Come here!"

Laddie's ears stood up and he looked around until he saw the white man. He looked at him and looked back at us. Then Laddie gave a loud bark and dashed to the car.

I cried and begged Laddie not to leave me, but after talking with the man, Bubber explained that Laddie really belonged to the Chief of the fire department and there was nothing we could do. I watched the car drive away with Laddie on the back seat, his long pink tongue hanging out the side of his mouth and one paw lifted in a wave.

For a while we did not have a dog. One day, however, Mama went out on the front porch to bring in the baby and found a little black fox terrier stretched out under the carriage. She tried to chase him away, but he followed the baby carriage indoors and made himself at home. Mama managed to get rid of the dog before Papa came. The next day she went out for the baby at the usual time and there, under the carriage, was the same little black fox terrier.

That night the dog refused to be chased and Papa found him curled up on the top of the back-porch steps. Papa inquired around the neighborhood and learned that our new friend belonged to a neighbor who did not care if the little dog never came home. We called him Snowball—in honor of the small round white spots on his back.

Snowball was squatty, but he could get about. He had brown markings around his eyes and his nose was pink. He was old, for a dog, when he came to our house. He was always thirsty, too. But that was because I could not remember to keep water in his tin drinking can. His tongue was as pink as Laddie's, though not as long. And though I fed him and gave him water when I remembered, Snowball was Ida Mae's dog and seldom strayed far from the baby's side.

One day when Aunt Emma came to visit and there was more than the usual nip in the air, Mama wheeled the sleeping baby in from the porch and left her in the parlor, still in her carriage. We went to the kitchen for midday dinner and I settled down to enjoy Aunt Emma's cheerful laugh as she and Mama talked about old times down in Chambers County while they ate collard greens, candied yams, and egg bread. I always liked to listen when Mama and her friends talked about their girlhood, so I did not hear the noise at first. There was a scratching sound, followed by a loud angry bark, then more scratching and whining. Mama opened the door and found Snowball crawling on his stomach and crying like a sick baby.

"This dog is hungry," Mama decided and fixed a plate of food for him.

Snowball sniffed at the food and ran back to the front of the house. Mama closed the kitchen door and came back to the table. She had hardly picked up her fork, when Snowball started scratching and whining again. When Mama opened the door again, the dog managed to get his paw hooked in the hem of her skirt and pulled her toward the front of the house. Then we smelled smoke—all three of us at the same time—and ran down the narrow hallway, with Snowball leading.

A curl of smoke oozed out of the parlor. There, on the floor in front of the fireplace beside the carriage lay Ida Mae, the scorching ruffle of her long dress in the ashes beneath the grate. She had managed to wriggle out from under the safety strap of the carriage and onto the floor. Mama grabbed the baby and Aunt Emma tore off the burning dress, while Snowball puffed and panted and danced around. Ida Mae yawned through it all.

That night Papa left a lot of meat on his steak bone for Snowball. Every time I thought about his bravery I put more water in the little dog's can. All of the neighbors heard about the rescue. Snowball was not only a hero, he had won himself a happy home.

He was the only dog Mama ever took to her heart. They were
friends until the end, which was the end of an era for us.

As spring and summer wore on, we all became more devoted
to Ida Mae's faithful little companion. The happiest hours were
the evenings, and the time spent in church. Snowball was *there,*
too. We never knew where he went while we were inside. When
we came out of the church he was always waiting. He would run
along in front of us, puffing and panting; when we caught up
with him, he would run ahead again. By the time we got home,
he was on the back porch lapping water from his can or, if the
can was empty, pretending his tongue was parched. Once Papa
even threatened to use his walking stick on me, if I kept forget-
ting to fill Snowball's water can.

Though the cold weather robbed our house of its outside
beauty, it also drove us inside to each other. On chilly evenings
we sat around the fireplace in Mama's room. I usually stretched
out in front of the fireplace behind Snowball, who was always
close to the fender. Papa held the baby while Mama did her
hand sewing, singing as she stitched. Though tone-deaf, Papa
loved music passionately. He enjoyed all kinds of music and
took me to every recital that came to town. The spirituals meant
most to him and Mama sang them over and over. These evenings
were never complete until he had heard:

> "Give me that old time religion
> Give me that old time religion
> Give me that old time religion
> It's good enough for me.
>
> It was good for my old mother
> It was good for my old mother
> It was good for my old mother
> And it's good enough for me...."

I often had to blink away the tears when Mama sang, "Just
Break the News to Mother," and "In the Baggage Coach Ahead."
When I was seven years old I went to school. Old Slater was

only a couple of blocks from our house—a block and a half if I cut through the back alley and crossed the Tidewater car line.

The children in my class had been repeating a chant about "yaller is roguish, but black is honest," and calling me "cat-eyes" for about a week before I understood that they did not like the way I looked. In Mama's mirror my reddish hair, gray eyes, and fair complexion showed me as I had always been and I wondered why the children had started calling me names. The same children teased me because I was so tall for my age and said I would "never see seven again" until I was "a hundred and seven." I decided that getting to know boys and girls who teased and said mean things about you was all a part of going to school. It never occurred to me to fight back, because Mama said only "common people" fought. Whenever the children started pulling my long thick braids some of the older girls who went to our church always showed up in time to rescue me.

This was also the year I told my first story, planted my first tree, and saw my first snowstorm. The snowstorm and the story happened the same day.

It was seldom that we ever had heavy snow in our part of Alabama, and the morning after the storm (which was not really a storm) the teacher asked each of us to come to the front of the room and tell what our thoughts had been when we woke up and saw the ground covered with snow. I waited until all of my classmates had finished, then I told how my first thoughts had been of how I would get to school with so much snow on the ground. I told how Mama had sent for the hired man to come and dig a path through the mountain of snow. The children's eyes got bigger and bigger as I described how I walked through a tunnel the hired man made and then built a snowman as tall as our house before I trudged to school in my huge boots. Then I stood in front of the class waiting for the teacher's approval.

Slowly the teacher walked over to me. She was smiling, but her smile did not make me happy. "Now, Ellen," she said, "don't you think you've just told us a *story?*" The children knew she meant I had told an untruth.

My classmates lost no time. "Ellen tells stories! Ellen tells stories" began a chant that some of them sang until I was in the third grade. By that time, I had silenced some through physical combat, and others by outdoing them in scholarship.

The sight of a little girl with her face pressed against a windowpane always brings back memories of what began on that Arbor Day when every child in my class received a tree to plant as part of a "city-beautiful" campaign. To me, the sapling looked like a switch and switches meant whippings. So I threw it behind one of the old brown flap-top trunks that sat in our hall. Mama discovered it, and since the trunk was closer than the peach tree behind the coal shed, she gave me several whippings with the little stick.

One day I decided that getting whipped with a tree was just too much. With a knife I cut away the top that Mama had broken on my legs. I got the shovel from the coal house and dug a hole in the middle of Mama's nasturtium bed in the front yard. There I planted the tree and packed the earth about it with my hands. Then I watered it and forgot it for the rest of the day. Next morning my tree was still standing and, as the days passed, caring for the sapling became a wonderful part of my life.

That winter, Mama was sure my nose would be flattened forever, so hard did I press it against the windowpane in our parlor when sweeping rainstorms lashed the tree. Neither lightning nor thunder nor Mama could tear me away. Though I watched and prayed, the sapling could not survive spring sleet on top of the winter winds, and bowed its head in temporary defeat.

Mama had little patience with the tears I shed over my broken tree. She cut away the injured top, and showed me how to put thick splints around the tree for protection. By May the tree was still standing, though it was—and still is—crooked. One morning I looked out of the window and saw tiny green shoots all over it. In a few weeks there were young leaves. Mama examined them and said the tree was a catalpa. From then on we grew up together, my tree and I.

The summer before I was eight I spent with relatives on a farm. It was the Sunday before school was to start when I came home. There on the front porch was Papa—with a new mustache. A nurse in a white uniform was sweeping leaves off the steps, leaves that had fallen from my tree. Inside I found a new baby— another sister—named Elizabeth after Aunt Lizzie next door. I did not want *her* either. But she was little and blue and did not look at all like Mama. Instead of feeling angry at her for being born, I felt sorry for her. Ida Mae was at Nannie's, so I took over added chores and became Sister Ellen to one more.

"Little Sister" was really the sweetest baby. Ida Mae treated her like another toy. Yet the baby seldom cried at Ida Mae's roughness.

During warm weather I would put Ida Mae in the front of Little Sister's carriage and wheel them both across the street to the tennis court where we played croquet at night. Mama always saved her hand sewing for the evening hours, so Papa would come over to the court and join in the croquet games. He was very proud when I won, even though he was often my opponent.

The tennis court was the closest Sixth Avenue came to having a playground—colored Sixth Avenue, I should say. Only two blocks away, at Sixteenth Street, just across from the Baptist Church, there was a beautiful city park. Although we had to walk through this park to reach the business district, we were not permitted to sit on any of the benches, or lie on the grass or drink water from the fountains on scorching hot days. We could not even get close enough to the flowers to get a good smell.

Most of Papa's customers knew his children by name. He saw to that. I half-loved and half-dreaded the visits to the barber-shop because I never knew what to say when Papa told his customers my name, grade, what marks I made, and everything I did. Yet I loved the smell of the barbershop, the white cleanness of it, and the proud love in Papa's eyes. I loved the kindness in the customers' voices when they told us to be sure to put the dollars they gave us in the bank. The ones who gave us quarters always told us to buy ice cream or candy.

By the way these men spoke to Papa, I could tell that they respected him. Papa told us several polite things to say, when they commented on our grades or our appearance, but I never thought up anything to say by myself and my cheeks always burned when Papa was talking about me. Two of Papa's friends, Mr. "Lige" Chandler, who had known Papa as a boy, and Dr. Henry Edmonds, are best and most fondly remembered.

When Papa's white friends from Mama's home visited Birmingham, they had a habit of taking their bags to the shop and coming out to our house for one of the Chambers County dinners Mama cooked. Papa would make reservations for them at one of the white hotels and get the bootblacks to deliver their bags. Later I learned that it would have been against the law for them to stay at our house.

One of the best loved of our local white visitors was "Miss Sally B." Mama had sewed for her before she married. Though she did not have time to make clothes for Miss Sally B. after we came, nobody but Mama was allowed to make the red flannel wrappers trimmed in black grosgrain ribbon that she wore each summer while vacationing in Canada.

Miss Sally B. was really the wife of one of Birmingham's wealthiest men. Her father had once been governor of the state and she was just as important in the social and civic life of Alabama as she was in our personal lives. But there were other reasons why she always seemed like a fairy godmother to me.

It was Miss Sally B. who gave me the beautifully embossed silver spoon with my name engraved on it, from which I first ate. It was Miss Sally B.'s chauffeur, Alphonse, who gave me my first ride in a shiny limousine that looked like the fine cars I saw pictured in storybooks.

I never saw Miss Sally B. frown, not even the day when she left her daughter to play with me and returned to find we had helped ourselves to a watermelon in the icebox and the fronts of our dresses were dripping with red juice. Miss Sally B. just threw back her beautiful head and laughed until she had to untie the chiffon veil draped about her sailor hat to wipe the tears from her eyes.

I always loved a parade—especially if the parade was part of a civic or patriotic celebration, because then all the public

school children took part. The girls wore white middy blouses
with red ties and pleated blue serge skirts; the boys were dressed
in blue suits, white shirts, and red ties. Though always in the
rear, with our variegated coloring and patriotic dress, we provided a brilliant ending for these demonstrations.

Because I was larger than most girls of my age, I usually carried the American flag for my class. As we stepped along to the
martial music provided by the Industrial High School Band,
spectators lining both sides of the street often broke into applause. I stepped a little higher and held my head a little more
proudly. Bearing the colors, I could afford to wrinkle my nose
at the girls who taunted me about being a "no-nation nigger."

Not only was I carrying the flag of my country, the same flag
our teachers had told us inspired Francis Scott Key to write *The
Star-Spangled Banner,* but by the time we marched down First
Avenue (and the skin had rubbed off my knock-knees) I knew
Papa would be standing outside the barbershop with his friends
and customers. Out of the corner of my eye I would see him,
immaculate in a white jacket, as he would point me out and say:

"That's my girl! See her? That one there, carrying the United
States flag!"

Papa always brought me an extra large bag of fruit or a special
gift after these parades. I have often wondered what became of
the little round lavender boxes of chiclets that Papa used to
put on top of our three bags of fruit. For years I have poked
around in delicacy shops and fruit stalls, but never have I found
those little boxes of wafer-like chiclets with violets on top of the
round lavender tin. If I could not remember the taste so well I
would be inclined to think this memory belonged with my snowstorm story.

There were numerous parades around the time I was in the
fourth grade, because that was at the time of World War I.
Though we carried huge signs in the parade about fighting for
democracy and why everybody should buy bonds, the Negro children were still put at the end of the procession.

The biggest parade took place when the first Negro soldiers
went away to war. Mama and her friends distributed soap and

washcloths to the soldiers. That day something happened in Birmingham that had never happened before. They let us sit in the Sixteenth Street park. We could even drink water from the fountains and smell the flowers.

The first grade teacher at Lane Grammar School, Miss Katie Sheffield, boarded at our house. Ida Mae, a little blonde minx with a cherubic face, began spending the day at school with Katie and before any of us realized what was happening, she was going to school on the South Side instead of to Slater like the rest of the North Side children. Katie often had to stop in town, and she would send Ida Mae home with an older girl. They had to cut through the path we used in Sixteenth Street park. Each day they met the boys from Industrial High School. Ida Mae, we later learned, had developed a reputation as a juvenile "shimmy queen." For the fee of a quarter she would stop in her tracks and do a shimmy-she-wobble that stopped the park traffic. Nickels and dimes merely brought Ida Mae's version of balling the-jack. We never knew whether or not she split the fees with the girls who brought her home, but it seems this had been going on for some time before word got back to Mama. After Mama heard about it, Ida Mae had difficulty sitting down.

That spanking was not the sum total of Ida Mae's punishment. After hearing that she had pulled up her dress and showed her knees in the park exhibitions, Mama and Papa decided to send Ida Mae to Slater, since that would be closer and I could look after her. The following summer Papa stopped cutting her hair. It grew like wild grass—and was just as straight and stringy.

The third day after Ida Mae's career at Slater began, she ran home in tears long before the dismissal bell rang. Her face was dirty and her hair was mussed up. Between sobs, she told Mama the children had been pulling it.

"But you are home now and everything's all right." Mama comforted her. "Why are you still crying?"

"Because they said I don't know who my papa is," she blurted.

"What are you talking about?"

"They-they said my papa is one of those white men who stand in front of the stores on Second Avenue."

"You crazy little child," Mama pretended to be amused. "Of course you know who your father is. Don't you see him every night? Come wash your face. And don't ever again let me see you crying because somebody tells you that you don't know who your father is."

Remembering my first days at school, I felt bad because I had not been near Ida Mae to protect her. Though I tried, I was no match for the children. But by the end of the year she had developed great fistic skill. Then Mama decided it would be safer for her to go to the school at Acipco, a suburb of Birmingham.

In an attempt to explain the actions of the children who taunted us, Mama told us they were "common" and that we should avoid them. Instead of realizing that suffering and humiliation had bred a belligerent attitude in these children or that our resemblance to the whites who were responsible for their plight was a constant source of irritation, I grew up thinking the world was full of "common" people like them and "uncommon" people like us. "Common" people were to be avoided.

That summer we went to Lafayette in Chambers County for a visit with Mama Ida. Lafayette never seemed strange to me because Mama Ida's letters always kept us informed about everything that happened at the long old house. Every year around Thanksgiving I knew it was time for most of Mama Ida's potted plants to be put in the flower pit with the windowpane top in the side yard next to the strawberry patch. I could close my eyes while Mama read from my grandmother's letters and see the ancient walnut trees in the front yard, heavy with their green fruit; later, I could almost hear the brown nuts drop to the ground. I knew Mama Ida would gather them in her gingham apron and put them on the porch next to the flower pit to dry out in time for Santa Claus. I knew how each new calf looked and we laughed over the red hen who insisted on laying eggs in the bushes. When Mama got to the part in Mama Ida's letters where she said it was time to say good night, I knew she would finish the letter and then undress in the room where my grandfather's picture hung on the wall. And I knew she would look up at that picture before she blew out the oil lamp and said her prayers.

I think of this particular summer in Lafayette as a summer full of vanilla ice cream, made from boiled custard, and Brunswick stew. Mama's family were Methodists and their church was up the hill from Mama Ida's house. All of the church clubs gave socials that summer and raised money by selling refreshments. Being a visitor, I was often "treated" and no sooner was one dish of ice cream finished, than someone else would offer another.

Numbers of transient soldiers returning from war passed through this little town. They ate at the home of one of my playmates and every time I visited her, I was met by the smell of the Brunswick stew that was being served in her mother's dining room. With the rest of the children, I would stand outside the windows and peer at the uniformed soldiers while they ate and the aroma of their unchanging menu drifted outside. The sameness of the smell was disappointing. Fortunately, the soldiers were never the same.

Many things were the same, though, in that town. The same uncommon people, who looked and acted like us, lived in town. The common people, who did not look or act like us, lived out in the country or on the other side of town. The people we knew could not help but look alike because nearly everybody was related, admittedly or otherwise. Perhaps that is why I did not think much about Uncle George and Uncle Robert being white. Aristocratic Uncle Robert did not look too different from his Negro son, one of Birmingham's leading insurance executives. But Uncle George had dark hair and blue eyes and seemed more mysterious. Mama Ida washed and ironed their clothes, mended their socks, and mothered them generally.

Smith's Park, at the far end of Sixth Avenue, was just a big field with railroad sidings, but to us it was like fairyland when the circus came to town. For weeks beforehand, billboards and abandoned store fronts were plastered with gaudy posters announcing the approaching event. More fun than a visit to the big show itself was a trip to Smith's Park on the day the circus trains rolled in. While the roustabouts were unpacking and the circus folk were setting up their living quarters, we stood around gaping, laughing, playing, and talking with friends. Most of the people who lived on both sides of the park were Negroes, so we usually had the place to ourselves.

Though no business was supposed to be done on the Sabbath, nobody seemed to mind that the concessionaires had always set up shop by the time church was out. There was plenty of pink cotton candy to be had and orange soda was the popular drink. The girls were satisfied to walk around and talk, but the boys bought as many gaily colored whips as they could afford and made a game out of chasing us. The boys seldom put much strength behind the lashes they gave the girls on their legs, but there was a boy in my class who was the one exception. He called me "fox Tarry," because of my hair, and his whip always left long red welts on my legs. He smiled when he was chasing me, but I knew he wanted to hurt me and I always outran him before he saw that he had. He was one of the first to talk about "no-nation niggers" and point to me.

I think of this boy every time I see a circus poster.

The summer when I was eleven we went to visit Mama's oldest sister, Elon, in Eutaw, Alabama. Aunt Elon's husband, a Methodist preacher, was presiding elder of the Eutaw district, and they lived in a big old white house across the street from the church and next door to a cemetery. There were three cousins, two boys and a girl, and we had wonderful times raiding melon patches while they were still wet with dew, picking blackberries, and frightening each other with ghost stories about what went on after dark in the graveyard next door.

That September I started my last semester at Slater School and my new teacher inspired me to reach for the moon. We had only been in school a few days when she told us to write a composition on the most interesting experience we had during the summer. I could not write about raiding watermelon patches;

blackberry hunting was tame. Until the night before the composition was to be turned in, I could not think of a subject. I just sat with my pencil and pad in my hands and looked out the window. Suddenly I noticed a calendar on the wall. On the calendar was a picture of an Indian camp scene. A wigwam stood among a cluster of russet-leaved trees with a thick forest in the background and a lake in front. Before the wigwam smoldered the embers of a campfire. A full moon shone on the lake and an Indian brave drifted downstream in a canoe—his oar raised. I thought about a camping trip we had planned, one that got rained out. I closed my eyes and rushed the Indian on about his business. Then I grouped my family about the fire and we told stories and sang songs until it was time to wrap up in our blankets.

The next day I turned in a descriptive composition on a camping trip outside Eutaw, Alabama. After the papers were corrected, the teacher picked my composition out and asked me to come to the front and read it to the class. I did and the other children were as quiet as could be. I could not understand why nobody said anything after I finished and I looked around at the teacher. Her plain, irregular-featured ebony face was beautiful with a glow that was new to me. Years later, I saw the same look on the face of a nurse who held a newborn baby in her hands. She left her desk and put one arm around my shoulders. For a moment I wondered if I had been caught in another "story."

"Someday," she said, ending my suspense, "someday Ellen is going to be a writer!"

I was to graduate from Slater at midterm. It was agreed that I would finish the year at Industrial High School. After that, I would go away, either to Fisk University at Nashville, Tennessee, or to Talladega College at Talladega, Alabama. Both institutions had preparatory schools and many of the children from Birmingham attended one or the other. Most of the Baptist people sent their children to Spellman Seminary and Morehouse College at Atlanta. Tuskegee was not as popular as people from the North supposed. At least, fewer city children went to Tuskegee then.

That Negro parents had to sacrifice and send their children to boarding schools before college was because of the emphasis that the Birmingham Board of Education placed on industrial education for Negroes at that time. Many parents felt that our local high school did not measure up and that their children would be handicapped by attendance there. So, most of the conversation at our house was related to the choice of a school for me to attend the next year.

Since Talladega was nearby and a Congregational school, too, it was only natural that the president, Dr. Frederick Sumner, often spoke at our church. Papa told him about our problem, and he took time out on his trips to Birmingham to tell me of the advantages of attending Talladega. Also, one of my best friends, Alice McCarroll, was going there. So we decided that it would be Talladega for me the next year.

At neighboring churches, someone was always lecturing on Africa. In those days, I heard more about Africa than I did about America. For years, Aunt Annie's son, Edward, and I had played at being African missionaries. I was always the lady preacher and he was always the doctor. I saved the natives' souls and he cured their tropical fevers and saved their lives. We could get other children to play the part of the natives at first, but in the end they would always get mad when we refused to change places and let them be the preacher and the doctor. They said that we thought we were white.

While I was in the midst of a rag and bottle selling campaign to raise money for Africa, the Henry Curtis McDowells, a young couple who had gone to the "dark continent" soon after finishing Talladega, started writing letters to the membership of the Congregational Church at Birmingham. Through these letters, they brought Africa right into our midst. I came to know their African friends by name and worried about them when letters were slow. I felt ashamed when I sat down to a good meal or put on a new dress because the little African boys and girls had to eat wild animals and run around half-naked. I sold all the junk I could find under our house or anywhere in the neighborhood and gave my pennies to the missionary fund.

Each letter from the McDowells painted a more touching picture of the Africans' hunger for the story of Christ and their delight in His teachings. I felt sorry for all the times I had gone to sleep during a sermon and promised God I would not talk in church or take part when other children were marking certain passages in the Bible and giggling as they passed it from one to the other.

One night at a prayer meeting I made a decision. I decided that the only way I could atone for my sins was to give my life to God and go to Africa to teach and care for the poor heathen. After a soul-stirring hymn, I rose and told the gathering of my determination. Papa was so happy he cried. I told them that the years spent at Talladega would be shortened by thoughts of the fruitful years ahead. But I had no idea of the changes that were just around the corner of my life.

chapter 2

THE YEAR OF CHANGE

My last term at Slater School was spent wishing I was not there. I was the youngest member of my class, with the exception of Alice McCarroll, but I was also one of the largest. All of my other friends had either gone to Industrial High or were enrolled in one of the preparatory schools. During Christmas and spring vacations, the dreaded question, "What's your school?" followed every introduction. Alice, who came from a musical family, was always at the piano with a crowd around her and that left me the sole representative of Slater.

The "great migration" was still in force and hordes of Negroes were moving northward. During World War I most of the people from Birmingham who went north were laborers. Industrial corporations sent their agents into southern communities to recruit manpower and the railway stations were choked with their rich harvest.

Papa claimed that all the big companies had to do was send special trains down, back the coaches into Terminal Station, and say: "All aboard for Detroit, Akron, Columbus, or Pittsburgh!" and Negroes would fill the cars. Once he took me to the station to see one of these "excursions" being loaded.

I remember thinking how funny most of the men looked in their store-bought suits and yellow-tan brogans. Some of them wore new overalls and caps with red bandanna handkerchiefs tied about their necks.

I heard a man in the crowd with us yell, "Hey, Henry! Where you going?"

Henry, on his way to board the train called back, "Man, I'm going to Destroy, Michigan!"

The men who were leaving looked eager and happy. It was the women, especially those with babies in their arms, who seemed frightened when they waved good-by as the train pulled out slowly and the men crowded to the coach windows. The women's faces would brighten when one of their men called out, "I'll send for you as soon as I get my first pay."

I heard Mama and Papa say that most of them did send for their families after their first payday, too. Much too often they sent for their families before they had found a place for them to live, and the cities to which they had moved suddenly discovered the "race problem." We heard that an organization called the Urban League had been started to help Negro workers who had gone north to adjust to their new surroundings.

Though most of the people who accepted the propositions offered by the labor agents were from the mining towns and steel mill districts outside Birmingham, it was not long before they were followed by merchants and a small number of the professional people that we knew. They, too, sent for their families and I went to the station to say good-by to my friends one by one.

The discontent of Birmingham Negro parents mounted as their friends wrote back and told how their children of high school age had to be "put back" to lower grades in the schools of other cities because they had had no Latin or French and found it impossible to keep up with their classes in mathematics. Talk about these matters was common, but the boys and girls who went to I.H.S. paid little attention to it; I.H.S. was our school and we loved it. We loved our principal, Professor A. H. Parker, too, and we were proud of Professor Whatley's band, which furnished music for all the civic, fraternal, and social affairs of importance.

It was impossible for me to ever feel new or strange at I.H.S. because Professor Parker, and his assistant, Miss Orlean Kennedy, were Papa's friends and they belonged to our church. Sometimes this was a disadvantage, especially when Miss Kennedy called

me out of line as we marched out of the auditorium to the tune
of John Philip Sousa's "The Stars and Stripes Forever," and
shook a bony finger in my face, saying:

"If I see you talking in chapel again, I'm going up to the
barbershop and tell your father."

She always spoke loud enough for the band boys on the stage
to hear. Like Mama, Orlean Kennedy chastised those she loved
and I had a special place in the big heart she shared with the
hundreds of boys and girls who passed in and out of the school.

It is these days I think of as my "white bread days" because
Mama, to remind me that life would not always be carefree, used
to say:

"You don't know it, but you're eating your white bread now."

When the doctor told Papa he needed a rest and should take
a trip, we all agreed that the house would seem strange without
him. Though we often spent the night at Nannie's and during
the summer Mama took us on vacations, Papa was never away
from home at night when we were there. Mama told us that
Papa had a "bad heart" and that was why his friend, Dr. Henry
Bryant, had also told him to stop smoking and suggested that
he should not drink the eggnog or homemade wines Mama
served on holidays and festive occasions.

Papa decided he would use his vacation to go up to Chicago
and see some of his friends who had moved there. He waited to
leave until spring when the weather warmed up.

Every night while Papa was gone, around the time he usually
came home, Little Sister and Ida Mae would get very quiet and
I knew that they were missing him. I missed him, too, because
there was nothing to look forward to, no surprise gifts each
night, no sacks of fruit with the little violet boxes of chiclets on
top waiting for us when we woke up on Sunday mornings. There
was nobody to say "Ellen, you come in this house and do your
night work" in such a stern voice that the neighborhood boys
would tease me about it the next day. Though Papa was away
for two weeks, Snowball never failed to wait for him each night
at the corner.

Mama was sewing in the dining room one day when a telegram came. We gathered around the machine as she tore open the envelope and read: "HAVING A FINE TIME. SEND PICTURES OF YOU AND CHILDREN. CASSIE WANTS TO SEE MY FAMILY. LOVE, PAPA."

"Who is Cassie?" we asked.

"A friend of your father's," Mama said and pressed her lips in a thin line which meant there was no need to ask any more questions.

That night after Mama put the younger children to bed she told me that Cassie had been Papa's sweetheart before she came in from the country. There had been a misunderstanding and, according to rumor, Papa's pride had been hurt to the extent that he presented Cassie with a one-way ticket to Chicago. He took her to the railroad station and made sure she was on the train which carried her out of his life and left room for Mama.

The day after the telegram came, Mama took the three of us uptown to Cloud's Photographic Studio. Mr. Cloud posed us so that Mama was seated with one of the children on either side as I stood behind them, leaning slightly forward. Looking at the picture now, I can imagine how Papa must have smiled when he showed his old girl friend the likeness of his beautiful wife and three healthy children. Later, Cassie wrote me: "You look so much like Bob I feel I know you already. . . ."

The first thing Papa told Mama when he got off the train was that we were going to move to Chicago. A friend of his from Atlanta had bought a barbershop in Chicago, and Papa was going to rent a chair. Mama said she was not sure she wanted to move. So Papa told her he would give her a trip so that she could go and see for herself.

Papa was the Birmingham Barons' number-one rooter and Mama and I suspected that the decision to move was made less painful because Papa's friend, Rube Foster, who owned a Negro ball club, lived in Chicago. Every time Rube's team came to Birmingham to play against the Black Barons he visited with us. Rube was a huge man, and I was always fascinated by the way he devoured the enormous meals Mama set before him. Papa used to look on in envy as Rube poured himself a glass of home brew so that there was only a little foam on the top. Papa could not eat heavy meals any more; neither could he drink home brew.

"I've got to educate these three gals," Papa would say. "I don't ever want them to have to live off of corn bread and fat back as I did when I was a child."

Rube Foster and Papa used to talk about their friend, C. I. Taylor, who had moved to Indianapolis from Birmingham. Mr. Taylor owned a baseball club, too, and Papa said he would be seeing him as soon as we moved. I did not know, then, that Foster and Taylor were pioneers in Negro baseball.

Though Papa would be close to his baseball friends in Chicago, I knew he would never forget the Birmingham teams and would miss going out to Rickwood Park, sitting behind third base and talking to the players who came over to speak with him during the warm-up period. Papa always took me to Rickwood when he wanted company, because Mama did not like baseball and he would buy me ice cream, popcorn, candy—anything that would keep me from asking him questions after the game started. As I grew older I used to wish Papa would not yell so loud when he was pleading with the players. But they were wonderful times and we would both miss them.

Mama and Aunt Annie stopped in Indianapolis and visited the Taylors on the way home from Chicago. When they got back to Birmingham Papa knew he had proved his point because Mama was ready to move to Chicago as soon as arrangements could be made. She had us wide-eyed over the wonder of all the amusement parks she had visited and all the shows she had seen. She told us about State Street where all of the business places were owned or managed by Negroes. She said there was even a big bank on State Street run by a Negro man named Jesse Binga. One night after the other children went to bed she told me that Cassie Brown had given a luncheon in her honor at the Vincennes Hotel.

Mama and Papa decided that I would go to Talladega the next school year and the family would move to Chicago the following spring. Papa had a long talk with Dr. Sumner, the president of Talladega, and I was told to write for an application blank so that I might apply for entrance to the preparatory school.

Then my friend Lena came home from Rock Castle, Virginia, where she had been attending St. Francis de Sales Institute, a Catholic school for Negro girls conducted by the white Sisters of the Blessed Sacrament. At the time Lena went away there had been a lot of talk because the Catholic Negro families in Birmingham could be counted on one hand and nobody understood why Lena's people sent her to Rock Castle. When Lena came back in June, a sweet girl graduate, she brought some romantic stories about her alma mater along with her diploma.

Everything I had ever heard about Catholic churches and schools had excited my imagination. Mama had told me about the times she went to Mass with her Catholic friend, Mamie Sims, and that if Papa had not come into her life she might have been a Catholic. When we were alone Mama had described the ritual and ceremonies. When Lena added a description of the many beautiful cherry trees on the campus at Rock Castle, the strawberry patches where the girls could pick as many berries as they pleased, and told me about the handsome brown boys at Belmead (St. Emma's Military Academy) who came calling regularly, she was sowing seeds on prepared ground. I wrote the Mother Superior at St. Francis de Sales and requested a catalogue.

Mama was impressed by the fact that St. Francis de Sales would cost less than Talladega and we had long secret talks about this change in plans. Neither of us had the courage to tell Papa, but when he requested the application blank from Talladega I had to confess.

Papa thought I was joking when I first told him that I did not want to go to Talladega because I preferred St. Francis de Sales. When he realized I was in earnest, he refused to discuss it and forbade me to mention the matter to anyone else. But it was two against one and by the time the letter of acceptance came from Rock Castle, Mama and I had won him over—but on one condition. Papa withheld consent for me to go to St. Francis de Sales until I promised him I would never become a Catholic.

Friends and neighbors were shocked when they learned I was going to a Catholic school. Papa told them that Catholic nuns were thorough teachers and that he was not worried about me because I had promised never to become a Catholic. After all, he reminded them, the family would be moving to Chicago in the spring, and if this arrangement did not work out satisfactorily I could leave St. Francis de Sales at the end of the school year. His explanation did not stop the criticism; it only reduced it to whispers and dire prophecies behind his back.

The criticism worried Mama more than it did Papa. But the more she worried the faster she sewed; going away to school always involves new clothes. I had not inherited my mother's nimble fingers and my help consisted solely of sewing name labels on the wardrobe Mama assembled.

Often that summer, Papa would talk about Chicago and his plans for our future. His family had been Congregationalists as far back as he knew and he reminded me that if I broke my promise to him everybody would blame him for allowing me to go to a Catholic school. Papa spoke often of his old teachers at Trinity College in Athens, Alabama. They were courageous white women who had given up comfortable lives in the North to come South after the Civil War and teach newly freed Negroes under the auspices of the American Missionary Association. He always said that he and Nannie owed whatever they were to those teachers. We talked about my ambition to go to Africa as a missionary and he told me that the members of our church were depending on me to fulfill this pledge and would do everything they could to help me.

Papa was always talking about how much others had done for us and I never dared to mention the fact that Mama complained he gave every penny he could get his hands on to the church. Besides contributing one tenth of his earnings, Papa begged large donations and cajoled his wealthy white customers into buying fine clothes for the preachers. When his good friend, Reverend J. C. Olden, was transferred and a young divinity student came to occupy the pulpit, Papa practically had to support him because our membership was small and not many came to church during the hot weather.

The warm feeling of companionship and confidence that flavored those talks as we walked home from Shipman's Pharmacy with the children running along in front, licking away at their ice cream cones, later became part of a series of memories that troubled my dreams.

I was to leave for Rock Castle on August 27. One month and one day before, my friends gave a party out at Aunt Annie's. I said good night to my escort at my door and tiptoed inside the house. I gave my new dress a hug as I hung it in the closet, then undressed and hopped into bed with the kind of smile on my face that you can feel up to your cheekbones.

According to the clock, I had been in bed about two hours when I was awakened, in the midst of a strange dream, by a scratching sound.

Ida Mae, who was in bed with me, sat up. "I hear something," she said, as the scratching continued.

"I do, too," I whispered and put an arm about her.

The moon was shining in the window and we could see how frightened Little Sister looked when she jumped out of the little white bed that had once been mine.

"Call Papa," she begged when I put my other arm about her. "I'm scared, Sister Ellen."

Mama and Papa were in the next room with their door ajar, but Mama had told me that we were never to do or say anything that would excite Papa. The children were trembling and I was afraid they would start crying. Our electric lights were switched on by pulling a string that hung from a bulb in the middle of the ceiling and I always had a hard time finding the string in the dark.

"Papa," I called softly. "Do you know where I can find the flashlight?"

"What do you want with it?" he asked.

"I-I want to get up," I said.

"For what? You must have a reason for wanting to get up. Are you sick?"

"Tell him we heard a noise!" the children begged.

"Don't be stubborn, Ellen, tell me why you want the flashlight. Don't be so stubborn!" he said when I did not answer.

Mama must have suggested that I might have private reasons for wanting to get up because he finally told me that I had left the flashlight in the dining room, contrary to the order he had given that it was always to be near our bed for use in an emergency. Ida Mae and Little Sister hugged each other for protection when I left them.

At the door of our bedroom I faced a hall window, the window over the old brown trunk behind which my tree had lain before it was planted. I thought I saw a huge shadow in the window. Then the shadow moved and I screamed.

"Papa, come quick! I just saw a man working at the window screen in the hall."

My sisters ran to Mama while Papa hurried to me. He looked out the window but nobody was there.

"Wait until I put on my house shoes and get a gun," he said. "I'll find out who's prowling around here this time of the night."

When he went back to his room the moon was shining on the bed where Mama sat, holding the children as she tried to comfort them. She had on a white gown and one thick long braid was thrown over her shoulder as it had been the first day I saw Ida Mae.

Papa got his gun and went out between the houses. The bottom of the screen had been cut, which explained the noise that had awakened us, but our night visitor had vanished. After looking around the back yard, Papa came in and told us to go back to bed.

I could not sleep. The children were as close to me as they could get. Each time I turned, they turned. Then I heard Papa ask Mama to get him some medicine. After a while I heard her say, "That girl has caused all of this trouble and now she's gone back to sleep. She had no right to call you!"

I threw on a robe, tucked the children in, and reached the door of their room just as Papa said, "Mama, who else was there for her to call? If she had called you and you had gone out there the man might have knocked your head off."

"I'm not asleep," I said. "Are you sick, Papa?"

"Just a little indigestion," he answered. "I think I'll sit **up.** Mama, you had better call Henry."

Mama telephoned the doctor and told him to come at once.

The indigestion got worse and Papa had a hard time breathing. I stayed with him while Mama went on the porch to wait for Dr. Bryant. Beads of perspiration were popping out on his forehead and I began fanning him with a palmetto fan we had brought home from church. The choking sensation was so great he could not talk and he motioned to me to stop.

"Cuts . . . cuts my breath," he gasped. Then he pointed toward the front porch.

"You want me to go to Mama?" I asked and he nodded.

I had never seen my mother so excited. Her hair was loose and she was pulling first one side then the other. "Why doesn't the doctor come?" she asked over and over. "He probably thinks I'm just excited, but this is different. I'm so afraid. It's . . . it's almost like in the dream."

I remembered that the previous morning Mama had been interrupted telling me about her dream when Papa came to the dining room for breakfast. She said she had dreamed that Papa had a heart attack and died. Before they took his body away she pulled the cover back and looked at his feet. She said his feet looked like gray marble and was describing the sensation she had when she touched them.

"Look here, Redhead," Papa had spoken up and we knew he had heard the conversation, "I've told you before not to be dreaming about me because too many of your dreams come true. I'm not thinking about dying. I've got three gals to raise. That's one of your dreams that is not coming true."

"I'll go and get the doctor," I told Mama quickly. She gave no indication that she heard me and I could not wait.

I thought about how the boys in our neighborhood always

said, "Ellen can run like a Injun. She runs with her head down
—watch her!"

My head shot out as I went into a crouch. I ran up Sixth
Avenue, across Fifteenth Street, up to Sixteenth, then past the
church and halfway down the block to the doctor's house. I
made the top of the steps in one leap. The doctor answered the
bell with his bag in his hand. I refused to get in the car with
him, though. I had to run back to Papa.

When I lifted my feet they felt as if weights were tied to them.
I stopped and tried to pray, but when I looked up at the sky
which had been so bright with moonlight a few minutes before,
the moon was behind a dark cloud. I felt as if the ceiling of the
sky had come down and pressed against my head, hard and cold
like metal. The doctor passed me in his automobile. I could not
call to him; nor could I run any longer. I just walked down
Sixth Avenue until I came to our house.

The doctor's maroon touring car was parked by the curb. All
of the lights were on and people seemed to be everywhere. The
young preacher from our church was leaning against the banister on the front porch. Nobody was saying anything; they
were just standing around—waiting. Then I heard a short shrill
scream. I knew why I could not pray the prayer that God wished
to go unanswered.

I leaned across the gate and lost track of time. I felt someone
patting my back; then another figure appeared and I heard the
young divinity student say, "Your father is in a coma. Come with
me."

Papa looked as if he were asleep but his skin was gray and he
was breathing heavily. The doctor, who had his hand on Papa's
pulse, told someone to go in to the next room and get Mama.
We could hear the children whimper when she left them and
joined the little group standing around Papa's bed. Then she
lifted the cover to look at Papa's feet. I felt them and they were
cold and hard like marble. His breathing became heavier and
heavier; then he gave one long shudder and lay still.

"He's gone," the doctor said, "but I've been expecting it for some time. If this thing had not happened tonight, you would have found him dead in bed. His heart had given out."

Someone started to pull the sheet over Papa's face, but I turned it back and begged them to leave me alone with him. Then they took Mama to the children. I smoothed his bushy eyebrows and brushed back the few strands of hair on the front of his head. I touched his lips with my fingers. They were still soft and I wished they would part and say, "Ellen, come in this house and do your night work."

I knelt beside him and prayed that wherever he was he would hear me as I promised to do all of the things he had told me he wanted me to do. I kissed him and felt his face grow cold beneath my touch. Water trickled from the corner of his mouth and I knew that death had won. I covered his face with the sheet and closed the door.

As I left the room, I could hear Little Sister talking to a neighbor. "Miss Gracie," she was saying, "will you give me and my mama and my sisters something to eat? We haven't got no more Papa."

Snowball waited on the steps of the front porch until the next day when they brought Papa back in his casket. I held the little terrier in my arms so he could see his master's face again but he squirmed out of my arms and curled up beneath the casket where he remained until they took the body away. Then he followed the procession to the church and waited outside as he had done on Sundays before.

Ida Mae and Little Sister were dressed in white. While we waited for the cars to take us to the church I heard someone say that the children looked like little angels. I wore the white silk blouse and skirt Mama had worn the night I recited "The Prodigal Daughter" at our church. Mama was dressed in black, according to the custom of the times, and wore a heavy veil to conceal her grief from the public.

I had never seen the Congregational Church crowded before the day of Papa's funeral. Though the faces of the people seemed blurred I knew that great numbers of his friends were paying their respects with the kind of dignity that he had always expected without ever demanding it.

Snowball stood by the hearse as preparations were made for the trip to Woodlawn Cemetery. I held out my arms to him but he ran away and lost himself in the crowd.

I remember the dull thud when the earth hit the wooden box, and Nannie's sharp wail, which tore through the air. Then, except for words of benediction, all was quiet as the last male of the Tarry clan was returned to the earth from which he had sprung.

The day after the funeral the talk that had been buzzing around me started penetrating. People were saying I had frightened Papa to death. Some of the old women said I had not seen a man at the window; I had seen the black figure of death. With the torn screen, the doctor's words, and Papa's "... who else was there for her to call?" I should have been comforted, but it was an added sorrow which I carried in tearful silence.

As painful as was the longing in our hearts, it was the physical act of waiting for Papa each night, then remembering that he would not come, that was hardest.

All of the white shops staffed by Negro barbers were closed the day of Papa's funeral. It was the next night that we saw Snowball trot up to the corner where he always waited. I stood at the gate and watched him as he looked up and down Sixth Avenue and I saw Aunt Lizzie's husband, Tommie Thompson, who looked a lot like Papa, walking down the street. When he reached the corner, Snowball pounced on Tommie and tried to lick his face before he saw that it was not his master. For a second it was as if the little dog were suspended in mid-air. Then he fell to the sidewalk in a limp heap and dragged his body from the corner to our yard, whining like a baby. The men who were watching shook their heads and the women cried with us.

chapter 3

THE CASTLE AND MY PRISONER

One month after Papa's death I went to Rock Castle. The way my friends fell silent when I approached made me know that my responsibility for his death was still being discussed. I was glad to get away too because I hated listening to the stream of friends who came in and out of the house giving Mama advice on how to raise us.

Snowball's grief was among my crowded thoughts as the train carried me to Rock Castle. But as the landscape changed from state to state, I found myself reluctantly thinking a little of the place which was to be my future home.

From the time a tall man who looked like a moving-picture Indian said, "I'm Frank. The Sisters sent me," a new world began to unfold. As Frank carried my trunk to the river's bank, I stood on a hill overlooking the historic James River and watched the train I had just left chug off in the opposite direction. He took my bag without speaking or giving any indication as to how we would get across to the majestic red brick building I could see on the other side of the river.

What looked like a dozen or more broad planks anchored at the edge of the water turned out to be a flatboat. The big lump at one end of the flat unfolded into an old Negro man who made me think of Stephen Foster's "Old Folks at Home." There was a cable overhead but he pushed the shore away from us with a long stick and I closed my eyes as the flimsy craft glided across the rocky stream. When we came to anchor I saw a well-groomed

horse hitched to an empty buggy. Frank carried my luggage to
the buggy, then motioned me to a seat. The entire performance
had taken place without a spoken word.

As the horse trotted along rutted roads I wondered where the
houses were hiding. All around us was vacant land. The "Castle"
as Lena had said the school was called, had seemed so near when
we were on the river, but as we rode along it seemed to be
moving away from us. We passed one or two farm houses and I
tried to ask questions, but Frank acted as if he did not hear me.
The dreams about going up to Virginia to a Catholic school
where the Sisters taught pretty fancywork and I could eat straw-
berries and cherries all day and flirt with handsome boys from
Belmead began falling apart. I wished I were back on Sixth
Avenue where the houses were close together and Mama and the
children were on the front porch while I stood at the gate—and
Snowball stood on the corner—waiting for Papa.

I looked down at my new black button-top shoes from Rich's
shoestore and they were still shining. The lady at Pizitz' who sold
us the Copenhagen blue sweater I was wearing over a darker dress
had told Mama it was the "latest thing." I had stood in front of
the marble-topped mirror in the hallway at home and decided
that my blue felt hat looked better turned up in the back and
tilted to one side. My appearance was all right, I thought; it
must be that I talked or acted differently from the way people
in Virginia talked and acted. The man beside me never spoke.

The horse turned off the road and we entered a winding lane
overhung by stately maples still lush in leafiness. Suddenly the
Castle was coming at us. Frank tightened the reins, turned a
corner, and I got a full view of St. Francis de Sales. My first
impression, after the lovely ivy-covered building, was of girls.
They were hanging out of windows, on porches, steps, and lawns.
They waved and I waved back. I saw girls everywhere except at
the front of the building.

Frank helped me out of the buggy and rang a bell. A pale,
ethereal-looking Sister opened the door. Sister called me by name
and took me to a reception room where she left me. I had never
seen such shiny floors before and I scraped my foot lightly on

the hardwood to break the stillness. I peeped out the door and looked down a long corridor until I heard distant footsteps. Then I ran back to my chair.

"This is Anna," was the way Sister introduced the tall amber-colored girl with pale freckles and dreamy gray eyes that lighted up with friendliness. "She will see that you get a late lunch and show you to the dormitory."

Anna did more than Sister had promised. She took me into her heart and helped me over the roughest spots.

"You'll like it here," she said.

I thought the period furniture in the dining room was pretty, but best of all I liked the sideboard that looked like Mama's. The woodwork and chairs were shiny like the floors and the table cloth was as white as scraped snow. The windows opened on a porch which Anna said overlooked the back courtyard.

Anna was from Natchez and she asked about Lena. I wanted to ask about the berries and cherries Lena had told me about, but I was afraid it was the wrong time of the year. I thought it was also too soon to ask about the Belmead boys.

An attractive brown girl stuck her head in the window.

"Is that the new girl? What's her name?" she asked.

"Her name is Ellen," Anna answered, "but if you don't get back to the bakery you'll get some marks." The girl hurried away.

Anna told me that her friend's name was Inez—she pronounced it "Enaize"—and that she was from Cornwells Heights, Pennsylvania, which was where the "Mother House" was located. As she talked, I added a few new words to my vocabulary.

We walked up the corridor and Anna let me poke my head into the Sisters' refectory. In contrast to the room where I had eaten, it was bare. There was a long wooden table that looked as if it had been scrubbed with ashes and the plain chairs on which the Sisters sat. Only the floor was shining. Everything else was dull and plain. Anna explained that the Sisters took a vow of poverty and that was why the room in which they ate was stripped of all but necessities.

Happy chatter rose like a sweet song as soon as Anna opened

the huge oaken door that led us out of the Sisters' part. The pleasant noise grew louder as we walked past the barn-like dining hall where a cluster of girls was putting away the luncheon dishes. At the top of a flight of slate steps we entered the recreation room where a chubby girl with a sailor's cap sitting down on the back of her bobbed blond curls was banging out a tune that sounded to me like the blues. The girls standing around the piano stopped singing long enough to ask, "Is that the new girl?"

"Where's my room?" I asked when Anna opened the dormitory with a gold-colored pass key and I saw row after row of beds. "This looks like a hospital."

"We have alcoves," Anna said as we stopped by one of the beds. "You pull the curtains on these rods around the beds and you are private. This will be yours."

That night in the girl's dining hall I sat at a table with Anna, Inez and three other girls. We kept silent until after grace when a Sister hit the side of a tin water pitcher with a spoon. There was a loud buzz and in a few seconds I had learned the meaning of "boarding-school reach." While I stared at the hungry activity around me, Anna heaped my plate and warned me that I would know lean days unless I, too, learned to reach. During supper we heard carriage wheels on the driveway. I was told that more new girls were coming in.

Anna and Inez took me to the baggage room, where I claimed my suitcase. The girls were impressed, when we went to the dormitory and they watched me unpack the bag. I was glad Mama had made my pleated blue serge skirts and the white middy blouses out of the best material she could find. I had everything on the list that Mother Superior had sent and Anna and Inez commented on the quality and cut of my clothes. I had almost finished unpacking when Inez picked up the black leather book still in my bag.

"What's this?" she demanded.

"That's my Bible," I said proudly. "The Ladies' Missionary Society gave it to me."

"This is not a Catholic Bible," she said.

"I'm not a Catholic," I answered. "I'm a Congregationalist."

"Anna, I'll see you in the recreation room," Inez announced as she turned and went out of the dormitory.

Anna helped me to arrange my personal belongings in the alcove, then told me about the "robery" in which I would hang the clothes that were in my trunk. Neither of us mentioned the way Inez had spoken when she saw my Bible and found out I was not a Catholic, but we both knew she had given me my first snub. That night in the recreation room the "old girls" asked me a lot of questions about how it was "out in the world" and how people acted "down there in Alabama." I was glad when the night bell rang.

After prayers we went to our alcoves and as I prepared for bed I thought about all the new words and phrases I had heard that day. Before I pushed back the end curtain at the foot of my bed and retired, I took my Bible from the drawer of the washstand. Just as I marked a page I wanted to read I saw a tall, willowy nun glide past, who looked like a graceful swan draped in cumbersome black. I crawled to the foot of the bed to get a better look but she pulled out the light before I could see her face. That night I dreamed Papa was standing over me with one of his ground-gripper shoes in his hand.

I was only half-awake that first morning when a Sister walked through the dormitory and started the day with a prayer. I barely had time to wash before Anna came, fully dressed, and handed me a white veil.

"What's this for?" I asked.

"To wear, on your head," she answered.

"I don't want to wear a veil," I objected. "I want to wear my hat."

"We all wear veils to Mass," she said. "We'll both be late if you don't hurry."

A Sister walked down the aisle ringing a bell and the girls began forming a line at the door. Anna and I were last.

As we filed into the chapel I thought the gray marble altar must be the most beautiful one in the world. The floors of the chapel looked like a wide taffy-colored river. I had once gone to Mass with Lena, but the priest prayed so fast I did not even recognize the "Our Father." The first morning at St. Francis de Sales the priest spoke more slowly and Anna shared a prayer book with me. One side of the page was printed in Latin and the other in English, with a picture now and then which explained what the priest was doing. The girls sang, bells rang, incense burned, and the sun shone though the stained-glass windows in brilliant rays. Only my sleepiness and hunger detracted from the beauty of the scene.

Later that day I met several girls from New York, and many from Philadelphia, Washington, D.C., and Richmond, Virginia. There were others who had come from towns in Ohio, Illinois, Missouri, Georgia and Florida. Some of them had not left the Castle for years, I learned. They were the ones who had asked me about "out in the world." I discovered that summer vacations were spent on the campus and many of the girls would not leave the school until after graduation.

When I asked about Belmead, the girls pointed to a distant building about a mile away and told me that was a part of St. Emma's Military Academy for Negro boys. It was located at Belmead, which had once been a huge estate and the girls always called the school by the name the estate had borne.

Frank Waldron, who had met me at the station, was the only male employee allowed any contact with the girls and I later learned he never spoke to any of them. The only other man I had seen was a priest.

Though Inez enjoyed making me feel uncomfortable, I liked her and did not feel too badly when I learned she had told most of the girls about my Protestant Bible. It was like rubbing salt on a wound, though I had already begun to feel guilty because each night when I tried to read my Bible the tall willowy Sister Callista, who was in charge of our dormitory, put the lights out. I still thought a lot about going to Africa and I kept dreaming that Papa was standing over me trying to tell me something.

Then a letter came from the ladies of the Missionary Society with a gift of more money than I had ever had in my life and I decided I was going to read my Bible even if I had to read it by moonlight. I went to Mass each morning, and catechism class when I was told to; I deserved some time for my own religion, I thought.

The next night when Sister Callista put the light out I put my Bible down and told her how I felt. I could see the girls around me peeping out of their alcoves.

"I'm sorry," Sister smiled, "but you will have to do your reading during the day."

And though we both knew there was no free time on my daily schedule, there was nothing I could say. I fell asleep trying to read by the pale light from my window.

Anna's friends became my friends, but I shared my newness with Kathleen and Katie Mae from Tuscaloosa, Alabama, Mamie from Cincinnati, and tiny Elsie from somewhere out in Texas. With the exception of Elsie, we were all Protestant and were thoroughly scandalized when the Catholic girls danced on Sunday afternoons.

It finally happened! One brisk Saturday afternoon I saw two boys. When they drove up in a one-horse rig it was like a bugle calling the girls to arms; the porches and windows were suddenly full of them.

"They are Belmead boys," one of the girls explained as we watched them go into the bakery and drive away carrying a little box. "They came over for altar bread."

That was as close as I came to any of the handsome Belmead boys Lena had told me about until the following December. I had a surprise coming.

Anna tried to stop Inez the day she said, "Ellen, are you going to be a *convert?*"

"I don't know what you are talking about," I answered and walked away.

That night when Sister Callista came to put the light out I asked her: "Sister, the girls are always talking about *converts.* What do they mean?"

Sister explained that the girls were referring to those who

study the teachings of the Church, accept them, and become Catholics.

"I want to get converts for my own church," I told the startled nun. "I'm going to Africa to be a missionary. I can never be a Catholic, you know."

Sister did not know, so I told her about my promise to Papa. I also told her about our church at home and how the ladies of the Missionary Society were expecting me to come back home and work with them before I went to Africa.

"It's late," Sister reminded me when I had finished. "You had better go to sleep now. I am sure you will be a credit to your father and your friends."

When Inez found the opportunity she repeated her question. I told her that Papa had been a Congregationalist deacon and, because I wanted her to like me, I told her how I had made the promise to Papa and about the circumstances under which he died.

"You mean he had heart failure because you screamed?" she asked.

Anna told the Sister in charge that I was not feeling well and I was allowed to go to bed early that night. When I did fall asleep, I dreamed Papa was dying all over again.

Bit by bit I built up a wall of resistance to the Catholic practices that were a vital part of the daily routine at St. Francis de Sales. I made no secret of my attitude and repeated my vow never to become a Catholic.

In December we held a bazaar and the boys from Belmead came. We were not allowed to speak to them, however. Nor could we dance with the boys. All we could do was look at them. When the music started, they danced on one side of the room and we danced on the other. Speaking to the boys was punishable by expulsion, the older girls told me.

"It's hard to believe," I sneered, "that the Sisters would expel a girl for talking to a boy when they allow you all to dance on the Sabbath."

The older girls were too busy answering the boys' glances with their eyes and hands to bother about my remarks. The new girls looked on in awe as the others managed to enjoy themselves in spite of the restrictions.

I advanced one step up the Castle's social ladder when the girl who kept books for the Sister in charge of the storeroom became ill after Christmas and I inherited her job. Sister Inez, who joined the Sisters of the Blessed Sacrament soon after the community was founded by the Reverend Mother Katherine Drexel, received all spending money and credited it to the students' respective accounts. The storeroom was a combination students' canteen and general store. There were other girls to help with the selling, but I had to keep the books up to date and post the balances on a huge card which was periodically hung in the dining room.

There was no salary attached to my job but there were many benefits. Sister Inez soon discovered that my appetite and Castle fare were at variance. She saw to it that I had extra pieces of fresh fruit and when I insisted that I had to work through meal-time, she went foraging in the Sisters' refectory or appealed to dear little Sister Michael, who presided over the kitchen like an exacting but lovable queen. During the afternoons when columns of figures conflicted with my daydreams, I opened a jar of fig newtons or Lorna Doones and looked out the window at the tops of the Belmead buildings while I thought about Mama and the children. In this happy fashion I got fat.

Though I had to study harder than ever before, my marks were only slightly above average. Sister Robert, our principal, kept a firm hand on me without revealing the concern which later brought matters to a head. She was never discouraged by the fight I made against all that was offered me. She knew that gradually a feeling of peace had begun to push back my doubts and confusion.

In spite of my convictions, daily Mass was comforting and inspiring. My spirit soared each morning when the priest stood at the foot of the altar and said in Latin:

"I will go unto the Altar of God, at which the God-man is both the High-Priest and the victim of the Sacrifice. I come to Thee, dearest Lord, confessing that I have sinned exceedingly; humbled and ashamed, yet confident in Thy fatherly pity. Create a clean heart in me, O my God, and take not Thy Holy Spirit from me. O Blessed Mother, who didst stand at the foot of the Cross when Jesus was suffering for us, be with me now that He is being offered up in sacrifice."

In the gospels I recognized familiar passages and during the Credo I repeated the Apostles' Creed as it had been taught to me back home in Sunday school. When the priest offered the bread, then proceeded to mix the wine and the water in preparation for the coming of Our Lord, I was filled with awe by the beauty of the act. With the ringing of a bell, my heart echoed the words of the Sanctus:

"Holy, Holy, Holy, Lord God of Hosts. The heavens and earth are full of Thy Glory. Hosanna in the highest. Blessed is He who cometh in the name of the Lord. Hosanna in the highest. . . ."

With the next tinkling of the bell the priest extended his hands over the bread and wine, recalling the Last Supper, and I bowed my head in the presence of "My Lord and my God! My God and my All!"

The proper meaning of transubstantiation was to come to me later. During those first troubled months it was enough for me to know that Christ broke the bread and drank the wine with His disciples at the Last Supper and said: "This is my Body— This is my Blood. . . ." Because the disciples had believed, and because I believed what they had passed on to me, each morning a miracle took place in front of my eyes and Jesus was present upon the altar before which I knelt.

When the Catholic girls went to the communion rail, I begged God to enter my unworthy heart and felt no less loved than they. With the words: "The Lord be with you—*Ite, missa est*—Go, it is ended," I felt He was with me wherever I went that day.

I came to understand how my mother had been impressed by Catholic ritual and decided that sometimes I would go to Mass and Benediction after I graduated and went back to Birmingham. My criticism dwindled and I was happier in my school work.

There were still obstacles to hurdle and a new meaning for the word "retreat" was one of them. I had always thought of soldiers falling back in retreat and never knew that the word had a spiritual meaning. When the girls told me about a week-long "retreat" each year during which they kept silence, read spiritual books, and listened to sermons and talks given by a priest who came especially for this occasion, it sounded, I said, like the equivalent of a Protestant revival. At least, I thought, I would get time to read my own Bible.

That year a Reverend Abraham Emerick, S.J., conducted the retreat for the students at St. Francis de Sales. Father Emerick was a venerable man whose simple oratory illuminated age-old dogma and theological teachings. He brought the men and women of Biblical days into our midst and their lives, inter-woven with the life of Jesus, became a living thing.

Sister Inez gave me a little book for my first retreat. When she placed *The Prisoner of Love*, by Reverend F. X. Lasance, in my hand, I had no intention of reading it. Thumbing through the foreword I came to a quotation from St. Augustine which said: "Do not, O reader, condemn a book until thou hast finished the perusal thereof; for it may be that after having done this, thy blame will be less severe!"

The little book became my constant companion and its simple words gave new and precious meaning to many of the practices I had questioned. Through the miracle, which I had come to believe took place during Mass at the solemn moment of Con-secration, whereby the bread and wine was changed into the body and blood of Our Lord, the same Christ who died for me came down and remained on all the altars of the world—a prisoner of the love He bore for all mankind. Before, I had believed "the Word was made flesh" to be only a phrase whose purpose was to fill out the sermon of the minister telling me that I should be good and do no evil. Father Lasance's little book told me that it meant Jesus was in the Tabernacle waiting for me to adore him, waiting to comfort me and quiet my doubts and my fears.

Father Emerick, too, talked about Our Lord truly present in

the Tabernacle, waiting to be adored and received into our
hearts. Suddenly God seemed closer than ever. Instead of being
a God I worshiped on Sunday, He had become a God I wanted
to worship every minute of every day. He was my prisoner of
love—always waiting. I longed to march up to the communion
rail and whisper, "Here I am. Please make my poor heart your
abode."

"If only," I wished as the retreat drew to a close, "Papa had
never asked me to make that promise."

The night before retreat ended the dream came back. Once
more Papa was standing over me, his hand raised as if to strike.
I screamed in my sleep and aroused the dormitory. The next
morning I was allowed to stay in bed and Sister Robert came to
see about me. After dinner she took me to Father Emerick. At
first I was self-conscious, but the priest talked to me about
Alabama and in a little while I was telling him about Mama and
Papa and the children. I told him about our church, too, and
about the promise I had made Papa just before he died. In the
months at Rock Castle I had come to feel so close to God, and
if being a Catholic meant that I would retain this feeling for
the rest of my life, I said, I wanted to be a Catholic.

"But I can never break the promise I made Papa," I insisted.
"He was always proud to say that his word was his bond and he
would expect the same of me. I knew it was wrong of me to make
the promise because I didn't really mean it at the time. I thought
I could change him later on. Then when he died there was
nothing I could do."

Through the years I have cherished the picture of the elderly
priest as he sat in silence for a few moments after I had finished
my story.

"Your father," he said, "must have been a good man. We
must hope and pray that he is with God. In His presence all
things are made clear."

Father Emerick told me that any loving father would wish his
child to worship God and be happy. He said he was sure Papa
would not want me to carry these doubts and fears in my heart
for the remainder of what he hoped was a long and useful life.

"But Papa disliked the Catholic Church," I reminded him.

"Your father did not know the Catholic Church. And most men are suspicious of things unknown. What about your mother? As a minor, you must have her permission before you can be received into the Church."

"We don't have to worry about that," I laughed. "Mama used to go to a Catholic church with a friend of hers. I *know* she will give her permission!"

"Here at St. Francis de Sales you are safe," the priest said gently, "but when you go home you may have to suffer for your Faith. Are you sure you understand all that this may mean to you?"

I was sure that I had found a peace I had not known before and in the safety of the Castle no suffering that I might be called upon to endure seemed too great a sacrifice for me to make for my Faith. Father called Sister Robert, who had been in and out of the room during the interview, and told her about my decision. Though she expressed surprise, Sister Robert must have known that she had been the hidden lamp whose light had shone through when my night was darkest.

The girls often used the word "cheap" to describe a person's chagrin, but when the news was passed along that I was going to become a Catholic, not one of them made me feel "cheap" or reminded me of the many criticisms I had made. It was hard to tell Sister Callista, to whom I had repeatedly vowed that I would never become a Catholic, but she did not seem at all surprised. It was my classmates who seemed happiest, although many months passed before I learned why. The Walker sisters, who occupied the alcoves on either side of me had a special reason to be pleased. With my decision to become a Catholic, my night-mares ended and the two girls slept in peace thereafter.

I wrote Mama a long letter concerning what Father Emerick had said about my promise to Papa. I told her about my decision, too, and begged her to reply by return mail so I could join the instruction class that was currently being prepared for Baptism.

A month passed and I did not get a letter from home. I was afraid Mama was sick or something was wrong with one of the children. I wrote another letter and I was so happy when Sister Robert brought me an answer that I grabbed the envelope and started reading before I looked up. Sister waited as I read.

"Mama must not have gotten either of my letters, Sister," I cried. "She didn't even mention my request."

"I am sure," said Sister Robert, who censored all mail, "your mother received both letters. Evidently, she wants time to think over your request. You will have to wait and pray."

Neither of us had any idea of how long I would have to wait and pray.

Not all of my time was spent in prayer, however. Spring came to the Castle and the countryside was a thing of beauty. Though the trees budded earlier in Birmingham, there were more of them at Rock Castle and I was filled with wonder at the profusion of green things. I finally found the strawberry patch Lena had told me about, but the berries were hot and gritty and looked prettier than they tasted. I thought the cherry blossoms were beautiful until the other flowers rioted in their eagerness to burst into bloom at the same time. There was a field so full of daisies and black-eyed Susans that they were flush against the side of an old red barn. A stream so narrow we could have crossed it with one wide step ran through the field providing water for the sleek black and white cows which spent most of their time nibbling at the grass between the flowers.

Memories of this field have always been associated with Beatrice, the Walker sister who slept on my right. There was a huge rock in the midst of the flowers and many a day when falling shadows forced us indoors and I stole my last long look, I saw pretty, red-brown Beatrice sitting on the rock looking into space. Years later I remembered and wondered if even then Beatrice had not known more about "out in the world" than the rest of us.

Days, weeks, and months passed, and Mama established a record for ignoring a given question. Over and over I wrote: "May I become a Catholic? I must have your permission because I am a minor." But not one letter from home contained a word to indicate that Mama knew what I wanted. My classmates suffered with me. It was only after we became seniors, though, that they told me I was about to become the first Protestant graduate of St. Francis de Sales and that they did not want to be the precedent-breaking class.

Just when we were ready to despair, Mama answered my question. She said she could not, in all conscience, have given me permission to become a Catholic until she was convinced that I knew what I was doing. She reminded me that I was at an impressionable age. She had withheld permission until my letters indicated that my desire to become a Catholic was more than the whim of a growing girl. She agreed with Father Emerick about the promise and reminded me that we could have persuaded Papa to release me if he had lived.

"If you are sure you will be a better person because you are a Catholic," she concluded, "you have my permission and my prayers."

Mama did not tell me that there was a reservation connected with her permission. That was her secret.

I had read *The Prisoner of Love* from cover to cover and studied my catechism and every other book on the Church which had been recommended. After an examination it was decided that I was ready for Baptism and that a special ceremony would be arranged. The Walker sisters were going home and wanted to be baptized before leaving and one of the Hazel girls, whose father was military instructor at Belmead, also became a candidate for baptism. The Feast of the Immaculate Conception, December 8, was selected as the day on which the four of us would be received into the church and make our first Holy Communion.

In spite of their devotion to each other, the Walker sisters were in constant conflict. Living between them was never a peaceful arrangement—not even during the three-day retreat before our baptism. The two sisters were opposites in appearance and temperament. Irene, the taller and older, looked like a pale Grecian goddess. Beatrice was always the Indian princess in school plays.

Our white dresses, shoes, and veils were put in readiness for the ceremonies before the retreat because we were expected to spend our time in prayer, spiritual reading, and reflection. I knew Irene and Beatrice always got their veils and stockings mixed but I thought they would settle their differences before retreat. When we were not in chapel, most of the time was spent in the privacy of our alcoves. During the very first hours of the retreat the girls exchanged notes and narrowed their quarrel to the ownership of one pair of white stockings in Beatrice's alcove. I had almost dozed off with a prayer book in my hands when I saw Irene slink past the foot of my bed. But Beatrice was a light sleeper and when Irene attempted to take the stockings in question, the fight was on.

The tussle ended on my bed and the last lick landed on my head. The girls apologized and went back to their own alcoves. I began reading again and dropped the prayer book to the floor just as Beatrice advanced on Irene's alcove. As usual, I was in the middle and got more licks than either of the girls, who came out of the fray with one stocking apiece. I donated a pair of white stockings to break the deadlock and on the eve of our baptism the dove of peace descended upon the mischievous girls. The last night the three of us slept in innocence and happiness.

The eighth of December is always an important day in the Church, but that year it was doubly important at the Castle. Gladys Hunter, a classmate, acted as my godmother and the Reverend Aloysius Roth, C.S.Sp., was my godfather. Despite the embattled retreat, Irene and Beatrice looked angelic and because of the Hazel girls a lot of important people came over from Belmead. After the ceremony, my classmates made no attempt to hide the joy they felt. Their prayers had been answered. I, too, was grateful. My Lord and my God had made my poor heart His abode.

June was in the meadows when we were graduated. Reverend Mother M. Katherine Drexel, who founded the Sisters of the Blessed Sacrament, came to St. Francis de Sales for the occasion. The Senior Class from Belmead came over and we were allowed to speak to them, but they still had to dance on one side of the room while we danced on the other.

The day before the graduates went home I slipped away for a last visit to the chapel where I had come to know my Prisoner of Love. Afterward, I found a door open that should have been locked and walked through to the still classrooms where so many hard days had been spent. I ran my fingers over the top of my worn desk and hugged the memory of the hours with Sister Timothy and Sister Robert. I could see a face for every seat and I wondered if any of us would ever meet again. I went downstairs to the music rooms where Sister Letitia had stood over me those last weeks as I played "Papillon Roses" or "Underneath the Leaves" on the piano in preparation for the homecoming when Nannie would say, "Let us hear you play something." The big door outside the music room slammed on me and I knew an important part of my life had come to an end.

Looking through the classbook now, I can remember the plans each of us made. Lucille was going to be a nurse; Gladys, another Lucille, Alice, and Ernestine would become teachers. Aloise just widened her pretty eyes when we talked about the future, and we knew some boy would soon make her his wife. I had long since announced the fact that I was going to be a writer. My classmates had watched me clip a coupon from a magazine which was an application for a correspondence course in creative writing. They knew I had sent it to Mama to mail with the required fee. They did not know that Mama, instead, had written that arrangements had been made for me to attend State Normal in Montgomery so I could get a certificate to teach as soon as possible.

We had talked for months about how happy we would be to leave the Castle, but when the morning came we were full of tears. Mother Mary Anselm, the Superior, gave each graduate a copy of St. Thomas à Kempis' *Imitation of Christ* in which our teacher, Sister Timothy, had written: "Cast thy care upon the Lord and He will sustain thee."

Sister Timothy rode with us to Richmond. Mama had given

permission for me to visit with a friend who lived there. But so many Belmead boys were at the station, Sister Timothy put me on the first train going in the direction of Birmingham. Until this moment I have never told Sister that Cupid outsmarted her and I got engaged to a Belmead boy from San Fernandina, Florida, before the trip was half over.

William was a shy boy and certainly not the one who had made the most eyes at me during the rare occasions when the Belmead boys visited the Castle. We held hands from Richmond to Hamlett, North Carolina, where we changed trains. I was still surprised when he stood on the steps of my train and said, "I've been liking you a long time. Let's get engaged."

The boys and girls on the Florida train were yelling for him to come on as the conductor had already called, "All aboard!" So I said, "All right."

"Will you wait for me?" he asked.

I nodded and William jumped off the steps and two of his friends pulled him aboard the Florida train. I thought that was the end of the engagement, but I had only been home a week when a letter came from San Fernandina reminding me that William was a man of honor who intended keeping his word.

When the train pulled into Terminal Station I saw Mama and the children standing with Aunt Annie as Sister Timothy had sent Mama a telegram stating that I would not stop in Richmond.

I could see an expression of disappointment on Mama's face as she looked at me. I knew that those fig newtons and Lorna Doones had added more flesh than was becoming to a girl of sixteen summers and I was sorry I had eaten them.

My sisters had grown more than I had imagined and they were full of questions. So was my Nannie, who was waiting when we reached the house. The friends and neighbors who came examined my diplomas but Mama did not look pleased until she saw the clothes I had made for graduation week.

I did not tell Mama that only Sister Robert's threat to hold up the diploma in Home Economics had made me overcome an old dislike for the sewing machine and finish the required clothing. All my life I had heard about how Mama sewed until one hour before I was born. Not only that, but the machine was linked in my memory with too many switchings for me to want to spend precious time stitching on one. Those were the first and last dresses I ever made.

Cousin Mabel, who had also been my music teacher, came and I went to the piano. She and Nannie beamed and bowed their heads with the music as I ran through my repertoire consisting more or less of "Papillon Roses," "Underneath the Leaves," and "Forgotten." But Nannie was always pleased with me and I had never had an occasion to doubt her love. I had no indication of what was to come or that there was something Mama had withheld from me.

"I'll stop by for you Sunday morning," Nannie said as she kissed me good night, "and we can go to church together. Everybody is anxious to see you. I hope you know how lucky you are to have so many friends who want to help."

Mama left the room hurriedly and I knew something was wrong. "Nannie," I said, "I have to go to Mass on Sunday morning."

"Mass?" she snorted. "You forget that foolishness! I'll be here for you to go to church and I'll expect you to be ready, too!"

Nannie left before I could reply. After she went home Mama admitted that nobody in Birmingham knew I had become a Catholic.

"You will just have to work it out yourself," she said. "After Papa's death I had so much to face I didn't have the strength to go through the ordeal of telling them. I have to think of Ida Mae and Little Sister now."

I remembered what Father Emerick had said about having to suffer for my Faith. It did not seem possible that Nannie, who had lavished love and understanding on me from the moment I was born, would be the one to strike the first blow. My sisters were too young to know what was happening. To conserve her strength, Mama had withdrawn and Lena was out of town. I was surrounded by so many strong family ties that I was afraid to confide in anyone. I was going to have to fight this battle alone.

For my armor I had only the cockiness of youth and a simple faith which had been a natural heritage.

"If only," I thought, "there was a priest or one of the Sisters nearby."

The next day was Saturday and I knew my time was short. I remembered having once seen nuns in the yard of a white Catholic school on the other side of town. I dressed Little Sister and we walked across Fourteenth Street to the South Side. We found the school and when I rang the bell a Sister came out in a brown habit that I did not recognize. I told her I was from St. Francis de Sales in Rock Castle, Virginia, that I was a Negro convert and wanted to talk with a priest at once. The Sister told me that I would find a church for "colored" about three blocks up the avenue. She served us cookies and milk and Little Sister and I walked up to Seventeenth Street where we saw a little white church that looked like a doll house. The door was locked and we went to the rectory. A Creole woman with iron-gray hair opened the door and smiled as she asked us in. She called the priest, a strapping red-haired Irishman whose smile belied his thunderous voice, and I met the Reverend Patrick J. Walsh, S.S.J. When we left the Rectory I knew there were two people in Birmingham who would be on my side.

The next morning I attended early Mass at the Church of the Immaculate Conception. It was supposed to be a church for "colored" but most of the people at Mass were white. They sat on one side of the church while the Negroes sat on the other. I saw Mamie Sims, who first took Mama to the big Catholic church in the heart of town, and her daughter. Then Miss Kate, the housekeeper for Father Walsh, introduced me to the other Negro Catholics who, to the best of my recollection, numbered ten—including the two Jones boys who served as acolytes. On the way home I smiled as I recalled the words of the distinguished old gentleman who had said, "We need some young folks like you in the church." He did not know that my need was the greater.

I was breaking my fast when Nannie came up the front steps. "Hurry and get ready," she called. "Be sure to put on one of those dresses you made. The folks at church will want to see how you look."

"I've just come from Mass, Nannie. I'm not going with you," I said.

"Get dressed and stop talking foolish," she urged. And I knew this was as hard for her as it was for me.

I could hear Mama singing in the kitchen, though I knew she must have heard us talking. Nannie was standing over me, waiting for me to speak and I realized it was the time of reckoning. I began, "You might as well know. . . ."

"Know what?" she snapped.

"That I am a Catholic and I am not going to church with you."

"You mean you joined the Catholic Church? After you promised Bob you wouldn't?"

"Wherever Papa is, I am sure he understands, Nannie."

"Sure, he understands," she laughed. "Those old women got you up in that school and made you do this!"

I tried to stop Nannie but her hurt turned to rage. "Your father, my dead brother, must have turned over in his grave this morning," she declared. "You've disgraced the family and everybody who believed in you!"

Nannie must have read a book containing all the accusations that have been hurled at the Church from the time of St. Peter. She let them fly that morning—in detail, and with gestures. Nannie was telling me about the awful things that went on in "that little black box" (the confessional) when I left the room.

chapter 4

BELATED HERITAGE

Most of the members of Papa's church felt that I had been unduly influenced. They said it was unfortunate that Mama had allowed me to go to Rock Castle so soon after Papa's death. They also said I would soon "see the light" and return to the fold. Though the majority shared the opinion that this change was merely a part of my adolescence that would soon be forgotten, there was one man in Birmingham who paid me the compliment of referring to my "conversion". P. Carlfax Rameau was a scholar who boasted of being an atheist. Mama said he was a "mystery man" but Papa said there was no mystery about Rameau. He was a labor agent hired by industrial corporations to keep Negro workers happy.

I remember the Sundays when he sauntered down Sixth Avenue in a frock coat, gray striped pants, a derby sitting on his head so as to show his mixed gray hair to the best advantage, with gold-rimmed glasses perched on his thin copper-colored nose. Rameau was really anti-Christian instead of anti-Catholic. When he questioned me, I found good use for all of the information I had culled from the catechism and the religious instruction with which the Sisters had crammed me. The attacks from other quarters were child's play compared with the verbal duels with Rameau. And though we were always opponents, we always parted friends.

As charges flew thick and fast, I came to appreciate the tonic value of laughter. When a woman I had always respected said

58

she could not understand how anybody would "leave the Congregational Church to go over on the South Side to some old Catholic Church nobody ever heard of before," I realized it was ridiculous to argue the point and thanked God for blessing me with a sense of humor.

It was impossible, though, to laugh away the fact that Nannie seldom came to our house and that, on her rare visits, she did not speak to me. Mama who had never exchanged a cross word with her sister-in-law and Cousin Mabel, tried to effect a reconciliation. But Nannie thought she was right—and so did I.

Nothing seemed to be the same in Birmingham. Snowball was dead, most of the girls I had known were away and every boy I asked about had left town. The difference was that the girls went away to school with the understanding that they would return after graduation; the boys left with the hope they would never come back. Some of them, I was told had "gotten in trouble," but nobody explained what the trouble was. Then I started making new friends and a steady stream of letters from San Fernandina made me look forward to happier days.

Mama had made arrangements for me to enter State Normal, but I was anxious to get a job and earn some money before it was time to go to school again. Cousin Mabel, who was using her vacation from teaching to conduct a survey for a Negro insurance company, solved this problem by hiring me as her helper. I made $15 the first week and bought a complete new outfit. I also bought some reducing pills. Fortunately, I stopped taking the pills before they did any good or any harm. Without the fig newtons and Lorna Doones the excess fat melted away.

After Mama decided that I was old enough to go to the movies with boys, my favorite pastime was a trip to the Lyric or the Champion Theaters. I enjoyed going "up town" to a show but after a while I noticed that the boys who escorted me did not seem happy when we were in the theater district. One of them told me the reason.

"I get sick and tired of these white people staring at you," he said.

"I haven't noticed them staring at me," I said.

"I know you haven't. You go around smiling at them like you think they want to be friends."

"If they look at me, why can't I look at them?" I asked. "I'm not mad at anybody."

"I know you're not. But you should be!"

"Why should I be mad?"

"Those crackers stare at you because I'm black and they think maybe you are white. The day one of them decides you are, it will be just too bad for me. This is a rotten town!" he exploded. "If I had any sense I wouldn't be here."

Afterward I sat on the front porch and thought about Rock Castle and how everybody had seemed to love everybody. Now, I thought, I was home and Nannie and many of our old friends were angry because I had become a Catholic. Even the boys who took me to the show found cause to complain. My sisters played by day and slept by night. Mama, who sewed away from home, was tired when she came in and there was little opportunity for any exchange of affection.

"If only," I wished, "things were like they used to be."

It was not long before I stopped yearning for the things which were gone forever and set my feet on a winding road; it led up the side of a hill that turned out to be a tall mountain.

Like most industrial centers during the mid-twenties, Birmingham had enjoyed an era of prosperity. The business district had spread out until it touched our neighborhood and only a few of our friends were left. Most of them had moved to Enon Ridge or Smithfield and the new people who moved in were unknown to us. Not only did we have new neighbors next door in the house where Aunt Lizzie had lived, but, according to Mama, they were a "wild bunch."

I felt like a real grown-up lady when I finally won consent to go to a party without a chaperon. I was more than a little excited when one of the boys who took me out borrowed an automobile and called for me. Mama was giving my escort her final instructions on what time I should come home when a car drove up. A light was flashed on our porch, then on the house next door before the driver stopped alongside a parked car that belonged to a man I had heard our new neighbors call "Shorty." Anxious to be on our way, we promised to be home "early" and started down the steps.

"Wait!" my mother screamed as two white policemen jumped out of the automobile with drawn guns and moved toward Shorty's car.

"Get out of there!" we heard one of them call to the two Negro men sitting in the parked automobile.

"And get out with your hands in the air!" yelled the other. "You boys got corn in this car and we gonna find it tonight!"

"Well, what you standing there like dummies for?" the first officer continued. "You *have* got whisky, haven't you?"

"No, sir!" the Negroes cried, their arms high in the air.

"We'll see," the officer said as he and his partner started searching the car.

Watching from our vine-covered porch, it looked as if the policemen were trying to turn the automobile into something for a junk dealer's yard. Cushions were thrown in the street, tools were scattered about and we could hear boards being ripped from the floor, although it was already evident that the zealous enforcers of Birmingham's dry law were laboring in vain.

"We didn't get you tonight," one of them said, wiping the sweat from his face. "But we've had a tip on you boys and we'll catch you yet!"

The rare sight of two white men working so hard—and in vain—must have amused Shorty, the smaller of the two Negroes, and he giggled.

"So it tickles you, eh?" shouted one of the officers. "Well, laugh this off!"

There was a succession of thuds as the butt of the officer's revolver cracked against the little Negro's skull again and again. He raised his arms to ward off the blows, but they came too fast and with too much force. He fell and his body lay crumpled and still on the pavement as his friend stood helpless, his black hands high above his head.

"Guess that'll teach him not to be so smart the next time,"

laughed the other policeman as he walked over to the prostrate form and gave it a kick. The Negro groaned and the white men laughed louder.

I suddenly realized this was not a bad dream. Shorty was real and so were the two men standing over him, especially the one who had raised his foot again.

"You dirty dog!" I screamed, "you're kicking a man who's flat on his back!"

A hand was clasped over my mouth. "Shut up, you little simpleton!" Mama muttered. "Don't you know they could do the same thing to you and I couldn't do a thing about it?"

Shorty groaned again before I could grasp the full meaning of what my mother had said to me. She tried to block me but I ran around her, down the steps, and into the street where Shorty lay with his attackers towering over him. I could hear words coming out of my mouth but I was past fear. The officers peered at me for a second, then ordered Shorty's friend to "get" and he ran up the street.

The men were still laughing when they drove away. Suddenly, I saw that the street was in darkness except for the corner light. The porches were empty, front shades were drawn. Mama was behind the vines and my escort was leaning over the fence retching as he vomited out his fear. There was nobody in the street but Shorty and me.

At that moment words and phrases which had lurked in the nether regions of my consciousness took on meaning. I knew that Shorty and I were alone; nobody wanted anything to do with us at the moment. They would say we were "hotheaded," that we didn't "know our place." Shorty was only half-conscious, but for the first time in my life I knew who and what I was. Without Papa, Mama could no longer shield me and I knew what it must have cost her to stand by and see the veil snatched from my face. I was a Negro come of age! All my life I must have looked at things which I had refused to *see*. Now I both saw and understood.

My legs felt weak and I sat on the curb. I remembered the

boy whom I had first heard whisper "race riot." Soon after, I remembered, I saw Papa put a gun in the drawer of a table in the parlor. Then came the parade in the middle of the night. A Ku Klux Klan parade, they said.

I remembered how Mama took me out of bed and carried me to the parlor where I saw Papa, in his old-fashioned night shirt, standing by the front window. He was as still as a statue and his fists were clenched. There had been the clatter of horses' hooves as the light from a fiery cross held high by white-robed men on horseback flashed a warning of destruction to all Jews, Catholics, and Negroes. Papa had opened the table drawer. As the reflection from the burning cross lighted up our room, it glistened against the steel of the revolver in his hand. Mama tightened her grip on my arm but I broke away and pressed my nose against the windowpane, the better to see the men who rode white horses and carried fiery crosses. After the last clop-clop died away there was a long stillness.

As I sat there I thought about the time I had crawled in the back of Miss Sally B.'s limousine and sat beside her while Alphonse, the chauffeur, held the front door open.

"Leave her alone," Miss Sally B. had said, when Alphonse tried to force me to sit in front beside him. She must have been well aware that this fiery night would come and that soon enough I would learn that Negroes did not sit beside white ladies in Alabama.

I closed my eyes and saw again the frightened faces of Negro mothers when white men stalked through our neighborhood, jingling money in their pockets. Now I knew why schoolchildren shouted, "Yaller is roguish, but black is honest." I knew why they taunted me with "cat-eyes," why the boy in my class said, "Hey, you! Fox Tarry!" like a string of dirty words.

Shorty stirred, then dragged himself to the curb where he sat with his head between his knees. We had never spoken in our lives. Tonight there was no need for words.

"Why," I asked myself, "did I ever think I was needed in

Africa?" Alabama was my Africa! Catholic or Protestant, white, black, or yellow, whatever I was, was wrong. I wanted to hide. But there was no hiding place and nobody to tell me why. The world—it could not be God's world. It was the white man's world and I was not white.

chapter 5

MY FIRST MISSION

I was glad when the time came for me to go to State Normal at Montgomery. A relative I had never met before, Ollie Brown, who was a faculty member, welcomed me to the girls' dormitory. Two friends from I.H.S. were waiting for me and we talked long after the lights were out.

The last half of the summer session started the day after my arrival. The old campus at the corner of Thurmond, Jackson, and Tuscaloosa Streets boasted a modern girls' dormitory, a frame administration building, and one or two other wooden structures. Ollie Brown took me to the home of the president— one street behind the school—where I met President Trenholm's wife, Ellen Brown Trenholm, whose father had been my paternal grandmother's brother. The family resemblance was strong and I felt very much at home with this gentle kinswoman. She was reliving her own days as a pioneer in education for Negroes through the activities of a brilliant young son, Harper Council, already a teacher in the school his father headed.

Montgomery, known as the "Cradle of the Confederacy," was little different from Birmingham. Most of the Negroes that I knew or would have occasion to know were teachers, doctors, dentists, nurses, postal workers, or preachers. Here and there one met a successful dressmaker, barber, or a merchant like Victor Tulane, who had been a trustee at Tuskegee Institute and a friend of Booker T. Washington's as well as a good friend of Papa's. There were one or two other merchants but I remember

65

"Daddy" Tulane best, because he used to come to the campus and bring ice cream and fruit for my friends and me. Many of the Negroes I never met worked as domestics in the homes of the wealthy whites or eked out a living as manual laborers. Montgomery had a larger rural Negro population on its outskirts than Birmingham and I met many boys and girls—teachers-in-training—from "out in the country."

The news that I had become a Catholic had preceded me and I soon found that sides had already been taken. The day I enrolled someone elected to tell me that the Birmingham Board of Education would never appoint a Catholic. At the time I had no way of knowing that this was a rumor based on one anti-Catholic principal's statement. Regular Protestant devotional services were held on the campus and another self-elected informant told me that I would not be allowed to go out to attend Mass. President Trenholm soon cleared up the latter point, but some time passed before I was to learn that the first warning was without foundation.

Birmingham was unchanged when I returned. After my friends and classmates had received appointments to teach in the public schools, Cousin Mabel made arrangements for me to substitute the following year. At that time substitute teachers were hired at the discretion of the principal and with the exception of two who had said they would never hire a Catholic, most of them were Cousin Mabel's friends. Meanwhile, Father Walsh appointed me to teach at the Knights of Columbus Evening School for Adults.

Rose Bernard, a niece of Father Walsh's housekeeper, came up from Mobile to teach in our parochial school, and lived at the rectory. We became friends, and when Lena came home from Spellman Seminary that meant I had two Catholic girl friends in Birmingham and we enjoyed doing things together. Most of my weekends were spent at the rectory with Rose so I would not have to make the long trip across town to the South Side. Lena, Rose and I sang in the church choir and assisted Father Walsh in any way we could, but I was restless. We planned little parties,

read books that we could discuss, and went for long automobile
drives with young men; but I had lost the gaiety which had kept
a smile on my face for so many years.

In the midst of a party, I might hear a peal of lusty laughter
and at the same time remember Shorty and the white officers
who had laughed as they kicked him while he lay helpless in
the street. I felt ashamed because I had been unable to protect
him, and hurt because I knew Mama must have hated to admit
that if the officers had done the same to me she would have been
powerless to protect her own child. I could not understand how
all of the good people that I knew—Negro and white—could go
about smiling when they knew that things like Shorty's beating
happened every day. I wanted to do something about it—how
or what I did not know.

Father Walsh was one of the few who was aware of all of this.
On Saturday nights he would let Rose and me sit with him as
he had his dessert and coffee. He listened while I said over and
over again that I would never be content as long as my people
were mistreated. His answer was always;

"Changes will not be wrought overnight."

After a few months of this he suggested that we might try to
organize the Negro Catholics into a club.

"At least," the priest smiled, "you'll be on the right road and
you will no longer have the feeling that you are sitting on your
hands."

During months of substitute teaching, I worked in schools
throughout Birmingham and its suburbs. There were many
mornings when I left a trolley car and walked past a spacious
brick building which served as an elementary school for whites.
My school was usually an unpainted frame building where I
would find forty or fifty little brown boys and girls packed in a
room. Sometimes two classes shared one room and, with rare
exceptions, toilet facilities for pupils and teachers alike were
outdoors. So was the water fountain. Rooms were heated by old
pot-bellied coal stoves. Lunches were brought from home in
brown paper bags, although a few of the principals arranged for
selling sandwiches, milk, and candies during the time I was

teaching. Few of the children I taught had any conception of the world beyond the mountains which hemmed us in, but Mother Nature and youth combined to give them a joyousness of laughter and the spirit of adventure which has to suffer multiple wounds before it dies.

The pupils in my evening classes were elderly men and women who were illiterate. The only signature that any of them could put on the enrollment card was an X. Most of them were domestic servants whose shoulders and hands showed their years of hard labor. There was always an air of expectancy in the classroom which blotted out the odors of the kitchens in which they cooked, or the yards they tended. The children I taught by day came to school because they were sent; my adult pupils came because they wanted to learn to read and write. Their gratitude was often overwhelming and each time I was confronted with a truant youngster I thought of the old man who kissed my hand and cried the night he learned to recognize and shape the first letter of the alphabet.

Mama was sewing away one day in the home of one of her old customers, when the elderly Negro cook tiptoed into the room and closed the door.

"Miss Eula," she said, "there's a lady at the Catholic night school who's gonna teach me to write my name."

It was only after this feat had been accomplished that Mama told my pupil who I was. Fortunately, the old woman was a Methodist and Mama started taking her to St. Paul's. After a few Sundays she fell into the habit of coming to our house when church was over for special instruction. Near the end of the school year I noticed a great deal of whispering each night when I entered the classroom and one Sunday I asked the old lady what was wrong with my pupils. She looked relieved, though it was difficult for her to express herself.

"Miss Tarry," she said, twisting her handkerchief and looking out of the window, "all of us have learned how to sign our names. Now we want to learn how to write a letter. I got a nice family down below Mobile and my madame, she writes for me now and then, but it ain't like as if I could write myself. . . ."

From the kitchen I could hear Mama's voice. "Count your blessings," she sang as she prepared dinner, "Count your many blessings—Name them one by one ..."

"Please, ma'am," the old woman touched my arm, "don't be mad at us. We know you got to teach what they tell you. And we don't want to get you in no trouble with the white folks, but could you just *show* us how to write a letter?"

The next school night when I told the class what we were going to do, the old man who had cried over his first "A" said, "Amen!"

Some of the others laughed, but they all turned the pages of their composition books to a clean sheet and prepared for a first lesson in letter-writing.

My pupil from Mobile had a head start. Two Sundays after her first letter was posted she presented me with a gift. "That's for this," she said, pulling an envelope from her pocketbook. "It's from my chillun. They sent it by special delivery. My oldest girl got my letter first. Then she run down the road and showed it to the others. She said it was just like when somebody gets religion, they was all so happy, 'cause that was the first letter I ever wrote them in my life!"

"Somebody else," I thought, "will have to teach the Africans. I have my hands full in Alabama."

The following summer was not unusual. Rumors persisted as to why I had not received a regular appointment to teach in the public schools. Mama decided to go to a man who had been one of Papa's closest white friends. Dr. Henry Edmonds was an outstanding citizen and a respected clergyman.

The day after Mama asked Dr. Edmonds to intercede in my behalf, I was called to the office of the Board of Education. Dr. Edmonds was leaving Birmingham that afternoon but he telephoned from Terminal Station while I was being interviewed.

"I am sending her to Slater School," I heard the man before me say.

So I was going to teach in the elementary school I had attended as a child! Later, I was told it had been the general opinion that my association with white teachers at Rock Castle had disqualified me for work in the Birmingham schools.

"Now that I know who your parents are," my interviewer declared, "all I can say is if you are half the woman your mother is and if you possess the sterling qualities your father possessed, then I will be proud to think I appointed you.

"Remember," he reminded me, "you did not create the race problem and neither did I. But it is here, and it is here to stay. I want you to go back to Slater School and teach those little Negro boys and girls how to stay in their places and grow up to be good useful citizens. If you ever need a friend, don't hesitate to come to me."

As I looked into a pair of the bluest eyes I had ever seen, I knew the man spoke in sincerity. Neither of us was responsible for the chasm between but for a few moments we were united in the act of meeting our respective destinies. Though I have never spoken to him since, in my thoughts, he has always been my friend.

The family was waiting to hear the outcome of the interview. Cousin Mabel, who had personally supervised my appearance for the occasion, was impatient when I walked into the house without speaking.

"What's wrong with you? Didn't you get the job?" she asked.

"I'm going to teach the fourth grade at Slater," I said weakly. I couldn't tell Cousin Mabel how many people had told me I would never get the job because I was Catholic, or about the official who said I was too far "above" the pupils, or about the principal who told me he could get me a job if I would only be "nice" to him, then chased me all around a classroom when I let him know that our ideas about being "nice" differed—because I could not tell Cousin Mabel all these things, I sat down and cried.

The ice was broken. Lena, who had attended a Baptist school after she left Rock Castle, had already been appointed. And since then I have never heard a Birmingham teacher's religious affiliation mentioned in connection with job qualifications. Like the chiclets in the little lavender box that Papa used to bring home on Saturday nights, I would think this, too, was a dream had I myself not been the principal character involved.

It was not long after my appointment that I came home to find Nannie at our house. She was talking with Mama. I greeted her and started to leave the room without waiting for the answer I had long ago stopped expecting. "Wait a minute!" Nannie ordered. "Mabel told me that you're going to teach at Slater. Carol Hayes is a good principal and he will expect you to be a good teacher. Just don't be giving him any of your smart talk or he'll tell Mabel." The rift was healed. I accepted with a grateful heart.

chapter 6

A COLUMN IS BORN

The first class over which I presided at Slater was housed in half of one of a dozen or more wooden shacks separated from the main building; another teacher used the other half. These two-room shanties faced a huge foundry across the street and had once served as homes for the Negro foundry workers. When I was a child we called these houses "the quarters." Each structure housed two classes of forty to fifty pupils. On cold days when air seeped in from broken windows or loose boards faster than it could be heated by the coal stove, it was hard not to think about the red-brick building which housed the nearest elementary school for white children.

I had become accustomed to changing classes while working as a substitute. At Slater I had a class of my own for the first time and it promptly won my heart. For most of each day, five days each week, those little boys and girls were my children and I was their mother. My lack of pedagogical skill was offset by the love which flowed between teacher and pupils. The sincerity of their love was proven many times.

Slater was only two blocks from our house and there were still a number of large boys in the neighborhood who had roller-skated up and down Sixth Avenue with me. Most of them had stopped going to school, but they had no jobs to occupy their time and made a sport out of heckling me. At noon recess I would see them talking with youngsters outside my classroom. It was not unusual, after classes were resumed, for one of them

to stick his head in a window and yell; "I wouldn't let *her* tell
me what to do. She ain't nothing but a little girl, even if she is
as big as a woman."

They varied their messages from time to time but only a few
of my children laughed at them. Joseph was one of the few who
repeated the taunts these older boys yelled at me.

Joseph, an albino, was two or three years older than the rest
of his classmates. He sat nearest the window and so had the best
chance to talk to the hecklers. Joseph had more than the usual
dash of mischief in him, and even if he had been in the seat closest
to my desk, he probably would have been a daily culprit. I tried
various forms of discipline with the boy before I discovered that
he respected only physical force, and I knew I would have to use
corporal punishment, which was permitted at the time. The day
of the showdown Joseph was behaving atrociously. The children
nearest him looked in the opposite direction, and I pretended
to be unaware of his noisy antics. When it became impossible to
ignore him any longer I called him. He refused to budge. I was
trying to decide whether I should punish him or send him to the
principal's office when he walked up to my desk and dared me to
touch him. I raised my strap the exact instant Joseph jumped at
me. The children were still screaming, "Don't you hit Miss
Tarry!" when I saw the red welt on Joseph's pinkish-white skin
where the strap had hit him between one eye and his nose.

"I'm going to get my father!" The boy pushed me away when
I tried to examine the mark. "He's going to put you in jail!"

Joseph ran from the room with the children's wails following
him. I knew I should have reported the incident immediately
but I could not leave the class in a state of excitement. Remembering how they enjoyed singing, I started one of the tunes
they loved and we sang until they were quiet.

I was in the midst of a reading lesson when the principal came
in with Joseph and his father and asked me to leave the room.

As I stood outside on the porch, I heard the principal ask:
"Do you know this boy?"

"Yes, sir!" voices cried. "That's Joseph. He's a bad boy! He
tried to whip Miss Tarry. He jumped on her!"

Through the window I could see the raised hands of two or three dramatic youngsters who offered to re-enact the scene from which Joseph had emerged with the mark on his face. Others volunteered to tell about Joseph's past wrongdoings. They were telling the truth and I knew they were trying to save me from the jail Joseph had threatened. But he looked so defenseless with the whole class against him, that I felt sorry for the boy.

The principal reminded the father that the same law which forbade teachers to beat children unmercifully also prohibited children from "jumping on" their teachers. Joseph's father left the grounds upbraiding his son for unbecoming conduct and I tried to explain to my superior what had happened.

"Come to my office as soon as school is out," was all he said.

After the bell rang and the children went home, the teacher in the next room came in to find out what had happened.

"I wouldn't like to be in your shoes," she said as we walked over to the main building.

"I guess this is the time when I really need a friend," I said, and I told her about the man who had appointed me and how he had said I could always call on him.

I found the friend I needed in the conference which followed— and I also found the beginning of a new career.

The principal disposed of the Joseph incident with a terse: "You've got some nerve tackling these big boys. Send them to me —I'll take care of them!" Then he exposed all the classroom weaknesses which I had thought were known to me alone.

From a shelf nearby he gave me a book, *Pedagogical Pep*. The author must have written it especially for imaginative teachers like me who found teaching dull when they followed the course of study furnished them. Carol Hayes is now supervisor of Negro teachers in Birmingham. Over the years I have heard much praise and many criticisms of him, but every child I later taught is in his debt.

When Joseph returned to school the scar had disappeared. Both of us had learned a lesson. And each of us tried to make up to the other for what had happened. I allowed Joseph to run all my errands and he bossed each work detail. In return, he was humorously obedient and we became fast friends.

The book the principal had given me to read was a good starter. It was reassuring to learn that my natural talents were tools to work with that could make lessons interesting to pupil and teacher alike. My remaining problem was to find a way to overcome the lack of race pride which I had discovered in my children. Each time a white visitor came to the classroom I read the nervous fear in their eyes. Afterward, spitballs seemed to fly faster and little girls seemed more inclined to quarrel with their seatmates.

The space beyond Red Mountain on the edge of town was a void to my fourth graders and I longed to give them a glimpse of the big, confused world I myself was discovering. They were promoted before I could accomplish much, but I was a better teacher when they left me.

With the exception of one girl who had gone to New York and taken a business course, all of the young women who were my friends taught school. At that time, only a few younger men taught. The handful who remained in Birmingham were either professional men or laborers. A girl with a regular escort felt it her duty to invite one or two of her less fortunate friends to accompany them to the social events.

Between the Negro people I knew in Birmingham and the Negroes I did not know there was little, if any, intermingling. The parents of most of the children I taught worked in the coal mines and steel mills or as domestics for the white people on the Highland. Few of us realized then that we lived off the money we received for rendering services to people with whom we would have been reluctant to associate. Our contact with white people was as limited as our contact with the Negroes we refused to know socially. We knew only our white supervisor, the saleswomen in the stores where we shopped, and the neighborhood merchants. Most of the young women I knew had comfortable homes and if the shortage of men had not been so acute, they would have been content to spend their lives in Birmingham.

The membership of the club we had organized at the Catholic Church grew as several Catholic families from Mobile moved to Birmingham. When we gave our first benefit affair and handed Father Walsh the proceeds to pay his coal bill, he reminded me that this was the way "big oaks from tiny acorns grow."

A new social club had been organized, and I was one of the charter members. It was from the latter organization that I suffered my first defeat at the hands of the caste system which dominated Negro Birmingham at that time.

The club, organized as a junior auxiliary to a group of older women, was composed of young professional women who claimed to have dedicated themselves to the task of eradicating some of the cultural lacks in our community. This aim was in keeping with my own need to "do something," and I was happy in this association until the time arrived for our first formal dance. We were preparing the guest list, and Mary, my friend from I.H.S. and State Normal days, agreed to invite a local business woman whose generosity we had both enjoyed when we were in school. I presented the name of a woman caterer who had always helped out at our small parties. When the club informed us that we could not invite either of the women—because they were "different," not "our kind," "not in our social circle"—I fought long and hard, but the club voted against me and our two friends were blackballed. I was just as helpless as I had been the night Shorty was beaten.

At the beginning of the next school year I was assigned to a fifth grade. My classroom was still in "the quarters," but a row or two closer to the main building. During the first few days when they were still being eased back into classroom routine, I discovered that I had a group of exceptionally bright youngsters. Though they had little more conception of the world beyond than had the others, I heard a group of small girls talking about what they wanted to do when they grew up, and that was a step in the right direction. It was the boys who seemed less sure of themselves. I worried about them.

Among the Negroes I knew, there was an unwritten law which said girls had to be educated. Boys from large families were allowed to go to work after finishing high school. I knew of cases where these working brothers helped send their sisters through college. I also knew that this custom had produced a widening circle of young professional women who were perforce thrown in the company of unskilled laborers, and that many unstable marriages had resulted. It was frightening to think that the bright-eyed boys whose classroom lives were in my keeping might one day add to the human waste which was all around.

In search of a window through which my boys and girls might snatch glimpses of the world beyond Red Mountain, I scanned magazines, newspapers, and books for mention of any and all achievements by members of our race. I pin-pointed distant cities where Negroes had migrated to enjoy broader economic and cultural opportunities, and shared with my children whatever knowledge I had of a given community. I led my young charges afield by easy stages from the known to the unknown. A member of an old Birmingham family had become a soloist in one of Boston's largest white churches. A young woman from another well-known family had become a member of the Williams Jubilee Singers. To tour the country with a musical group and to sing in a big, white church in Boston seemed wonderful accomplishments to children who had never been outside Alabama.

Around this time, a Negro insurance company in Atlanta sent out a picture calendar called "Our Hall of Fame." Small photographs of Negroes who had made outstanding contributions to American culture adorned the top portion of the calendar. There were likenesses of such men as Crispus Attucks, Peter Salem, Benjamin Bannecker, Booker T. Washington, James Weldon Johnson, George Washington Carver, W. E. B. Du Bois, Benjamin Brawley, and John S. Hope. Miss Lizzie Thomas, who gave me the first book of poetry I ever owned, worked at the Booker T. Washington Branch Library with Mrs. Earline Driver and the two librarians spent many hours helping me find books

containing biographical material about these men. Then I wrote
my own version of their stories and told them to the children.

In the beginning it was hard for my fifth-graders to believe
that Crispus Attucks, the first hero of the Revolutionary War,
was a Negro. But this prepared them for the story about the next
Negro hero, Peter Salem, who fired the shot at Bunker Hill that
wounded the British officer, Major Pitcairn. I set the alarm on
our old Big Ben and let it go off when I told them about Benjamin Bannecker, who made the first such clock ever constructed
in America. The shoes on their feet came in for careful consideration after they learned that Jan Matzeliger, who built the first
shoe-lasting machine, was also a Negro. They knew enough
about Tuskegee Institute to appreciate the well-known story
about Booker T. Washington walking many weary miles from
his home in Franklin County, Virginia, to Hampton Institute
and being told to sweep a classroom as part of his first examination. They enjoyed eating pecans, sweet potatoes, and peanuts
enough to become excited over the many experiments a former
slave, Dr. Carver, had made with these food plants.

The sketches of these famous Negro lives formed the basis for
a series of lessons in reading, writing, spelling, and composition.
With the help of one of my boys who was artistic, an attractive
bulletin board was constructed on which the pupils' compositions
were displayed. Though I had suspected that my principal was
pleased with the project, I was sure of it when he started bringing visiting officials to my room. By the end of the year both
teacher and pupils were convinced that Negroes could rise above
the handicap of race.

Slater and Industrial High School were both crowded to the
danger point and a new building was constructed to house the
high school. Professor Parker and Miss Kennedy, who had
devoted a half century to the education of Negro boys and girls,
were proud of the new building which was later to carry the
name of A. H. Parker High School. Lincoln, a new elementary
school which occupied the old I.H.S. site, was created, and the
intermediate and upper grades at Slater were to be transferred

to Lincoln. When school closed and I read the assignments in the Birmingham News, I learned that I had been assigned to the new school. The principal was one of two who had said they would never hire a Catholic teacher.

I did not go to the new school and I never went back to the classroom as a teacher. We moved from Sixth Avenue to Enon Ridge and it was not long before the little old house fell apart leaving only my tree standing as a reminder that so many lives were nurtured on that tiny plot of land.

During this period personal affairs occupied much of my time but I was still searching for a way to make my seventh grade teacher's prediction come true, that I would be a writer. I wanted to communicate with the world—to cry out against the outrage of racial discrimination and its attendant ills. But I knew it meant taking up another cross, and I hesitated. I reread Booker T. Washington, and studied everything by and about James Weldon Johnson, Du Bois, and Brawley that I could find in our humble library. One of my chief sources of inspiration, I remember, was the folksy articles by Bruce Barton which appeared in Sunday supplements around the latter part of the 1920's.

The study of journalism, I thought, might be a steppingstone, with books to come later. I dreamed of going to New York and enrolling at Columbia University's Pulitzer School of Journalism. But I had to start somewhere and a correspondence course was the first step. Then I went to a local editor and showed him the sketches I had written for my pupils.

Guillermo Talliferro, who edited The Birmingham Truth, read my stories and hired me. The Truth served as an organ for the Knights of Pythias and the Court of Calanthes; with an assured source of revenue, Tally, as we called the editor, could afford to experiment. From week to week my assignments grew and I became a combination reporter-columnist-editorial writer. Tally pushed me until I finally managed to sell ads, too.

One of the time-hallowed lacks which has handicapped my people has been the dearth of knowledge concerning our race

in Africa and in the time shortly after we were brought to
America. In a small way, "Negroes of Note," as my column was
captioned, helped to fill this need. Years later I was criticized
for having written "in defense of being a Negro," but at the time
I was happy to do so. One of the peaks of this happiness was
reached when my former principal suggested that other teachers
might do well to use the material in my sketches for classroom
work.

The published works of young Negro writers like Claude
McKay, Countee Cullen, and Langston Hughes encouraged my
awakening ambition. I regretted that more Negro women were
not writing or being written about. There is no doubt this tiny
spark was fanned when I read the life of Harriet Tubman, a
runaway slave who went back into the land of bondage time
and time again to lead loved ones to freedom. Harriet's exploits
gave me courage to write the angry editorials about segregation
and discrimination which appeared in the *Truth* under my by-
line.

In the midst of the excitement of the national elections of
1928, Theodore Bilbo, then governor of Mississippi and the
ranking anti-Negro spokesman of America, came to Birmingham
to speak on behalf of Alfred E. Smith, the Democratic candidate
opposed by Herbert C. Hoover. Some weeks earlier, the *Truth*
had carried an editorial I had written concerning the hue and
cry raised by white-supremacists when Mr. Hoover, as Secretary
of Commerce, had abolished segregation in his Washington office.

On the night Bilbo addressed an audience in Birmingham's
Municipal Auditorium, a bridge game was in progress at our
house on Enon Ridge. Earlier in the evening we had joked about
what Bilbo would probably tell the white folk to do with the
Negroes. During our game I turned on the radio and tuned in
on the rally. My friends decided they did not like the sound of
the Mississippi governor's voice and I cut it off. About the time
we thought the rally was over—and my partner played the hand
—I turned the radio on again.

"... And she should be burned!" we heard a man scream. Applause, whistles, and cheers followed.

"That must be Bilbo," one of the bridge players said. "He's really working up a lynching party tonight."

Only one trick had been taken, when the telephone rang.

"Are you all right?" the caller asked. "We were worried about you."

"Why should you be worried about me?" I asked my friend.

"Didn't you hear Bilbo's speech?" she asked.

"Only the last few words," I replied. "We were playing bridge."

"I guess it's just as well," the friend laughed. "He read one of your editorials and said you should be burned. From the way the crowd cheered the suggestion, we thought there might be some trouble."

Cards were over for the night; the telephone rang constantly. Friends, enemies, and cranks called to ask if I was alive and well, or to warn me that I would soon be toasting over a bonfire. I was told that the governor from Mississippi had read the entire article "Mr. Hoover and Jim Crow," which I had written weeks before. I took from my files a copy of the editorial:

MR. HOOVER AND JIM CROW

Through the South (and probably elsewhere), there have appeared recently in many newspapers criticisms of Herbert Hoover in regard to his abolishment of segregation in the offices of the Department of Commerce at Washington, D.C.

They say he took this step to win the vote of the Negro. Well, what of it? Perhaps he did and perhaps he didn't. If he did, is this the first time a presidential candidate has "gone fishing" for votes?

The writer's knowledge of Mr. Hoover is limited, having been obtained from papers and magazines. So you see we could scarcely judge his actions.

But perhaps Herbert Hoover believes that the same God that made him made Booker T. Washington. Perhaps he knows that W. E. B. Du Bois is a scholar of whom all America should be proud. Perhaps when Herbert Hoover sees the flag of this great country swaying gently in the breezes, the red stripe reminds him of the blood Crispus Attucks shed that his flag might exist. Yes, perhaps that's why Hoover chased old "Jim Crow" out of the offices of the Department of Commerce.

Three cheers for Hoover (whether we vote for him or not) and three cheers for the National Association for the Advancement of Colored People!

Some of the protesters may succeed in ushering the old crow in again, but any way (using a line from our own Countee Cullen's *Black Majesty*), we know joy had a day once and a clime!

The thing that seems to cause them so much anguish is that many of these workers (in the Department of Commerce) are white girls and they will have to work in the same rooms with our colored men.

No doubt they feel as do many of our black mothers down here in Dixie when they have to see their daughters take employment in some white doctor's office to help earn a livelihood knowing that white supremacy reigns.

They seem to become enraged over the idea of colored men being near their young women. Of course we get the inference. The poor fish, that's all a lot of bunk.

Why should their women's cold blonde charms so affect our brown men when our brown women's warm loveliness is so great as to even attract many of them.

And if it's the white skin they think our men crave, they (our men) have not to leave the colored race for that, especially down here in my own Dixie. Certain practices dating from the beginning of slavery produced these!

Perhaps Hoover knows all this!

That night as I read the article aloud none of us could understand why it had aroused so much ire in the statesman. Later, I realized I had touched his most vulnerable spot. The lone male in our party was a member of the family who set great store by a collection of firearms he had gathered through the years.

"Guess I had better grease the guns up," he laughed as he took one of them out. "I'll shoot the first white _____ who puts his foot on that top step."

The only concession we made to Bilbo's threat was to pull the shades. We waited until morning, but nobody came. I was not at the age to be fearful and my only regret was that Mama was disturbed by the incident. However, she took great comfort from the fact that her white friends had assured her she could count on them for help if the family was in danger.

"I've spent most of my life in Birmingham," she complained, "and I was never mixed up in any *mess* like this before."

Tally, the editor of the *Truth*, was as happy as Mama was unhappy. A veteran of Mexican revolutions, he had long been bored with the safety of the sanctuary which Birmingham afforded him. The thrill of knowing that we had aroused the ire of a confirmed white-supremacist, plus the increased circulation which the *Truth* enjoyed, put him in an encouraging frame of mind.

"As long as you can write editorials like that"—Tally patted his bay window—"I can print them. They can't scare me!"

Bit by bit the small reforms I advocated in the *Truth* came to pass. A cemetery where the older Negro families buried their dead and which had been allowed to reach a horrible stage of neglect was cleaned up. My clubs scheduled more book reviews, and more attention was given to Negro history. With each little victory, I became more aware of what I might be doing if only I were better prepared. I argued with myself; I prayed and thought of all that needed to be done. I could see and feel the lethargy which enslaved my people just as much as the unfair laws which gave them second-class citizenship. Even after I had sent for a catalogue and knew I could meet the requirements for admission to Columbia's Pulitzer School of Journalism, I was not sure how I would live if I left home. My only asset was a diamond ring which I could pawn, and I had a fear of being alone and hungry in a strange city.

The night I made the decision to leave Birmingham I was sitting on the front porch looking out over the lights of the city in the valley below. The moon was full and all the stars were out. The radio, just inside the window, was playing and Rudy Vallee was singing;

> "... Look down, look down
> that lonely road
> Before you travel on...."

The magnitude of the heavens assured me and I decided that somewhere in such a vast and beautiful universe I would be sure to find my niche.

chapter 7

NEW YORK

The New York-bound train jerked to a stop at the crossing opposite Sloss-Sheffield's foundry. The only other occupant of the Jim-Crow coach with its musty plush seats and dirty spittoons was a man who had gone into the smoker. I thought of all the times I had stood at the top of the mountain and watched the sky steal an orange glow from the rivers of molten lead which ran in and out of troughs at this foundry. Overhead was a bridge where we usually stopped the car to give visitors a closer view of the thrilling spectacle, and of the men who worked this industrial magic, their goggled eyes and half-naked bodies filling out the picture. This, I knew, was part of my way of life. Shorty was, too. So was the *Truth,* my church, Mama, Nannie, the children, and Cousin Mabel. So was Woodlawn Cemetery, where White Mama and Papa were buried.

"There's still time," I thought as I stood up, "to grab my bags and get off this train. I'll run back to the station and tell my friends that I'm not leaving. I'll not run away. I'm going to stay right here where I belong and fight!"

Someone honked the horn of an automobile. I ran from one window to the other. Long lines of cars were parked on either side of the train. I remembered all the times I had waited— impatient to be on my way—blowing the horn when the driver in front was slow to start after the train pulled away. A few hours earlier I had passed this same spot on my way to pick up a friend who was supposed to accompany me on this trip, only to find her dangerously ill and unable to travel.

I tried to move my suitcase but it was too heavy, and I was alone. Soon I would really be alone, for though the trip was to be broken by a visit at Rock Castle and Belmead, New York was my destination. Then I would be a thousand miles from all these things and all of the people who mattered most to me.

A dining car waiter who lived in Birmingham came through the coach. "You're traveling in style," he said. "Got a whole car to yourself. Anything wrong?"

"No," I lied, "nothing's wrong. I—I was trying to arrange my baggage. Would you push the big one back, please?"

The train started again and I knew, as I sank down on the seat, that there was no turning back.

It was a sultry August afternoon when friends met me at Union Station in Washington, and drove me around the city. Late that afternoon we went to a Marine Band concert given on the steps of the Capitol. When the white-uniformed marines played the familiar "Stars and Stripes Forever," I looked up at the red and blue of the flag. Crashing cymbals cut through the dusk, which was settling around us. Then somebody pushed a button and there was light where there had been near darkness. The band played "The Star-Spangled Banner," and I understood for the first time how the old women at Mama's church felt when they shouted. I was happy and I wanted to shout, too. Geographical boundaries were ignored. To me, this was the right side of the Mason-Dixon line.

"I'm free! I'm free!" I kept whispering to my friends, who could not understand my reaction to anything so commonplace as a Marine Band concert on the steps of the Capitol at lamp-lighting time. They all looked relieved when they put me on an excursion train for New York the following night.

August 11 is always a day of sober reflection and quiet celebration for me. It was on that day in 1929 that I finally crossed the Hudson River on a ferry, took a subway train to Lenox Avenue and 145th Street, then rode a trolley over to St. Nicholas Avenue.

From the one window in the room which my classmate had found for me, the buildings looked as gray as the sky above. New York had temporarily lost its enchantment.

The next day I counted the few dollars in my pocketbook and went out to find a job.

Glancing backward, I remember that nothing in New York seemed familiar. In Alabama we had already begun to feel the pinch of tight money, which we always expected during a Republican administration. In New York everybody seemed to be enjoying prosperity. Every third woman I talked with had two jobs and two men paying court. It was the latter circumstance which caused me to write Mama and tell her that New York was so wicked I was afraid God would destroy the city. The contempt with which so many New Yorkers spoke of Alabama worried me and I became angry when people complimented me on a dress and said, "Don't tell me you got *that* in Alabama. I didn't know they sold dresses like that down there."

I accepted the fact that I had an accent, since everybody talked or laughed about it. But it was more than the accent that got me into trouble at the corner grocery store. The clerks said they did not know I wanted white bread when I asked for "light bread." My requests for sweet milk and white meat required explanations also, but it was only after I asked a red-haired clerk named Pat for five pounds of Irish potatoes that I decided to check my lists with Mother Ysaguirre, with whom I roomed, before I went shopping. After overcoming these petty irritations, the two New York customs I found hardest to accept were the pew rent boxes at the doors of Catholic churches where a coin was dropped before entering and the men who remained seated on public vehicles while women stood. Years later I conceded that both were logical and practical.

I had never looked for a job before in my life and now that I was actually on my own the prospects were bewildering. I spoke to the people with whom I lived and to a classmate who lived upstairs in the same apartment building and they suggested that I look in the help-wanted ads. But most of the ads for young women wanted young white women and the others were for "settled or mature Negro" women to cook, nurse, or keep house. I saw one or two for a "Light colored girl to keep a small bachelor apartment. Work pleasant," but my friends said I would not like that kind of job. Wherever I went people laughed at my accent and I began to wonder why I ever had come to New York. The prospect of going to school was not enough to cancel out my disappointment.

My classmate told me to stop asking people what they did for a living. The musicians I met and the pretty girls I saw on the street late at night who, I was told, were show girls seemed to be the only Negroes I knew who were proud of their jobs.

I went to the stores on 125th Street, the shopping center for Harlem, but all of the salesgirls were white. And I did not see any Negroes working in the department stores downtown.

I rode on the subway and sat wherever I wanted. I ate in restaurants and drank sodas at the lunch counters downtown, too. I did not see any signs saying "colored" or "white" but a few days after I came to New York I learned that these signs were stamped on the minds of many of the men concerned with employment. For the first time in my life I was thrown into contact with "working people" and I began to suspect that most of the professional people I knew would have felt just as lost as I did. My friends did not encourage me to go to any of the Negro papers. They said I would never make any money that way and I knew I had to have money to live and to go to school.

Gladys Hunter, who stood with me when I was baptized, was teaching in one of the Harlem schools conducted by the Sisters of the Blessed Sacrament. During her vacations Gladys worked for one of the large chain restaurants. My money was gone and Gladys suggested that I take a job as a waitress at a Barclay Street store. My rent was due and though I wondered what the people in Birmingham would have said if they had known, I had no alternative. I kept reminding myself that Mama often said, "Honest labor is no disgrace."

It was difficult for me to understand the curt chatter of the customers and more difficult for them to understand my relaxed drawl. I never laughed at them, though many of them made no attempt to conceal their amusement when I spoke. I had never seen so many people rushing around as poured in and out of the store during lunchtime. I moved slowly and it took me a few days to understand that fewer customers meant fewer tips.

My feet became tender and swollen from long hours of standing and I had to go to bed each evening as soon as I got home. Each time I counted my daily tips I was reminded that it would take me a long, long time to save the $1,057 which the information bulletin listed as the minimum estimate of expenses for one year of journalism at Columbia. Two weeks of supporting myself in New York forced me to concede defeat. I knew I would have to wait another year before I registered for the course that had lured me to New York.

My expenses seemed exorbitant, but this was because my earnings were so meager. Lucille had secured a room for me with a family from Honduras, who had only been in New York a few years. The older brother, Bobby Ysaguirre, a musician, was seldom home, and his sister, Florence, ran the household. Mother Ysaguirre was a Carib Indian whose children had been fathered by a Spaniard who spoke "real Castile." Her two grandchildren, Doris and Constance, supplied the homelike atmosphere to which I was accustomed.

It was Mother Ysaguirre who bathed my swollen feet each night and showed me how to stretch the few dollars I brought home. Though her English was broken and mine was Alabama-grown we had no difficulty understanding each other. She introduced me to tropical foods which were cheap and filling, and initiated me into the art of bargaining with shopkeepers.

Flo, as they called her daughter, was an excellent pianist and life in the six-room apartment revolved around the grand piano which almost filled the living room. I usually sang to Flo's accompaniment. It was not long before we had an audience of young men who came visiting.

I soon learned that courtship in New York was different from courtship in Alabama. With the exception of Bill, who lived nearby, the young men made no attempt to hide their ultimate intentions, which did not include marriage. But I was twenty years old, weighed 118 lbs., and felt equal to the occasion.

I was fascinated by the beautifully dressed women I saw on the streets of New York. The waitresses with whom I worked only averaged a few dollars more than I brought home, but they dressed even more expensively than older teachers I had known in Birmingham, who had unlimited credit. After I paid carfare and room rent, and bought food each week, I despaired of ever having enough money to buy a dress. I was curious about how other self-supporting women managed and instead of asking one of them, I admitted my curiosity to a young man whom I had many reasons to trust. He was also a Southerner and one of the few Catholic men I knew.

"Most of them have help." He laughed in a way I did not understand then. He went on to tell me that most women in New York could dress well because they lived with their families, were married, or had some other source of income.

"There must be other women in New York like me," I persisted.

"That gives me an idea," he looked at me closely. "I may have something good for you."

"A good job?" I jumped at the suggestion. "What is it? What do I have to do?"

"You just wait. I'll have to talk it over with someone, but I'll let you know in a few days," he promised.

I told Mother Ysaguirre and Flo about the "good job" I was expecting and walked around in a state of expectation. It was the next weekend before my friend called. Everything was arranged, he said, so we were to celebrate my good luck by going to dinner and the theater. All the time we were downtown, my friend was vague about the details of my new job. He said he would give me the name of the woman I was to call when we got home. I asked about the nature of my duties but he said she would tell me everything, including how much money I would make. We were standing at the Ysaguirres' door when he said what he must have been trying to tell me all night. Even so, I must admit that he picked his words carefully when he told me about the blond, blue-eyed girl he was engaged to and that she had a benefactor who was a wealthy white broker. The broker had a business associate who wanted a girl, too. "Someone like you, you can pass," he said. "And who knows how to keep her mouth shut."

My feet were hurting, anyway, so all I had to do was pull off one shoe and advance on my unsuspecting friend, who had made such a fool of me. He also made good time down the four flights of steps.

Only Negro waitresses were employed in the restaurant where I worked. I was the youngest in the group and they knew all the tricks of getting the best stations and the best customers. The lunch hour, when the surrounding buildings dumped many of their occupants into our store, was the busiest time. Though my "Yes, ma'am," and "No, sir," made most of the customers laugh, my speech was also a mark of distinction. Within a few weeks I had built up a following of the more leisurely customers—all male. Even so, I never felt comfortable when they called me "Honey Chile" or greeted me with "How're yo'all today?"

My cousin, Edward Hutchinson, was finishing his course at Meharry Medical College in Nashville, and had been working in and out of New York that summer. He came to see me and told me that money was "getting tight" everywhere. I did not pay much attention to what he said until September 26, my birthday, when we heard the first serious talk about the Wall Street market. My customers seemed more preoccupied at each meal and my tips suffered. Then came the day in October when the newsboys on the streets shouted: "Extra! Read all about the Wall Street CRASH!"

For the next few days, nobody joked with me when they came in the store. Groups of men bunched around tables and ordered extra coffee. They sat and smoked longer than usual but they left smaller tips. A week or two passed and I was forced to start looking for another job.

Bill worked at the College Station branch post office around the corner from my St. Nicholas Avenue address. During World War I, Bill had lied about his age in order to enlist and when I met him in 1929 he was still saving money to go back to medical school. He and Sam, another cousin, had an apartment on Bradhurst Avenue. A young woman around my age, who was distantly related to Bill and Sam, kept house for them. Just before I met him Bill had been jilted by a girl he loved and from the start our conversation turned to books and our respective ambitions. After I met Bill's family, most of my Sundays were spent at their apartment in an easy chair with the books Bill lent me on a table at my elbow. I would go straight to their house after I left Mass at St. Charles' and breakfast was always waiting.

Bill and his family tried to be helpful when I started looking for another job. Sam read through the help-wanted sections and marked the jobs he thought would be of interest to me. Invariably, these ads stated that only white or American females need apply. Sam and Bill spent long anxious hours telling me that I was "American" and there was nothing wrong about my answering an ad for a "young white woman" because I was young and my skin was white. They lost patience when I said I did not want to sail under false colors and I felt hurt because they did not understand.

I continued to write "Negro" in the space on job applications opposite "nationality." I became accustomed to the change in expressions when interviewers saw the word Negro. Smiles froze and receptions which had been cordial became curt. Then came the stock reply: "We don't have anything today, but we'll keep your application on file," or "We will get in touch with you as soon as there's a vacancy."

Flo, who was an elevator operator in one of New York's oldest department stores, knew I was broke and she got me a job where she worked. The elevator girls were much more congenial than

the waitresses and when Bill invited me to my first formal dance
in New York, they shopped all over the store to make sure I was
correctly dressed for the occasion. Flo did not tell me until the
day we found the blue satin gown I finally selected that this
party would be the first affair Bill had attended since his girl
friend married. I could not afford evening slippers and one of
the girls lent a pair of hers. I wore a triple A and my friend's
slippers were C width, but they had to serve the purpose. Before
I left the store, the girls insisted that I let them see how the
evening dress looked on me and I became alarmed over its low
cut. Mama had warned me not to pull off my knit undershirt
during cold weather. She said she knew too many people who
had "gone into the decline" as a result of not wearing enough
clothes after changing climates.

The night of the affair, Mother Ysaguirre solved this problem
by massaging my arms and shoulders with alcohol, assuring me
that I would not catch cold. I made my New York debut at the
old New Star Casino.

Monotony is one of the evils that dog an operator on a bank
of slow electric elevators. Most of the customers knew that a
clause in the founder's will had stipulated that only Negro men
and women should be employed as elevator operators in the
store. On slow days when the up and down motion of the
elevator was lulling me to sleep, some customer usually pulled
me out of my lethargy by asking, "Who was white? Your mother
or your father?" In the beginning, I tried to explain my parentage, even when some frustrated bargain hunter said, "Did your
father and mother really get married?"

The girls who came to relieve me heard one or two of these
quiz sessions and gave me some sound advice. They told me that
when the next customer asked "Who was white?" I should say:
"My mother." At least that answer made them catch their
breath, though many of them could not resist the urge to ask
me the name of the shop where I got my permanent wave. I resented that more than the inquiries about my parentage, because
all my life I had been trying to brush the waves out of my hair

and they had persisted in spite of the hair tonic and water I used to try and get rid of them.

Most of the Rock Castle girls I met in New York had married. After Gladys Hunter added Brauer to her name and moved to Long Island I felt more alone than ever. My friend who lived over the Ysaguirres was a nurse and she was busy most of the time. Though Flo introduced me to her friends they were new and untried. Near me lived, I knew, Beatrice Walker, who had shared that wonderful December 8 in Rock Castle with me, but after I left the elevated train which brought me uptown each night I was so weary I kept postponing the visit I had planned to Bea's home. I had only seen her once on the street; she was so beautiful she reminded me of a brown velvet rose tinged with red. So I promised myself I would stop by her apartment the next Sunday on the way home from Mass.

But I never got to see her. A few nights after I made myself the promise I found a note stuck under my door. Beatrice Walker had been found dead. Another Rock Castle girl wrote that all of the gas jets were on when they found her, but she had set her canary outside the door of her apartment before she lay down.

Death has a way of suggesting an inventory, and I had to face the fact I could expect to be laid off any day. Already there had been cuts and we had heard that only a skeleton staff would be retained. Almost every night, Mother Ysaguirre told us about someone in the building who had lost a job.

People who had never "taken in roomers" began letting it be known that they had a vacant room. As men lost their jobs mothers who had been staying home found part-time work as house maids. I heard a lot of talk about the Negro being "the last to be hired and the first to be fired." Yet I was surprised at first that suicides were much more common among the whites until I realized that my people were used to hard times and that they were experienced in finding ways to dispel the fear, in "laughing to keep from crying." When I mentioned the fact that I had heard of not a single wedding or funeral, other than Bea's, a friend told me that few Negroes had enough money to get married and caskets were too expensive for them to consider dying.

Though the Ysaguirres treated me like a member of the family, I did not want to impose on their generosity. The school year was coming to a close and it looked as if another year would come and go before I could register. I had no energy for writing, and I was bored with the Saturday night parties my friends gave because I was the only one who had to go out to church the next morning. When I received the notice of dismissal I was not too sad because I knew I needed a new job and new interests. And I never worried too much until the last dollar was broken.

Jobs for Negroes were few and hard to find during the summer of 1930 and I seemed to have a talent for arriving on the spot just as the "No Help Wanted" sign was hung out. But among the memories of these uncertain days of employment agency lines, hot-dog stands, and apples that I bought from men who stood on corners singing "Brother, Can You Spare a Dime?" are also little acts of human kindness from unexpected sources.

There was a tiny luncheonette on 145th Street at Bradhurst Avenue. After a disappointing day of job hunting I would stumble down the steps of the El station on Eighth Avenue and walk one block west to get my evening meal. When there was only one nickel left I had to decide between a hot dog or a glass of milk. The West Indian girl who served as waitress and short-order cook was lacking in the social graces, but she was an expert at judging human nature. She watched me grow shabbier and hungrier each day as we grew friendlier. Each morning she would save me a paper that someone had left on the counter. She insisted that I eat even when I tried to tell her I did not have money for the morning toast or evening frankfurter and dismissed my protests with a frown so that she could serve a paying customer. Each time she fed me I remembered that if we both were living in Birmingham I would not have been allowed to invite her to my club's formal dance.

One morning she shoved a paper at me. It was folded to the "Help Wanted" page and she had marked an ad for a governess. No racial or religious stipulations were included. "That one is made to order for you," she laughed, "providing you tell them what they ask and nothing more."

She was right. From the information given in the ad it certainly seemed I had the necessary qualifications for the governess job. I was glad of the Riverside Drive address because I could save a nickel by walking to the interview.

I was greeted by a pleasant, youngish-looking woman with snow-white hair. I could tell she was impressed when I told her about my teaching experience and my newspaper work. Then she told me that her child, a girl of twelve, had received a brain injury at birth. She was unable to take care of any of her body needs and required constant care, which meant the governess had to sleep in the room with her. The child was also given to seizures or fits and whoever cared for her had to know what to do in these emergencies. It was a grim picture, but I was broke, my rent was due, and there was a piece of cardboard over the hole in one of my shoes. When the mother asked if I would take the job, I remembered what the waitress had said and agreed to do so before the woman had a chance to ask about my race. She assured me that her husband would abide by her decision.

I missed the Ysaguirres, and there were many unpleasant aspects to the job, but these were forgotten when payday came. I wrote Mama and told her about my young charge and the sorrow the child's condition had caused the parents. I told her that they had not been the least concerned about my racial background and mentioned how I had felt one day when a black woman sat near us on a park bench and the child started screaming because she said she was afraid the black would rub off on her. I insisted, however, that I was going to grit my teeth and stick it out because any Negro who had a job was lucky and I was so sorry for the mother. I put the letter on a chest of drawers I was using, intending to take it to the corner mailbox as soon as the child was asleep. The mother came in the room while I was busy and offered to mail the letter when she went to get a paper.

Two days later the woman came to me in tears. "My husband's business is so bad," she said. "I will have to let you go at the end of next week. You've been such a help I don't know what I will do without you, but I'll write you a good reference."

When I returned to the Ysaguirres I found a letter from Mama. She was pleased that I had a job where I could be of service, but cautioned me about not properly sealing my letters. I realized then that my employers had opened the letter I wrote my mother.

The next ad I answered was another one for a governess. It was placed by one of the few Wall Street brokers who was not broke by that time. He asked me to come in for an interview in his office. A clerk took my name and address as soon as I entered the expensively furnished suite. I was the first of six or seven applicants. The others were all well-dressed, poised white women who sat around the room smoking and reading magazines as though they were waiting for a showing of the latest Parisian fashions.

"This is just a waste of my time, he'll never take me," I thought and was trying to think up an excuse to leave the room when an inner door opened and a red-faced man of medium height with an unruly shock of auburn hair walked out. The clerk handed him the paper with our names on it and pointed out each applicant. He worked from the bottom of the list and I was the last one to be called to the inner office. He stood when I entered the room and motioned me to a chair.

"I could have let all the others go without talking to them," the man said, "because when I looked out there in that room I knew you were the only one who was young enough to get down on the floor with this rough kid of mine." He pointed to a handsomely framed picture of a robust baby boy.

I was so excited I just shook my head when he offered me a cigarette and lighted a cigar for himself as he told me all about his son and what an exceptionally smart and active child he was at the advanced age of two years. "He's talking already and I want you to start teaching him at once. What do you think?" he asked.

I explained that I had taught fourth and fifth grades and that my experience with two-year-olds had been limited. "But I'll do my best," I promised.

Salary, working hours, and conditions were settled, and I was getting happier by the second when my new employer made an admission. "You know," he leaned over and spoke softly as he looked in the direction of the clerk who was visible through the open door, "when you talked with me over the telephone you sounded like a darky."

"A darky?"

"Yes, all of you Southerners do. Particularly the ones from Alabama. Take Tom Heflin, for instance. He sounds just like my darky cook. I knew another man from Alabama once . . ." He went on and on.

I thought about all that Bill and his family had told me. I tried to keep my mouth shut, as my waitress friend said I should. My eyes never left the face of the man before me, but in my mind I was appraising a weekly pay check, a summer in Long Beach rolling on the sand with the baby whose picture rested on the desk, then a comfortable winter in a Park Avenue apartment with a warm coat, warm gloves, and shoes without cardboard over the holes. I even saw a bank account on which I would write the check which would enable me to go back to school.

When my daydream ended, he was saying, "With all their faults, you have to admit the darkies are loyal, though. Now take our cook . . ."

"I'm afraid you have made a mistake," I spoke quietly. "I *am* a Negro. You did not ask or I would have told you."

"You—you can't be!" he insisted as he left his chair and closed the door. "You just can't be! Look," he pulled back his sleeve baring a portion of his arm. "You are whiter than I am."

"I'm fairer than you, but I am still a Negro. Does it make that much difference?"

"Well, now," he began, "I'll have to take that up with my wife. Don't think I don't like the darkies, er, the Negroes. They are fine people! We treat our cook just like one of the family. It's just that we never thought of having a Negro governess for my son. But you leave it to me. I'll discuss the matter with my wife tonight and call you the first thing in the morning. I'm sure it will be all right. You'll hear from me tomorrow morning!" he called as I walked through the outer door, knowing he would not call.

I took the El to 145th Street, thinking I might sit on one of the benches on Edgecombe Avenue until I felt like facing the Ysaguirres. As I walked the block between Bradhurst and Edgecombe an elderly white woman approached me.

"Isn't it beautiful up there?" She pointed toward upper Edgecombe Avenue and the rows of apartment houses high on the hill overlooking the park. "I used to live there. It was even more beautiful then. But that was before the niggers came. They've ruined everything."

"It may interest you to know"—I advanced on my whipping boy—"that you are talking about me and my mother and my sisters and my father and my grandmother!" I screamed.

The woman ran up the hill toward St. Nicholas Avenue; a crowd of people quickly gathered around me.

"What happened? Did she try to rob you?" asked one of the men who had eaten with me at the luncheonette down the street.

"Nothing. It was nothing," I answered as the people looked at me in astonishment. "I'm just tired of looking at the promised land and then getting pushed away."

chapter 8

SUGAR HILL

A picture-ad in a subway train was responsible
for my next job. Once I had mastered the art of getting on and
off the right train at the right station, I fell into the habit of
entertaining myself enroute by reading the ads above the heads
of the passengers and selecting the merchandise I was going to
buy once I had enough money to go on a shopping spree. One
of the ads pulled me into a drugstore. It showed a beautiful
blonde girl combing tresses that sparkled with high lights. The
caption advised readers: "Use _____ Hair Wash and Bring Back
the Beauty of Youth." This struck a responsive note because the
hair tonic and water I used to try to keep my hair from being
curly had caused it to darken. I didn't look like the "Fox Tarry"
the boys at Slater used to tease. With everything else strange and
unfamiliar, I wanted to look like myself. So, the night before
I was to be interviewed for another job, I bought the advertised
product, washed my hair with it, and went to bed. When I looked
in the mirror the next morning I was a blonde.

After the first few moments of panic, I read the directions and
discovered the "wash" was a bleach and I had used it as an
ordinary shampoo. I ran to a little beauty shop near the corner
of 145th Street and St. Nicholas Avenue, but the beautician,
whose name was Teresa, insisted that all she could do was even
the various shades of blonde hair I had produced. Nobody in
the shop understood my agitation and Teresa asked me if I
didn't know that "gentlemen prefer blondes." I explained that

I was concerned about the job I needed instead of the "gentle-men."

That afternoon I got the job as an attendant in a white down-town club. The manager of the place, a round-faced, heavy-set man who wore rimless nose glasses, said he had another blonde girl working for him and we would make a good pair.

The beautician was right; the gentlemen I met did prefer blondes. My tips at the club were sufficient to care for my daily needs, there was always somewhere to go before or after work, and my daily bread ceased to be a problem. Once in awhile I stopped by the luncheonette to see my West Indian waitress friend, but I didn't eat her hot dogs any more.

"I'm used to this," she laughed. "I've seen them blossom out before. I'm glad you are doing so well—even if I have lost a customer."

I was weighing the idea of looking for a small apartment when Mama wrote about Ida Mae. Always a rebel, my second sister had announced that she did not intend to teach. She wanted to be a nurse. Ranking members of our matriarchal clan had vetoed Ida Mae's plans and nobody was sure what was going to happen. I remembered my promise to Papa and before the week was over arrangements had been made for my sister to leave Alabama State, where she was still in school, and join me.

Ida Mae arrived in time to be part of my second Christmas in New York City. The Ysaguirre apartment was not large enough to accommodate my new "family," and we parted with sincere regrets.

When I rented a room from one of the girls with whom I worked, I felt like a real woman of the world. It thrilled me to watch my sister, who had turned sixteen the past spring, glow with the excitement of seeing New York for the first time. Her red hair and sea-blue eyes attracted attention wherever we went and it was a pleasure to go in the shops along Broadway and buy her some of the small things I had so longed for when I first came to New York.

Ida Mae got a job in a clothing manufacturer's showrooms two days after she arrived. To my younger sister it meant only that she had come to New York and gotten a job. To me, it was a miracle.

Between spurts of apartment-hunting, I met a lot of young men who enjoyed showing the bright lights to a "country girl." My sister was not included in these night-life excursions, but she never complained. She understood that I was trying to protect her. As I made new acquaintances I saw less of Bill, since he never went out during the week and spent most of his Sundays studying.

Someone always seemed to be calling me to join a party of visiting dignitaries. I often think of one such group who came over from Philadelphia and Washington. I joined the party after work and we went to the Cotton Club on upper Lenox Avenue. The doorman told us there were no seats available, but the men said we would have been admitted if they had been white. Then we drove down to Connie's Inn on Seventh Avenue near the old Lafayette Theater building and were turned away again. After that we went to Small's Paradise and wound up at a smoky basement club on one of Harlem's side streets. One of the men in the party was a judge and I always remembered that he said Harlem and Africa were just alike: the Africans no longer controlled Africa and the people of Harlem were no longer free to go where they chose in Harlem. They had been teasing me about Alabama, so I reminded them that at least we knew where we could or could not go in my home town.

The Harlem speak-easy seemed most in keeping with the exciting things I had heard about the community in which I now lived. A soft-spoken musician who fell into the habit of accompanying me uptown each night after work introduced me to his family one night and to my first speak-easy the next. It was the Golden Grill, on the corner of 145th Street and St. Nicholas Avenue, where my companion rang a bell and said magic words that opened the door. There were soft lights and tables in the secluded back room. My friend ordered sherry and dropped a few coins in the record machine so that we could have music. The waiter said it was a slow night. We had the place to ourselves

and just sat and talked. The walls were mirrored and suddenly I saw myself sitting with elbows on the table, my chin
resting on the back of laced fingers, looking, I decided, just like
a movie siren. But the next day when I awoke with tom-toms
pounding inside my head I knew I was not really the speak-easy
type.

The girls with whom I worked had most of their social life
after working hours, too. Their escorts, who sometimes were the
patrons we had served, waited outside the club and there was
always a lot of curiosity as to who was meeting whom. Nobody
ever called for me but the young musician, and I was surprised
the night one of the girls asked me if I cared to ride uptown
with two friends of hers. That was how I met Johnny Yates and
his friend, Ray. They later introduced me to Johnny's brother,
Ted, a journalist who was writing for a publication called *The
Tattler*. The Yates brothers adopted me, and because of our
mutual interest in journalism, Ted and I formed a partnership
which still exists. Johnny, a mortician and popular man about
town, filled the role of adviser, and Ray became an on-again-off-
again escort. There were times when I resented the dubious
protection with which Ted and Ray insisted on surrounding me,
while Johnny sat back and watched, but I know now that they
did give me a wonderfully secure feeling.

I knew that my sister needed companions of her own age.
When we had an opportunity to move into the home of a
Birmingham friend who had an apartment on top of Sugar Hill
at 409 Edgecombe Avenue, I made the change. Edith Cook and
her husband, J. Lawrence, an arranger for the Q.R.S. Music
Company, encouraged Ida Mae to bring her friends to the house
and there was a lively bunch of youngsters in the neighborhood.
Ida Mae became friendly with two girls who were going to
Hunter College and I hoped these associations would encourage
her to go back to school.

Even though the depression made obvious inroads there was
an undercurrent of gaiety in Harlem which was a carry-over from
that period during the twenties so often described as the "Negro
Renaissance."

On Sunday afternoons my sister and the younger set went to a place on 134th Street called The Devil's Den. Sometimes I went along with them. Actually, the *décor* was the only thing in keeping with the name of this place. It was an ordinary dance hall with an elaborate array of grotesque masks, horned and otherwise, hanging on the walls. Flickering lights cast an eerie red glow over the room and its occupants. A jazz band—often of the washboard variety—produced the hot notes that kept the cheek-to-cheek dancers moving around the crowded floor on Sunday afternoons at The Devil's Den.

Among the most popular of the young men in this Sunday afternoon set were Roi Ottley, Alfred Campbell, Maurice Weeks, and Tony Hicks. Roi, who later established himself as a writer of promise with *New-World-A'Comin'*, a descriptive history of the Negro in New York, was still in college when we met him. Even then he had a facility with the language which he often used to confound the girls who gathered about him. One of Roi's female audience was usually my sister, Ida Mae, whom he addressed as "Child" and ordered about in a patronizing, fatherly manner which I suspect he regarded as a cave-man tactic.

Alfred Campbell, who called for his dates in a chauffeured Rolls-Royce, was the son of one of the leading ministers in Harlem. At that time none of us would have guessed that he was one day to follow in his father's footsteps. Neither would we have guessed that Tony Hicks would be the first of this little company to die or that Maurice Weeks was to become one of the capital's most able attorneys. When Maurice got an apartment on upper Edgecombe Avenue, the Sunday afternoon parties gained momentum and his buddies took turns playing host.

The first bad break came when Ida Mae lost her job, because of the seasonal slack in the clothing industry. She accepted work at the club where she had already helped out on occasion. Though we were usually on the same shift, I was not happy over this arrangement. I knew there had been whispers to the effect that I thought my sister was too good to associate with the other girls. I also knew that they teased her about asking my permission to accept the inevitable invitations.

One night when I was not working and my sister was, I went to a movie so I would be downtown when she finished. As I lined up in front of the ticket office the person in front of me turned out to be one of the men who frequented the club where we worked. He insisted on buying my ticket and took a seat on the aisle in front of me. We left the theater at the same time and when I told him I was going to meet my sister he walked as far as the door, tipped his hat, and went about his business. One of the girls came out of the employees' entrance just as he turned away.

A few days later my sister confronted me. "I didn't think you would do it," she said accusingly.

"Do what?"

"I didn't think you would go out with a *white* man," she cried.

There was no need to remind her that all white men were not scoundrels or to point to Mr. Lige Chandler, who grew up with Papa, or Dr. Edmonds, who helped me to get my first teaching job. I told her what had happened the night I went to the show and cautioned her about listening to pointless gossip.

I doubled my efforts to find another job for my sister, but my hand was forced before I could succeed. Someone reported a serious infraction of the rules to the manager of the club where we worked and intimated that I was the guilty party. I sensed a growing coolness toward me that did not include my sister. One night I was on a rear station, resting my back against a broad post, when I heard whispers and my name mentioned. One girl was telling another about a man who had asked her to arrange a date with my sister and how she was going to "open the poor kid's eyes."

I never asked whether my sister was aware of what was going on. "Get your street clothes on," I said without wasting time on details. "We're going home." And home we went without a job between us.

Though we seldom had more money than was enough to meet the day's needs, I was glad to be free of such a situation. We went from one job to another, but my sister was a pleasant companion and never complained. I knew that the young men who took me out made jokes about "my shadow," but we had to share social engagements in order to survive.

One morning when we had decided to sleep instead of looking for work, the telephone rang. Maurice Weeks was calling to tell us to come down to the Abyssinian Baptist Church and get a job which would pay $27 a week. Maurice said he was working with Roi Ottley, Richard Kennard, and Adam Clayton Powell, Jr., whose father was the pastor of the church. He explained that they had set up something called an Emergency Relief Bureau to care for the thousands of Harlemites who were out of work and he wanted Ida Mae and me to be investigators.

"If you think we are going to come down there and give you the chance to laugh about how you fooled us," I told Maurice, "you're crazy. Go away. Leave us alone. We're not biting this time."

But Maurice was dead serious. The first Emergency Relief Bureau really was in the Abyssinian Baptist Church. And before long Adam Clayton Powell, Jr., was considered Harlem's crown prince. When I learned all this I was sorry we had doubted Maurice and turned down his offer of a job.

The following fall Ida Mae went home. I could not blame her, though I still believed that New York was a city of opportunities and I was determined to find one of them. I moved to a smaller room farther down Edgecombe Avenue and adjusted myself to being alone once more.

If the struggle to obtain food, clothing, and shelter had not dominated my every thought, I might have been less surprised when Bill and the distant relative who kept house for him told me that they were in love and intended to marry after Bill finished his medical training.

We had a long talk together before Bill left New York for Chicago, where he was to study. "Partner," he said, "if I should die before we meet again, remember that I died trying to be a doctor." Bill did become a fine doctor after many weary years of personal sacrifice.

Jobs came and jobs went as the depression wore on. I followed rainbow after rainbow, but the pot of gold always vanished before I arrived. When I had to choose between staying at home and being hungry, or going to a party with someone I did not like and getting a good meal and enough sherry to make me forget who I was and why I had come to New York, I chose the party. I had learned to keep my mouth shut and if a prospective employer did not ask about my race I did not tell him. No party was too gay, however, to prevent me from arguing with the man or woman who made unwarranted or unfounded charges about the South. I was especially resentful of smug Northerners who advanced the theory that any Negro who was dumb enough to stay in the South should expect to be mistreated. With trembling fingers I could only cling to my belief in God and the hope that one day I would have the opportunity to write again and answer my friends who thought of Alabama as a land of savagery and ignorance.

Keeping up a front for the folks back home is often the hardest part of trying to make good in the big city. Letters can be revealing and I had to be careful about what I wrote Mama, because I had already failed in my efforts to provide a home for Ida Mae. Then there was Edna, the orphan girl who had kept house for us, who wrote constantly to remind me that she was still expecting me to send for her.

By 1933 I had gone through a succession of jobs, sometimes holding two poorly paid ones at the same time, and working extra wherever I could. I had managed to get an apartment in a swanky building on St. Nicholas Place and enough flashy clothes for Ted Yates and his newspaper friends to dub me "the Mae West of Sugar Hill." I met a whole generation of men and women who, like myself, had matured during a depression. Layer after layer of sophistication was piled on to hide the accumulation of disappointment and shattered dreams.

In the midst of this precarious existence I met a woman who was a caterer. Her business was flourishing as a result of the repeal of prohibition. She gave me a job, and after I added a little imagination to my brief experience as a waitress, it was a profitable association for us both. Her clients did not find my accent as comical as had the first New Yorkers I met. Instead, after they found out I was a Negro, most of them asked me if I could sing. We developed a regular cocktail party circuit and I met a crowd of people who followed me uptown to see Harlem.

The *Tattler* had folded but Ted was writing a "Nite-Life" column for another Negro weekly. Through this source I was always informed about the liveliest spots. The Nest Club, that Johnny and Ray talked about, was no more, but Dickie Wells's Theatrical Grill was a number-one favorite. Pod's and Jerry's was a popular after-hours rendezvous and for real southern fried chicken we went to Tillie's Chicken Shack. Night club owners curried favors with Ted because he mentioned their places in his column.

The old Yeah Man! Club on Seventh Avenue was one of the first places Ted named. The night of the opening special tables had been set apart for Ted's party. He introduced me to Anne Brown, the singer, and her husband Dr. Jack Petitt, and pointed out Libby Holman and Betty Deitz. Clarence Robinson, who had staged the Cotton Club shows, was in charge of the entertainment, but the different performers who came in and out of the club all got into the act. Minto Cato, who was with Andy Razaf, the composer, sang "Memories of You" and Broadway Jones accompanied her. Margie Sipp, who had one of the sweetest soprano voices I have ever heard, went from table to table entertaining and Detroit Red delighted the men with a lusty dance routine. Ted also named the Hotcha and numbers of other Harlem hot spots, but the christening parties were much the same. The smoke in the poorly ventilated rooms made me sleepy and I always had a headache the next day. But I never missed one of them.

I often marveled at the abandon with which the Negroes we saw in the night clubs cast aside the cares of the day. I came to understand that a good part of the Harlem population made a living from the uptown night life. For them, fun after dark was a paying proposition.

The sons of families whose name appeared in the Social Register brought parties of pleasure-seeking friends to Harlem and left a path of greenbacks behind them. Heiresses, actresses, and movie stars with their wealthy escorts and stagedoor Johnnies mingled freely with the Negro musicians, entertainers, and sporting-world figures in the various clubs and cabarets night after night. The after-hours spots were more intimate. One little hunchbacked Negro was said to have made a comfortable living conducting "tours" of these secluded spots, which the preachers of the community called "sin-dins."

Young white boys with a flair for music hung around the clubs which were frequented by popular Negro musicians after working hours. In the smaller places, the jam sessions which the Negro musicians and singers held in the early hours of the morning were something to remember. There were usually one or two white boys sitting around, listening, beating out the rhythm on the top of a table and tapping their feet. They hung around the orchestras at the Savoy, too. Then the white boys went back downtown and practiced playing like the Negro musicians until they grew up and started jazz bands of their own and competed with the Negroes who had taught them.

It was not until Mr. X came along that I realized I was dancing on wafer-thin ice. Mr. X was one of the most charming men I have ever met. He came to America from one of the Balkan countries when he was a boy, bringing with him an air of subtle mystery and romance, mixed with a spontaneous gaiety and love of music that hinted of warm gypsy blood. The first time we met he told an old folk tale over a stemmed glass of sparkling wine. The stories he unfolded from his Old World background fired my imagination, giving me a yen for the quaint places and customs he told me about. I had no idea then what an important role Mr. X was to play in my life.

The big night came unexpectedly. We were alone in my apartment. Something—a word or a phrase—in a story he was telling shocked me. He was surprised at my reaction and there followed a discussion of the difference between the European and the American sense of moral values. In the pretty language he always used, Mr. X admitted that he thought *"all* Negro girls" indulged in sex freely, with abandon, and boldly explored the many bypaths of love-making. I was never sure whether it was the inclusiveness of his "all" or the sting of being taken for granted which lashed me the harder, but it is still a remembered anger. That night when I closed the door on Mr. X I knew it was time to take another inventory.

My biggest asset was a stack of rent receipts. I seldom had a dollar more than my bills required and Columbia was further away than ever. Life had been so pleasant I had no idea I had drifted so far from my original objectives. I had noted that most of the secretaries I knew were regularly employed and lived more or less orderly lives. I started skimping. As soon as I saved up enough money for tuition, I enrolled in a midtown secretarial school.

My typing was improving and I was hard at work with Pittman when my doorbell rang one day and in walked Talliferro, my old editor, who had moved to Boston after the *Truth* folded. Tally was on his way to New Orleans for the winter. Always a heavy eater and free spender, he enjoyed flashing a fat roll of hundred dollar bills. Johnny and Ray stuck with Tally until his roll was flat and he was cashing traveler's checks. Neither of them were around when I took his temperature and discovered that I had a sick visitor. Tally had influenza and by the time he was strong enough for me to put him on the train for New Orleans I was so far behind in my school work and other obligations that I gave up the secretarial course.

"I didn't want to be a secretary anyhow," I rationalized. "I'm a writer and I'm going to write!"

Ted thought I attached undue importance to the need for a course in journalism. He said it would be much more practical for me to get a job on one of the newspapers and learn by doing. He suggested that I talk with some of the editors to whom he had introduced me. Soon afterward he brought the New York editor of a Negro weekly to the apartment, but aside from the fact that he was patronizing and ignored my previous journalistic experience, this man said most newspaper women were ugly and he didn't think I was the type.

My next venture was better organized. When I went to the office of Editor No. 2, I had typed up a work sheet, which I handed him along with a scrapbook containing clippings from the *Truth* and a sample feature story. After an interview which lasted for hours, he offered me a job as a society editor—without salary. When I explained that I had to live off my earnings he assured me that I could get money from the people I wrote about. He laughed when I insisted that such an arrangement was a violation of journalistic ethics. We left his office at the same time and he offered to drive me home. Instead, he drove up the Speedway to a roadside rendezvous and I came home via bus and trolley car.

The next week when his paper came out with the core of my sample feature woven into an article which carried his by-line, neither Johnny, Ray, nor Ted made the usual charge that I was "all worked up over nothing." When I told them what had happened, Ray was angry, but Ted and Johnny tried to answer the questions that were bothering me.

When I asked why I ran into so many embarrassing situations Ted said he thought my southern manner of open friendliness was misleading. He said I should be more direct and strictly professional.

"Living alone," he added, "is another strike against you."

Johnny, who spared few words, leaned back in a wing chair and blew smoke rings from a big cigar. "Men look at you," he said, "then they listen to you talk. By that time, they've seen the cornshucks that are still in your hair and they decide you're a natural pushover."

The boys had to draw pictures before I understood the important principles of male psychology which they were trying to explain to me, and realized I had to learn how to live in a world dominated by men. I determined to build up a stern exterior as an aid to survival.

While I was perfecting this new approach, the flame which had been ignited the night I saw a white policeman kick Shorty was rekindled. The mailman rang impatiently the morning he brought the airmail-special-delivery letter which supplied the

match. I had just had a letter from Mama the day before and
I wondered why she had written again. When I tore the letter
open, a clipping dropped to the floor. As I stooped to pick it up
I read: "... Edna Davis ... a Negro woman ... fatally wounded
by Detective ... for resisting an officer of the law...."

"Edna Davis," I thought. "This can't be *my* Edna Davis. She's
coming to live with me as soon as I can send for her. She can't
be dead. She's only eighteen years old."

My feet and legs felt numb, the way they had felt the night
Papa was dying and I tried to run back to him. I managed to get
to the living room and sank down on a chair. I read the letter.
It was, I soon realized, my Edna. Mama had pieced the details
together as best she could. She wrote that Edna had gone to a
party in a section of the city where we seldom ventured. During
the evening, a woman Edna barely knew became intoxicated
and when one of the other guests lost a pocketbook the drunken
woman was accused. When the woman failed to return the
pocketbook she was alleged to have stolen, her accusers attempted to beat her. It was then that Edna got into the fight.

According to the story Mama picked up, Edna knew her
drunken friend was innocent because she had seen another guest
actually steal the missing purse. Instead of exposing the thief,
Edna fought off the attackers. Three inches short of being six
feet tall, with a frame which was covered with sound flesh, Edna
had always reminded me of Africa at its proudest. When
angered, she was powerful and it was not difficult for me to
imagine her beating off a crowd of revelers. Then she took the
woman to the house where she had gone to live after I left
Birmingham. It was said that the angered party crowd called
police headquarters and told the officers to go to "913 North
Sixteenth Street. And you'd better go armed to kill because
there's a bad Negro woman there."

When the policeman walked into Edna's house she was in the
act of changing her shoes. We had often laughed about the way
Edna insisted upon wearing shoes one or two sizes too small, and
her first act upon entering the house was to slip off her shoes and
put on house slippers.

That night when the officers said, "Put up your hands!" Edna, leaning over her shoes, looked up to see what was happening. A bullet tore through her forehead, right between the eyes. And Edna Davis, aged eighteen, died before she had ever lived. "They say she died calling your name," Mama wrote. "I had to get down on my knees and thank God that you were not here, because if you had been in Birmingham that night I know they would have had to kill you, too." I closed my eyes and relived the day when I had told Edna I was going to New York. We sat looking at each other for awhile; finally, she said: "You go ahead and study. Maybe you'll get to be a real good writer. But be sure to send for me as soon as you get a place. You need me to look after you." This I had remembered all during the hungry, jobless days. Now Edna was dead and I could never send for her.

Now I really knew hate. I hated the white man who had killed Edna. I hated the Negroes who had sent the police to her house and, secretly, I hated myself because I had left her in Birmingham to be killed. Mama used to explain my ability to weep easily by saying that God forgot to close Papa's tear ducts and he had passed the trouble on to me. But my eyes were dry that day when Mabel, who for six years, had been my constant friend and companion, pushed open the door I had left ajar and walked in. I was still sitting on the side of the chair with the clipping in my hand. Without speaking, I handed it to Mabel.

Although Mabel was not a Negro, she shared my indignation. She knew how much Edna had meant to me and her sympathy broke my silence. She closed the windows and let me scream out my hatred for Edna's murderer and the system which allowed him to go free. Mabel got other friends to sit with me when she had to leave. She said later that they had tried to talk to console me, to tell me that I could not carry the problem on my back. But they were mere shadows and the only voice I could hear was Edna's, calling out to me for help, too late.

I thought of all the white friends I had known and loved as a child. How, I asked myself, could they live year after year in a town where men who had been entrusted with the task of upholding the law of the land openly defied God's laws and murdered helpless men and women whenever they chose? How, I asked, could decent people see these things and not cry out? It was weeks before I could follow a normal routine. I only laughed when Mama wrote that the NAACP was investigating the circumstances surrounding Edna's death, because I knew no white man would be punished in Alabama for killing a Negro woman. I went to the Sacraments but found no peace because the hate in my heart was sinful. I stopped writing Sister Timothy and the other white nuns who had taught me. I went to parties, dances, night clubs, and after-hours spots. Every white man I met became Edna's murderer. I half-prayed, half-hated, half-ate, and slept only when I was too exhausted to do otherwise—until another letter came.

When I read the second clipping I could only say, "God forgive me!" The detective who killed Edna had in turn been killed by an alleged criminal in the act of "resisting an officer of the law."

As another Christmas approached, it was good to be free of the heaviness of hate. Because we had always felt that Papa's heart condition had been aggravated by the loss of his life savings when the Penny Prudential Bank failed in Birmingham, I had a deep-seated distrust of banks and used to hide whatever money was left after my bills were paid under the Tree-of-Life rug on my living room floor. Mabel, who lived across the street, came over each day to make sure I was putting something aside. A few days before Christmas we turned the rug back. When we finished counting, for the first time I had enough to send gifts home for Mama and the family and dress myself up, too.

I bought a fur coat on the installment plan, a print dress, shoes, hat, and a black pin-seal bag with white doeskin gloves to wear to midnight Mass. Someone had sent me a corsage of fresh violets and I felt happy inside and out as I knelt in one of the rear pews at St. Charles. I was at peace with men of good will.

My first visitor on Christmas morning was a uniformed messenger who handed me a long box bearing the name of a Fifth Avenue florist whose display windows I had often admired. Inside were two dozen Marshall Neil roses, scarcely more than buds, with a card inscribed, "From Mr. X." The beauty of the roses had canceled out the last grudge.

As I turned away from the door, I saw the living room and foyer reflected in the gilt-edged mirror which hung between the two windows in the front room. The mirror had also picked up the high polish of the hardwood floors. In the background was a woman of average size and height, in a velvet negligee with long, full sleeves which were trimmed in fur. She was holding a box of pink roses.

"I may be broke again," I thought, "but this sure is real fancy poverty."

Soon after Christmas, Little Sister, who had finished State and was teaching in Birmingham, wrote that she was coming to visit me as soon as school closed. I was thrilled to think that I had a comfortable home in which to entertain her. My friends caught my enthusiasm and by the end of May they were all asking: "When is Little Sister coming?"

When Bill, the uniformed doorman at our apartment house, opened the door for us and tipped his hat I saw my sister's eyes dance with excitement. Inside the apartment she stood in the foyer and stared at herself in the living room mirror. She walked down the hall and peeped in the tiny but compact kitchen, then went to the bedroom where I had spent hours ironing the frilly pink bedspread and organdy curtains.

I was shocked when I discovered that my friends had been expecting to see a little girl in pigtails. Little Sister, who was two inches taller than I, far exceeded their expectations. By the time this adult version of her had been accepted, a rumor circulated to the effect that I had let it be known that only young "professionals" were eligible to visit my sister. That was one rumor I laughed away; most of the young professional men I knew were either relief investigators, carrying bags at Penn Station or Grand Central, or "running on the road." As the vacation passed, I soon realized I had little need to worry about who my sister would or would not associate with. The only practical offspring my mother ever had, she solved most of her own problems and opened my eyes to a few of mine.

One night after a party, when we were both in a relaxed mood, we talked about the future. Having chased so many vanishing rainbows, I was reluctant to commit myself. In commenting on whatever fuzzy plans I admitted, my sister said, "And you were the one who was going to do so much!"

I knew then that she preferred the militant Sister Ellen who used to write features and editorials advocating reform and civic improvement to the sophisticated sister she found on Sugar Hill. I had tried to dazzle her with superficialities, but she was like a child who had looked at a beautiful Christmas tree, then discovered there was no Santa Claus and become disenchanted. I consoled myself by reasoning that she had no idea of the world between the two personalities. She had never been hungry and broke in a rented room. She thought everybody who was anybody lived in modern Sugar Hill apartments. Due to the generosity of my car-owning friends, she rode on the subway only once during three months and never knew there were few New Yorkers who could match her record.

We both laughed over the remark, but the dart was firmly embedded in the center of the target. I could not deny the truth, and the truth was that I had allowed a depression and racial discrimination to change the course of my life. Suddenly, I heard Edna calling.

chapter 9

THE MUSIC WENT
ROUND AND ROUND

The apartment was filled with alternating echoes after my sister left: one voice was hers and the other was Edna's. One day I was defeated and the next I was obsessed by the desire to answer Edna's call, to offer a substitute which would blot out the nights when her voice had been drowned by Harlem jazz. I became critical of my friends and lost interest in parties. I choked on the smoke in night clubs and went to sleep during the entertainment, which seldom varied. I had nothing to show for six years in New York but a closet full of cheap clothes, a few pieces of furniture, and a stack of rent receipts.

The following New Year's Eve I sat with the friends who gathered in my apartment and watched 1935 die without shedding a tear. At the sound of the first whistle I excused myself to kneel before my crucifix and beg God's help for what was ahead.

The din of the whistles had faded when I rejoined my friends. Someone suggested that we should go out and we put on our coats and hats.

It was drizzling when we joined the crowd on St. Nicholas Place. Radios and jukeboxes were blaring a new novelty tune— "The music goes 'round and around ... Ohohoho-o-o-o ... and it comes out here. ..." We met more friends and went from apartments to corner grills and bars. Wherever we went the music was going " 'round and around." The repetition made me remember the time Mama took me to a carnival and we rode on a carrousel. Mama sat on a seat, but I insisted on riding a wooden horse. Each time the merry-go-round stopped I wrapped my arms about the horse's neck and refused to get down. Then Mama would buy another ticket and we would go around again. Mama finally got so dizzy she sat on the floor; when we stopped again she refused to buy another ticket. The man who owned the contraption let us go around once free and then he helped Mama to tear me off of my wooden horse.

We left Sugar Hill and went "down in the valley" to Harlem. The drizzle had turned into a light, soft snow that felt as if somebody was shaking feathers out of a high window. The streets were crowded and people were blowing horns, throwing confetti, and shouting: "Happy New Year!" Seventh Avenue was celebrating and every jukebox was playing "The Music Goes 'Round and Around."

Suddenly I knew I'd had enough. I had come down off the wooden horse on the merry-go-round.

A lone taxi came up Seventh Avenue. The snow was falling fast and it had gotten colder. The driver stopped for me. He had the heat on and it felt good to be inside. I thought about Mama's old saying about God taking care of fools and babies. I wanted to go home to Birmingham.

It was in the spring of 1936 when I told Ted and Mabel I was going to leave Sugar Hill. I had received a business offer for next fall from a friend who knew I had expressed interest in opening a combination gift and book shop. I needed to get away from New York and touch hands with people in the world outside of Manhattan who lived more normally. I needed to breathe fresh air so I could think more clearly.

My pulse quickened with the first sight of the red hills of Alabama. I had not realized how lonesome I had been for familiar scenes and faces. I muttered to myself against the social and economic conditions which made it impossible for me to live in Birmingham; then I smiled to think that I was still naïve enough to believe it might be possible—one day. As we approached Irondale where Allena lived, I watched for her house.

Dusk had gathered on the mountainside, but I could see the rays from the big lamp which always sat on her living room table.

At Terminal Station in Birmingham I followed the other first-class passengers to an exit, and went to the waiting room. I stood there a few moments wondering where my relatives were, since meeting a train is an obligation my family never neglects. A Negro redcap passed and I realized his was the first dark face I had seen because I was in the white waiting room. I heard a whistle and looked outside in the corridor where my relatives were standing opposite the "Colored" waiting room, beckoning for me to join them.

An Alabama sun was blazing and heat waves were dancing on the pavements the day Little Sister and I went shopping. Our last stop was a five-and-ten. We were tired and the moment I saw the lunch counter I knew I was hungry and thirsty, too. I plopped down in one of the "white" swivel chairs. When I turned to ask my sister what she wanted I saw a strange white woman sitting next to me. At the extreme end of the counter, her eyes flashing danger signals, my sister was beckoning.

"What happened to you?" I asked. "I thought you were behind me."

"Come on out of here," she snapped, "before you get us all in trouble." She walked hurriedly toward the door.

"What have I done now?" I asked after we were outside.

"Oh, you *know* they don't serve Negroes in there," she said. "Anybody would think you had lived in New York all your life."

"But I'm hungry and thirsty," I insisted. "And I think they would serve Negroes if any of them asked to be served. The waitress had already offered to take my order."

My sister gave me a knowing look which reminded me that I might have been ignored or forcibly ejected if the waitress had been sure I was a Negro.

"There has to be someplace we can stop and eat or get a cold drink of water," I said. "Even animals deserve that."

"You don't have to be so dramatic about it," my sister laughed. "You won't starve before we get to the drugstore in the Masonic Temple."

That summer I knew many days when no such incident marred our goings and comings. It was a deceitful kind of existence, though, because we had to close our eyes and minds to so much before we could act like normal human beings. It seemed to me that the interests of my friends covered such a narrow range. I often thought it was as if the mountains around us were encircled by wire fences with posted signs: "BEWARE! DO NOT TRESPASS UNDER PENALTY OF ARREST!"

In the Negro business section there were sides of certain streets on which my friends would not walk. "Nobody that we know goes over there," they explained. In spite of what they said, I saw familiar faces. And when I was alone, I walked on the side of Fourth Avenue between Seventeenth and Eighteenth Streets that Octavus Roy Cohen had made famous. The same poolrooms, barbecue joints, cafés, and barbershops that he wrote about in his *Saturday Evening Post* stories were still there, with a dozen or more jukeboxes added. The streets were lined with Negro men who seemed to have nothing more inspiring to do or nowhere else to go. More often than not, one of them separated himself from the crowd and reminded me that we had gone to Slater together or that I had taught him. It was plain to see that most of them were long since defeated, but more alarming was the bitterness and rebellion in their voices and their eyes. At the slightest provocation, it tumbled off their lips. At night I would wonder what would happen if a stray spark ignited their smoldering emotions before one of their own alerted the white community. Though these encounters usually left me frightened and unhappy, one of them left me ashamed, as well.

I was passing one of the Fourth Avenue poolrooms when someone called my name. A man wearing a leather jacket and a cap came out and I saw he was a boy who had gone through Slater into I.H.S. with me.

"I heard you were in town," he said as we shook hands, "but I didn't think I would get to see you."

"Why didn't you call or come out to the house?" I asked.

"You know how it is." He shrugged his shoulders. "You just bum around and before you know it you don't see the people you used to know any more. Things go wrong, you start drinking and hanging out in these joints and before long nobody you know wants to see you anyway."

"You always had so much talent in art," I said, and reminded him of all the opportunities given him to use that talent in school. "What are you doing now?"

"I pick up a few odd jobs," he admitted, "but there's no market for art work here—not for a colored man."

"Why don't you leave? I did."

"But you're different. Always were."

"We went to the same school, knew the same boys and girls, played the same games. How can you say I was always different?" I asked. "I didn't feel there was a market in Birmingham for what I wanted to do and I went to New York to find a market. Why can't you do the same?"

"You wouldn't understand," he laughed and took his cap off, then turned it around with the bill to the back the way he wore it when he was in short pants and, along with the other boys, chased the girls at the circus with whips. "It's easier for the women. But you'll always do things and I'll always be proud of you."

I thought of all I had *not* done during the years I wasted going to parties and night clubs and speak-easies and walked away.

A few days later I heard a younger version of the same story from a boy who had been a member of the second class I taught at Slater. He was the pupil who had helped me design and decorate the first bulletin board I had used for my children's stories about successful Negroes. "I guess you think I didn't try to go away to art school." He avoided my gaze as he talked. "But you're up there in New York and you don't know how it is down here. What can you do when you don't have any money and never make any more than you have to have each day?"

I thought of all the times I had asked myself the same question as I walked down New York's street. Then I gave the youngster the only answer I knew: "Don't give up. Keep trying and one day you'll get a break."

After the boy left I sat on the porch for hours looking down on the twinkling lights of a busy city. The sky above the foundry lighted up with the glow from molten lead, and I thought that in the midst of so many natural resources, there was so much human waste; that flight and defeat cheated a community which should enjoy abundance and progress. And what could I do?

A kind fate balanced the scales at this point by throwing in a touch of romance. Arthur, one of four eligible young men from New Orleans who came to Birmingham for a weekend visit, was a fast worker. A few moments after we met he knew all about me and exactly where I had been all his life. The rest of my visit to Birmingham was overflowing with letters and long-distance calls from New Orleans that did or did not come when I expected them. The letter that made me happiest was the one which extended an invitation to my sister and me to visit the Creole City. Little Sister reminded me that convincing Mama of the propriety of our trip would not be an easy task. Even after I arranged to have a girl friend who lived in New Orleans invite us to be her guests, Mama had her doubts. But we left Birmingham in high spirits. Little Sister was looking forward to a round of social activities, as she was not particularly interested in Arthur's pal, who had invited her. I was looking forward only to being in Arthur's company.

The Old World atmosphere of New Orleans fascinated me. Whether we were uptown, downtown, or "back-o'-town," our surroundings were pleasant as long as we were in New Orleans. It was not until the night we were leaving for home that I had any indication that the arrogant, assured air I had admired in Arthur was but a defense for the brooding bitterness which lies curled up in the breasts of most of the Negro men I have known. It was what came between us from the first.

It was after we reached the station for our return trip that

I remembered Jim Crow. I had not had an opportunity to see him in New Orleans but they told me he was in the coach behind the engine and we all walked down the track to meet him. The only other occupants of the car reserved for Negroes were a group of preachers who had been to a convention in New Orleans and were on their way home. It was obvious that they wanted to be friendly, and when the train pulled out Arthur was pointing in their direction and shaking his head. He need not have feared because I turned my face to the window and cried until the train stopped at Bay St. Louis, Mississippi.

A telegram from the friend who had made me a business offer was waiting when I arrived in Birmingham. Within a few days I was bound once more for New York and no tears were shed when I left Birmingham in 1936. I had found myself again.

Washington had become my Mason-Dixon Line and I felt freer with each mile the train traveled in the direction of New York. Mabel met me at Penn Station and staggered me with the news that she had married and moved to Long Island. I knew the stern, industrious man she had taken as a mate and I knew Mabel, but I hoped for the best.

My apartment would not be ready until the next day and I went home with Mabel. That evening Mabel's husband took great pride in showing me the apartment which he had furnished, with excellent taste, for his new wife. The rooms were half of a two-family suburban dwelling. While walking from the station, I had observed that the neighborhood was white. Though Mabel was white, her husband, a native of one of the Carribean Islands, was brown. But he never considered himself a Negro.

Before we went to bed Mabel asked me how I liked the apartment.

"It's beautiful," I said, "but how did you happen to pick this neighborhood?"

"I know what you're thinking," she smiled. "But it was the only place I could find. I transacted all the business with the woman who owns the place and we moved in. So far there's been no trouble. I've seen the neighbors staring at us, but if they don't bother us we don't bother them."

The girls had my apartment ready the next day and I was glad to unpack and get under way with my plans. Mabel stayed with me until it was time to meet her husband for the trip back to Long Island. The next day I went to the store in the mid-eighties in which my friend had proposed to rent me space for a combination gift-book shop. After consulting cabinet makers, publishers, card companies, and wholesale houses we both agreed that the space was not adequate for what I wanted to do. My friend was short of help and I agreed to work with her until she found someone to help her. Then, we said, we would look for a larger place.

Mabel found suburban life lonely after the excitement of Sugar Hill. She enjoyed shopping for the house and came in each morning with her husband and went back with him at night. When she tired of rambling through department stores she either went to my apartment for a rest or came by the store where I worked.

I had been working in my friend's store about two weeks when I discovered that beside being short of help, she was also short of cash. When an additional week passed and I did not get paid I realized I had gotten a bad deal again. I learned later that she had been depending on the rent I would have paid to make up for reverses she had suffered. Our association ended with her in my debt.

The morning that Mabel and her husband came to my house I was asleep. When I saw her standing over me I knew something was wrong and dreaded to get up and face it.

"We're house-hunting again," she announced when I joined them in the living room.

Mabel was making a special effort to be cheerful in front of her husband but I could tell she had been crying.

"If she's going to spend so much time in the city"—her husband seemed more stern than usual—"we might as well move back. At least we'd save carfare."

The husband and wife left together, but Mabel returned after a morning of futile hunting.

"Now, I'll tell you what happened." She began walking up and down the living room. "That frowsy old woman who owned the house made me so mad I wanted to slap her. At first, I held back when she tried to be friendly. Then I thought I might as well meet her halfway and we got so we would exchange a few words every time we met. The other day she told me she had something to ask me. She knows I come in town nearly every day so I thought she wanted me to make a purchase for her. But do you know what she asked me?"

"No," I said, reluctant to admit that I had a very good idea.

"She asked me why I married a nigger."

"And?" I prompted.

"And I told her she could take her old house and . . ."

"Don't bother to tell me the rest," I interrupted. "You must feel awful."

"I will *so* bother to tell you," Mabel screamed. "I listened to you when they killed Edna, didn't I? So why can't you listen to me? It's the same thing, the same lousy thing!"

Mabel talked and cried awhile before she admitted that she had not told her husband the truth about the conversation with their landlord.

"It's bad enough as it is," she said. "I couldn't bear to say that to him. I just said it was too lonesome out there and I wanted to move back in town."

After a week of hunting for apartments that were always "just rented" when her brown-skinned husband arrived on the scene, Mabel asked if they could stay with me until other arrangements could be made.

Nobody ever quite understood how we jammed Mabel's three rooms of furniture into my well-furnished apartment. It was a happy arrangement, though, since it required a minimum of housekeeping. Most of the furniture was covered with sheets and we only had eating and sleeping space to take care of. When more than one guest came, we had to entertain in the kitchen, but we made a lark out of it all.

After a month of living in a three-room apartment with six rooms of furniture in it, Mabel's husband suggested that it might be easier to find a large apartment that we could all live in together. There were only a few dollars left under the Tree-of-Life rug; such a move would cut my expenses in half. I agreed and we found a larger apartment in the Paul Lawrence Dunbar Apartments.

Mabel and her husband went to bed early the night before we moved. Everything but our beds was packed and I sat and looked around the bare apartment, remembering all of the faces that had drifted in and out during the years I had lived there. The bell rang and a boy from Birmingham came in with a package under his arm.

"I heard you were going to move tomorrow," he said, "so I brought you a bottle of wine to toast the new home."

He toasted the new home, but I toasted the end of an era of errors. I thought a prayer about the new job I was going to the next day. Perhaps I had not grown in grace but I felt I had grown in human understanding.

chapter 10

THE HOUSE OF FRIENDSHIP

It was good to live with people again and to think in halves when the bills came in. Gradually, I withdrew from my wider circle of friends and the few who came to my new home were Mabel's friends also. The Yates boys were among those few.

Ted sponsored me for membership in the Negro Writers' Guild, a group of journalists and creative writers who gathered periodically in a Republican club house on West 136th Street. It was at one of these meetings that I first met Claude McKay, the Negro poet-novelist who had just returned to America after living in Africa and Europe for a number of years. I had heard that Claude was a man of extreme moods, but he was at his best the night I met him. He was so attentive to me I felt guilty about the editorial I wrote in the *Truth* criticizing his *Home to Harlem* when it was published in 1928. The first few times I was in Claude's presence I remembered how I had accused him of selling his birthright for a mess of pottage and labeled the book a "gross and debased exaggeration of life in a Negro community." Then I forgot about the article.

Claude saw something I had written and asked if I had more samples. I was flattered to receive this attention from so famous an author and before long I was a pupil at his feet. He kept asking to see my scrapbook but it was in the bottom of an old trunk and I did not find it until one day when we had an appointment. I knew better than to keep Claude waiting and thought I would look through the book after I got to his house, but he was in one of his bad moods and snatched the book out of my hands soon after I was inside his door.

"You've got a good fist," he muttered as he thumbed through the clippings. "But I'm not sure it's strong enough yet."

I watched Claude as he read. His skin looked like polished mahogany and I wondered why his hair appeared kinky in most of the pictures I had seen of him. It was so pretty and wavy when he bothered to brush it. The little laugh wrinkles around his eyes belied the cynical lines at the corners of his mouth, which a silky mustache almost hid. Claude's expression did not change until he was almost at the end of the book.

"Now you've tightened your fist!" he cried, as he started pacing the floor. "That other stuff was just do-good business. Once you double your fist it's good and strong, but I think you have to get angry to do it. You need a lot of experience, but this"—he thumped the book with his forefinger—"is good stuff, even if you don't know what you are talking about!"

"I don't know what you are talking about, either," I smiled. "May I see...."

"Here." He pushed the book at me, his thumb marking the place.

"SELLS BIRTHRIGHT FOR MESS OF POTTAGE" was all I saw and I knew I had forgotten to remove the article about *Home to Harlem* from the scrapbook. Claude's eyes were like two augers boring in a hard surface. I grabbed the book and left as fast as I could. I heard him chuckling as I ran down the steps.

That was the first of many occasions when I saw Claude McKay set the stage, then pull the strings to see how his friends would react to a given situation. I was an excellent puppet for Claude and he never hesitated to use me. I often suspected that he set his observations down in a little black book each time he cleared the stage. In return for the uneasy moments he caused me, Claude gave me my first orchid and also introduced me to James Weldon Johnson, Countee Cullen, Langston Hughes, Harold Jackman, Roberta Bosley, and many other important people in the literary world of that time.

Claude was credited with being the leader of the revolt in Negro literature, but he was also a lyric poet of rare ability. He was born in Clarendon, on the island of Jamaica, near the end of the last century. He lived in various parts of the United States, but his happiest years were spent in France and Morocco. As early as 1912 his *Songs of Jamaica* had been a medal-winner and the book I had criticized, *Home to Harlem,* had won the Harmon Gold Award. Like Carl Van Vechten's *Nigger Heaven,* the book had created a sensation, particularly among Negroes like myself who knew nothing of the life Van Vechten or McKay wrote about. Claude is best remembered by many for his *If We Must Die,* which is said to be "the most quoted and reprinted poem of this generation."

Every now and then someone said he had heard that Claude had once been married, but he seemed bitter whenever any discussion of love or courtship arose and there was nobody who dared to ask about his past.

In self-defense I had to acquaint myself with Claude's likes and dislikes of people and things. High up on the list of his many peeves were: "yellow Negroes," "people who spout religiosity," and "the Reds." He could say "you Catholics" with so much contempt it was useless to do anything but utter a silent prayer for him. That all of these prayers were answered is part of a later story. Despite my color and my religion, Claude opened closed windows for me and taught me the meaning of craftmanship. I was grateful but he forbade me to say so. He always said, "Gratitude! I *hate* the word."

James Weldon Johnson, the poet, author, and diplomat who was also the first Negro professor to lecture in white universities, was occupying the Spence Chair of Creative Literature at Fisk University in Nashville, Tennessee, when I met Claude. All my life I had heard of Mr. Johnson, for he had attended Atlanta University at the same time that several of Mama's friends were there. With his brother, J. Rosamond, he had been a part of the first Negro song-writing team on Broadway. The Johnson brothers had written "Lift Every Voice and Sing," sometimes called the "Negro national anthem," for a Lincoln's Birthday celebration before they left their native Jacksonville, Florida, and had also collected a book of Negro spirituals. I was familiar with James Weldon Johnson's *Saint Peter Relates an Incident, God's Trombones, The Autobiography of an Ex-Colored Man,* and *Along This Way.*

I had heard that during the Negro Renaissance the home of James Weldon Johnson and his attractive wife, Grace Nail, had been one of the first gathering places in Harlem of the great literary minds of that time—colored and white. Through mutual friends I learned that Mr. Johnson had also been a sort of father-confessor to Claude and had straightened out many of the controversies with people in literary circles which Claude was said to have instigated.

I felt highly honored when Claude McKay invited me to accompany him to a meeting where James Weldon Johnson was to be the speaker. I especially enjoyed the warm human quality of Mr. Johnson's talk and detected a humor I had not discovered in his writings. After the meeting was over, Claude asked me to join them for refreshments and we went to a little place which was owned by one of Claude's West Indian friends. Mr. Johnson had been a guest in my Aunt Annie Hutchinson's home when he went to Birmingham to lecture for the Periclean Club, and I told him how much pleasure Mama Ida had gotten from reading the autographed copy of *Along This Way* which he had given her. Then we spoke for a while of people he knew in Birmingham. Claude was pouting. When I could ignore his sullen glances no longer, I asked him if anything was wrong.

"Just look at you," he blurted. "You're sitting up here as white as alabaster. Why don't you buy yourself some brown powder?"

Though I was familiar with Claude's hostility toward light people, this unwarranted attack in front of Mr. Johnson left me spluttering.

Mr. Johnson raised a restraining hand and shook his head as his deep-set eyes twinkled. "Claude," he said, "don't you think it's a little too late for Miss Tarry to do anything about her color?"

Claude was contrite, but the night had been spoiled. To make up for it, he promised to have a party the next time Mr. Johnson was in town—if he had any royalty money. "And you will be the only woman I'll invite," he laughed.

Soon after this incident another member of the Negro Writers' Guild who had known Claude in Jamaica told me how the young poet acquired his dislike for fair complexions. According to his friend, Claude had once been a policeman. His immediate superior, a stern, uncompromising, sometimes unreasonable task-master, was a mulatto. The indignities—real and imaginary—which Claude suffered at this man's hands left their mark. I can also imagine that Claude, dressed up in a policeman's uniform, was not an obedient subordinate.

When Claude's friends heard that he had been offered a chair at one of the Negro universities they were delighted. He was writing a new book and working on the Federal Writers' Project, but we felt the new offer was more in keeping with the living standards of a man of his achievements. I was shocked when a mutual friend told me that Claude was going to refuse the offer.

"Why?" I asked. "Does he dislike teaching?"

"No. He says there are too many strings attached to the job," the friend told me. "He claims the board informed him that living quarters would be furnished for his family and that they have taken it for granted that he is married."

"If he feels that marriage is one of the qualifications necessary for this job, why doesn't he marry?" I asked.

"He can't decide between you and ——." My friend said the name of a well-known woman once rumored to have had a torrid love affair with Claude. "He says you are *too* white and *too* ambitious, and she is too promiscuous."

"If he'd ask me," I laughed, "I could tell him a few more reasons why he can't marry me. Reason number one is: I'm not ready to go to jail for killing a distinguished Negro poet!"

It was impossible to stay angry with Claude. Soon afterward he sent for me. He wanted me to talk with one of the supervisors on his job. Negro writers were gathering material for a book about New York which was to be published by the WPA.

Once before Claude and Ted had insisted that I come down to the Federal Writers' Project, which was housed in the American Express Building on 42nd Street across from the *Daily News*. By the time I had applied for the job, a relief status was necessary. Although I was eligible, I had discarded most of my rent receipts when I moved from Sugar Hill. The broken sequence of the receipts, plus my thick southern accent, made it difficult for me to prove I had been in New York for the required time.

Claude banged his fist on a desk. "If you were a member of the Party, you'd be working. But I'll show them a thing or two. They can't beat me. I'll get you on."

"What party?" I asked.

"The Reds!" He spat out the words. "They've gotten control. But I'm going to get them out somehow. And I'm going to get you a job, too."

"Claude, I don't know anything about the Reds," I told him. "Where I come from it's the whites we have to fear. However, I don't think they had anything to do with me not getting a relief status. I hate questioning. I've never been good at filling out applications and usually hide receipts and records so well that nobody can find them."

"You Southerners," he laughed, "are so naïve. I know these dirty Communists."

Later, I learned that Claude had a very good reason for hating "the Reds," but I thought there were times when he carried this hatred to an excess.

I was not on familiar terms with anyone in any of the social work agencies and the priest I had talked with had little or no conception of the problems of our community. Through a social contact I met the minister of the local Congregational Church and told him about some of the problems I was encountering. The kind old preacher agreed that it would be easier for me to study if I was engaged in work which was related to my field. When I told him about my experience with WPA, he offered to take me to an Emergency Relief Bureau office and intercede.

The preacher kept his promise and I found that he was highly respected by the workers at that district office. However, when he proceeded to deliver a sermon concerning certain workers who yielded to pressure from Communist groups, a crowd gathered and I was so embarrassed I forgot most of the answers I should have given when I was questioned about the length of my residence in New York City. The encounter left me so discouraged I would have gone back to waiting on tables if Claude and Ted had not kept prodding me.

I was away from home more and more, and Mabel did not hide the fact that she was suspicious of some of my new friends. I wanted to invite them into our home but neither Mabel nor her husband cared to meet people.

Internal friction broke out in the Negro Writers' Guild. Many of the older and more solvent writers complained that there were too many unknowns in the Guild. In answer to their charges, Claude started planning to build a prestige organization around James Weldon Johnson. Sometimes we suspected that Claude had not bothered to share all of his plans with Mr. Johnson, but we hoped it would all work out. Everybody knew that Claude was not a good organizer, but those who were qualified were afraid he would get angry if they offered their services. The preliminaries dragged on for months, but we had an excuse to get together almost every week.

Claude had quarters in the home of Augusta Savage, the sculptress who lived in a private house on West 136th Street near St. Nicholas Avenue, which was said to have belonged to the late actress, Florence Mills. Augusta's paying guests were either writers or artists who studied in her little art colony. Claude's place was furnished with rugs, stools, statues, tapestries, and paintings he had brought back from Morocco. It was here that we held our meetings and I was sitting on one of the tapestry-covered divans discussing the advantages of a writers' guild with one of the group when I heard Claude yell: "I'm Claude McKay, I don't want to write any *little* stories! Let Miss Tarry have it."

"What are you going to give Miss Tarry now?" I had learned to meet Claude's storms with calmness. "All she wants is a job."

"I'm going to get that, too," he said. "Jimmie has promised to straighten that out. But now he's telling me about some scholarship for a writer who wants to do stories for children. You go and take it. I write novels!"

"All right. I'll take it. Just tell me where to go. From here on, I'm not turning down anything."

"Good," he grinned and shooed his friend, whom he called Jimmie, in my direction. You tell *her* about it," Claude said, "and leave me alone so I can get this writers' business on paper."

Jimmie told me that the Bureau of Educational Experiments was setting up a Writers' Laboratory under the distinguished educator and writer, Lucy Sprague Mitchell. The Bureau was making an effort to have as many ethnic groups as possible represented. A scholarship was being offered to a Negro who was a writer and had teaching experience or vice versa. He instructed me to write Mrs. Mitchell at the Bank Street headquarters and asked me about the job difficulties Claude had mentioned to him.

"Several people have suggested that I see a James Baker, who heads the ERB office in this district," I told Jimmie. "But I can never get past the reception desk. Do you know him?"

"Very well," he said.

"What kind of person is he?" I asked. "He's certainly hard enough to get to."

"We're very much alike," he laughed, "because *I* am James Baker. Claude has told me about your case already."

After Jimmie patiently explained how I must establish the fact that I had been a resident of New York City for a number of consecutive years, it was easier for me to take the grilling I went through before I acquired the status which enabled me to get a job as a writer-researcher on the Federal Writers' Project.

Claude and Ted Yates were happy that I was working with them, though Claude insisted that "the Reds" had tried to keep me off the project because I was his friend and a Catholic. Once he made up his mind, he would never admit he was wrong. The day when he would was still to come.

Mama was delighted when I wrote and told her I had a research job and was in line for a scholarship. Mabel was less impressed than I had expected, but she had seen so many of my dazzling ventures fail I could not blame her.

Arthur, my New Orleans friend, was making progress, too, and I felt flattered that he wired me the day he was promoted and became head of his department.

During the weeks which followed I learned that Jimmie Baker was the husband of Augusta Baker, the librarian in charge of children's work at the 135th Street branch library. Augusta had talked with Margaret Wise Brown about the Writers' Laboratory and passed the information on to Jimmie. I found Augusta to be a pleasant, energetic young woman who bubbled with enthusiasm when the subject of books for children was mentioned. She knew about Claude's reaction to the scholarship offer and, though all concerned would have been pleased to know that a name writer represented the group, she was glad I did not allow it to go begging.

I like to remember my first impression of Lucy Sprague Mitchell. She was wearing a cotton dress and comfortable flat-heeled shoes, and a narrow black ribbon band kept her hair in place. From a cotton bag of the catch-all variety she extracted our correspondence. Mabel had insisted that I should dress up for the conference and I kept thinking I could have discarded the high-heeled shoes I was wearing for my old oxfords because I soon understood that the only thing Lucy Sprague Mitchell would ever expect from me was "books for children that children will read and enjoy." In a few weeks I was the lone Negro member of the Writers' Lab and two of the most important years in my life began.

Next to Mrs. Mitchell, my dearest friend at Bank Street was "Brownie" as we called Margaret Wise Brown. In jest, I often chided her for coming all the way to Harlem to find me for the Lab.

"I wasn't looking for you," she grinned. "I was looking for a Negro who looked liked a Negro and up you turned!"

We laughed when I told her what James Weldon Johnson had told Claude and we agreed that it was too late for me to change. Anyway, my southern accent made up for the lack of pigmentation and everything I said seemed to amuse the other members of the Lab. I did not mind, however, since they laughed with me and I never was the butt of any joke. It reached the state, though, where Mrs. Mitchell would not allow me to read my manuscripts in workshop sessions because she said I did too many tricks with my voice. I worked hard to show my gratitude for the opportunity to learn how to tighten my fist and build a story. And there was much for me to learn.

My schedule also included classes at the Cooperative School for Student Teachers (now Bank Street College) and observation at the Harriet Johnson Nursery School and the Little Red Schoolhouse. Since I was a product of public, state, and convent schools, I was bewildered by my first contacts with progressive education. The children in both schools came from ultra-modern homes and their frankness, particularly that of the nursery school children, was in direct contrast to my mid-Victorian upbringing. The day I walked into the Little Red Schoolhouse and heard the activity noises and saw children and pets running up and down the hall I had doubts as to how long I would last. But my conversion to progressive education, with certain reservations, was not a lengthy process. Norman Studer, who taught the thirteen-year-olds, was a great help, but it was the youngsters who really made me see a good reason for all I had originally viewed with critical eyes.

Claude succeeded in getting all of his plans for a Negro writers' organization down on paper and called a meeting at his house. It was a Sunday afternoon affair and most of the people who had figured in the Negro Renaissance were there. The editor who had made a pass at me and then copied my feature story accepted another introduction. Many of the prominent librarians were also there, including Augusta Baker and Roberta Bosley. I was talking with Ted Yates and another writer, Arnold de Mille, when Claude announced with dramatic pride that I had been granted a scholarship by the Bureau of Educational Experiments, which entitled me to study creative writing for children under Lucy Sprague Mitchell.

Most of the guests had been served with highballs but the only noisy one in the group was a famous illustrator. "Who the heck wants to write for brats?" was all he said, but the meeting turned into a debate.

Augusta Baker tried to talk, but the artist shouted her down. Then her husband, Jimmie, took the floor in defense of children and their need of a literature they could understand and enjoy. In the midst of the confusion Claude lost his temper and James Weldon Johnson walked out. The organization Claude had planned for so long fell apart before our eyes. I was the richer, though, because Augusta and Roberta Bosley drew closer to me and I acquired two of my most valued friends. The artist who started the argument now has a "brat" of his own and has bought dozens of copies of my juvenile books for his child and her friends.

Though I observed the letter of the law, visits to my Prisoner of Love were infrequent, and brought misgivings and doubts. Slowly, my temporal needs were adjusting but a thin crust of spiritual indifference plagued me. A number of Protestant church groups had invited me to work with them on civic projects, but I felt a need to identify myself and associate with members of my own faith. The only time anyone from a Catholic church had been to my house was during a Catholic Charities Drive and I felt left out of a circle in which I belonged.

All this I wrote to my former teacher, Sister Timothy, who was stationed at the Mother House in Cornwells Heights. I gave her a résumé of what my life had been like during the years she had not heard from me. I spared myself nothing and, after admitting my many stumbling and futile efforts, asked for help so that I might find direction. Sister Timothy wrote two letters, which she posted by return mail. One of them went to Reverend Michael F. Mulvoy, C.S.Sp., then pastor of the Church of St. Mark the Evangelist on West 138th Street, and the other letter came to me. It was good to be reminded by my teacher that, like every other girl who had ever attended a school conducted by the Sisters of the Blessed Sacrament, I was remembered in daily prayers. Sister said she added special prayers for her pupils who did not write because she said she knew that was when they needed prayer most. The letter ended with a thought which has consoled many a racked soul.

"Remember," Sister wrote, "Our Lord fell while He was carrying the Cross. He, too, fell more than once. But each time He pulled Himself up, picked up the Cross and went on to Calvary."

Within a few days I had been summoned to Father Mulvoy's office and I left the meeting happy in the knowledge that I had acquired a rare and understanding spiritual advisor who recognized the existence of an area where the spiritual and temporal complement each other.

Father Mulvoy's fiery red hair and matching freckles were well known to Harlemites, who called him "the blackest white man in Harlem." He talked to me at length of his efforts to induce white employers to hire Negroes on the white-collar level, particularly in the 125th Street area where Negroes were not employed at that time. He also told me of the rebuffs he had encountered in his efforts to persuade the utilities companies to employ Negro girls for their Harlem offices. He was slight of build but tall, with a straight back that showed no signs of bending, and I had to lean towards him to hear when he said quietly: "These things will come, but it will require time and hard work. That's where you come in. I have a group of young women who assist me—they call themselves Omicron Omicron—and I'd like you to work with them. I'll send you a card for the next meeting."

Father Mulvoy was a priest-social worker and every recognized social agency in Harlem considered him a valuable friend. Harlem's needy looked to him as a child to its father and he made it his business to acquaint himself with the problems we faced. He knew that we did not want pity or charity, but an equal chance to acquire the necessities of life and to preserve human dignity. He did not work for us, he worked with us and became one of us. The very esteem in which Harlem held Michael Mulvoy made him a target for people who had no conception of what he was trying to do. He was one of the first priests to convince Protestant Harlem that the Catholic Church was interested in the Negro.

Father Mulvoy's card of invitation came and I became a member of Omicron Omicron. The girls were a jolly group. They had dedicated themselves to the task of raising funds to support Father Mulvoy's civic work. Though I was not in the parish, I started going to St. Mark's Church. It was almost like being in Birmingham again to walk out of church and meet friends who were glad to spare a pleasant greeting.

Omicron meetings were usually held in the church hall, but sometimes we scheduled our social meetings in the homes of members. Several of the girls had cars and after the meetings Father used to take us to an ice cream parlor on Seventh Avenue and 138th Street for treats. One cold, snowy night when a carload of us arrived at the place before Father and the girls who were riding with him, I stood in the snow and looked up Seventh Avenue, remembering the New Year's Eve when I had been there alone. It was good to be a part of wholesome environment and to feel protected once more.

My new interests left me little time and I seldom saw Mabel and her husband except at mealtimes. They made plans to buy a home in one of the outlying suburban communities and I looked for a smaller apartment, which I found on lower St. Nicholas Avenue. My new home was near the subway, inexpensive, and easy to furnish. Though there was little chair space, my friends cheerfully sat on the floor. It was a far cry from Sugar Hill—but so was I.

When the school year closed I had been granted a scholarship for another year. My friend, Arnold de Mille, also received a scholarship and joined the Lab in the fall.

Work on the Federal Writers' Project, where we were gathering material for a book on the history of the Negro in New York, opened many new avenues of research to me. If I learned nothing else, I learned to make intelligent use of available library resources. My assignment was the Underground Railroad and I spent long hours in the labyrinthine stone building at 42nd Street and uptown in the Schomburg Collection, which was housed in the 135th Street branch. As I waded through documents which recorded the deeds of my favorite heroine, Harriet Tubman, my old interest in the life of the Underground Railroad's most daring conductor was revived. Lives of men like Frederick Douglass, David Ruggles, Isaac T. Hopper, Elijah Lovejoy, and the other brave abolitionists, writers, and statesmen who cried out against the evils of slavery and risked their lives to cheat the heartless men who trafficked in human flesh, became my daily fare.

Most of the talk about politics which I heard on my job flowed around or above my thought levels. We were told that the American Writers' Union protected our jobs but Claude told me never to attend any of the meetings and I didn't until the night when Emil Ludwig spoke. I had read the famous biographer's book on Napoleon and I enjoyed the speech. But the trend of the meeting before and after he spoke seemed focused on raising funds to send aid to Loyalist Spain. Though I recognized the need to broaden my horizons I clung to Mama's saying about charity beginning at home.

"What about Alabama?" I asked a woman who attempted to appoint me to a committee. "The crackers are still killing my people down there and nobody is raising a finger or lifting a voice to stop them. The only thing I know about what's happening in Spain is what I read. But I *know* what's happening in Alabama. When you get ready to raise money to fight Jim Crow, call on me."

As I left the meeting hall I noticed a tall, pasty-faced white girl who seemed to be active in most of the union affairs. She was holding court and I recognized several of the men around her. "I've been so busy working for the Party," she said shrilly as I passed, "I haven't had time to take a bath."

Claude listened attentively the next day when I gave my report on the meeting. "Now you see how dirty those crooks are," he said. "They've gotten control of the union just the way they control everything they get in. I hate them!"

We went to another part of the building and Claude introduced me to an elderly gentleman named Banta, whom he told about the meeting.

"When they see you talking to me," Mr. Banta said, "they'll go to work on you, too. But let me know whatever you hear. We must stick together."

I thought Claude and Banta were exaggerating when they talked about "the Reds plotting a revolution." I attributed it partly to their advancing years and I did not intend to enter any conspiracy with them. Later I saw a picture of Mr. Banta in one of the dailies. He had testified before some committee concerning Communist activities. I only wish I had listened to these two men with both ears so I might more intelligently answer charges made against Claude when he can no longer defend himself.

On paydays Claude, Arnold de Mille, Ted Poston, and I would stop at a grill on Eighth Avenue off 42nd Street where they served a free lunch with a round of beers. Ted Yates was so busy he seldom joined us. From time to time other writers came to these sessions, and one day when Claude was either pouting or had been detained I heard the story which partly explained his hatred for Communism and "the Reds."

During Trotsky's regime, I was told, the Communists made many attempts to woo the Negro literati. Even the most uninformed members of the Comintern who read Claude's "If we must die, let it not be like hogs / Hunted and penned in an inglorious spot, / While round us bark the mad and hungry dogs, / Making their mock at our accursed lot. . . ." could tell that these words had been torn from a heart crying out against injustice. Claude was labeled a likely prospect and invited to Moscow. Always eager to investigate, he accepted the invitation. There were few, if any, Negroes in Russia in 1923 when Claude was there and his presence added weight to the Communists' protestations of racial equality. He went everywhere at the State's expense, was taken up as a sort of mascot and given luxurious quarters in which to live and work, so he could be trotted out and put on exhibition at a moment's notice.

"They tell me that they picked him up and bore him through cheering crowds on their shoulders when he first arrived in Moscow," our informant said. "He was treated like royalty. Then when they started telling him what to write—well, you know Claude. He knew it was time for him to leave."

In the introduction to *Selected Poems of Claude McKay*, his friend, Max Eastman, too, mentions Claude's sojourn in Russia and the disillusionment which followed.

It was on another payday in this same tavern that I first heard the story of the motion picture depicting the horrors of lynching in the United States which the Russians were making when one of their officials returned from a visit to America and called a halt. A large company of Negro writers, actors, actresses, and singers had been given a trip to Russia to make up the cast. In the midst of the filming, a Russian dignitary ordered all work on the movie to stop. He informed his associates that Russia would never gain diplomatic recognition from the United States if the film were released. The picture was never finished, but even more interesting is the manner in which this abandonment of what was supposed to be an ideal was accepted by the Negro cast. They realized that they had been pawns and it is my sincere hope that one of them, who, I was told, acted as spokesman for the group, will one day write the story.

A few Sundays after I heard about this, Father Mulvoy spoke to me after the last Mass. "Ellen," he said, "there's a white woman across the street at Number 48 who came down from Canada to help me with the social work of the parish. She escaped from Russia during the Revolution and knows all about the Communists. I'm counting on you to help her. Go over there and meet her."

"She should meet Claude instead of me," I thought as I crossed 138th Street to Number 48 and rang the bell beneath the name of Catherine de Hueck. After climbing three flights of steps I found myself in a one-room apartment dominated by a handsome blonde woman of large stature. I saw many stacks of books.

"I'm Catherine de Hueck," the woman smiled after I explained that Father Mulvoy had sent me. "You are wondering about the books, aren't you?"

"Why so many of them?" I asked. "And what are you going to do with them?"

"My friends sent them from the Friendship House Library," she said.

"Where *is* Friendship House?"

"Why, you poor child," she said. "*This* is Friendship House. You must come around Monday night when the Newmanites meet here."

Looking around the room I wondered where the Newmanites or anybody would sit. Except for a small space on a couch pushed against a wall, books were piled on all the furniture. I might have asked the woman many of the questions which were running through my head, but the telephone rang. While she was talking, I decided I needed more information on the De Hueck woman and the Newmanites before I visited her Friendship House again.

"They're probably a bunch of tea-drinking youngsters who think its smart to come to Harlem and tell us how to run things," I thought as I left. "I wonder who she thinks she is with that 'you poor child' stuff. Guess she's just another one of those white people who feel St. Peter will throw open the pearly gates as soon as they tell him they've been working for the 'poor dear Negroes'."

Father Mulvoy, who sensed my misgivings, told me that the Newmanites were Catholic students from nearby colleges and universities who were banded together in social action groups called Newman Clubs. He further explained that the "Baroness," as he called Catherine de Hueck, was a White Russian who had seen most of her relatives shot down during the revolution. She had managed to escape, make her way to England, then to Canada and finally to New York.

I went to the Monday night meeting. It would be truer to say the meeting met me as I climbed the steps. Boys and girls were standing on the stairway, leaning against the banisters, sitting wherever they could. With the exception of one gray-haired woman they called "Flewy," and the Baroness, I seemed to be the oldest person present. Many of the books I had seen previously had been put in wooden cases that were under construction around the walls. The gray-haired woman was passing tea and cakes, and the others were talking about the Negro and his problem. I sat on the floor next to an attractive Creole-looking girl, who I soon learned was from New Orleans. Across the room was one brown-skinned boy. Though the others were talking about my people I could tell that few of them had known or associated with Negroes.

I could catch phrases like "the Fatherhood of God, and the Brotherhood of man" or "the Negro and the Mystical Body" which indicated much more depth than I had attributed to these youngsters. Then the Baroness talked about "Christ in the Negro" and along with all the others in the room I came under the spell of Catherine de Hueck. I had entered the room a Doubting Thomas and left as an ardent disciple. I was convinced that Friendship House needed me and many other Negroes if it was to be the Catholic Center the Baroness had said was needed to combat the forces of Godless Communism in Harlem. But I would have to get more Negroes to help me and we would have to explain to these well-intentioned white boys and girls that, instead of working *for* the Negro, they would have to work *with* us.

Friendship House soon outgrew the little flat and mushroomed into a library and three other store-front clubrooms on West 138th Street between Lenox and Fifth Avenues, with an apartment over one of the clubrooms which we called "Madonna Flat." The "B," as we affectionately called Catherine, insisted that the only way for white workers to know the Negro was to live with him. Though she offered the zealous white boys and girls who joined the staff no salary, she gave them food, clothing, and shelter from whatever donations came in. The "B" could woo an audience into the palm of her hand and then separate her listeners from enough money to carry on the work of establishing an interracial center in the midst of a Negro community where whites and Negroes could come together and discuss America's No. 1 Dilemma.

Catherine de Hueck lectured in Catholic schools, universities, and seminaries on Christ and the Negro. She talked to church groups and women's clubs. She begged for money, scholarships, jobs, or willing hearts and hands. The Catholic students and their older brothers and sisters who heard the "B" describe the conditions under which the average Negro in Harlem lives out his life came to Friendship House to see for themselves. In the early days there was lovely Jane O'Donnell, from Quakertown, Pennsylvania; Charlie Ward, the beloved "Mr. Charlie" from Rochester, New York, who befriended all the gamblers, bootleggers, and unfortunates; Ann Harrigan, later to become assistant to the "B," came over from Brooklyn; and Betty Schneider came all the way from Minnesota. We had no way of knowing then that the two Jewish lads who worked with us would later join religious orders and dedicate their lives to the cause we all served.

There were no bookcases for the library. Neither were there tables and chairs, but an artist named Tom Keating turned himself into a carpenter and piece by piece the furniture was soon in place. There were volunteers like myself and staff members to be fed at dinnertime. Olga La Plante, who had come from Canada to help, always managed to stretch the soup so there was enough for everybody. When good friends like Father George Ford of Corpus Christi parish, who was Chaplain to Catholic students at Columbia, brought steaks on days when the cupboard was bare, we rejoiced.

Lecture by lecture, the "B" talked up the $10,000 neeeded each year to support the work. Herb McKnight, who was the one

Negro in the room the first night I attended a meeting, was the first of a score of Negro boys and girls who went to college on scholarships the Baroness arranged or financed. It was after we had grown enough to put on parlor airs that the veteran journalist and author Eddie Doherty, Thomas Merton, later to write *The Seven Story Mountain,* and Mary Jerdo, who wrote *Harlem Novice,* came to Friendship House.

Beside the Martin de Porres Library, which also served as a meeting place, there was a clothing room in an old store across the street, a clubroom for the Cubs, and another for the C.Y.O. The "B" said that Friendship House, as a Catholic interracial center, was "an experiment in social action." In preparation for this work, she had made a survey of Communist propaganda in Canada and the United States and to obtain the necessary information had lived with the Communists for a year. As a result of her experiences she knew that the Negro was one of the Communists' objectives and she hoped through Catholic Action to cheat them. Because of methods and procedures which ofttimes seemed unorthodox, many criticisms were leveled at the "B" and Friendship House. There have been times when I have been one of the most severe of these critics. There are few who are familiar with the work, however, who can deny the fact that Friendship House held the line in Harlem for the Church until all America, and particularly Catholic America, was awakened to the Communists' designs on the Negro.

Perhaps it is in the area outside the realm of Friendship House's objectives in which it has made its greatest contribution. As a clearinghouse for information concerning matters pertaining to the Negro, the center has been invaluable to students, writers and social workers. As a meeting place where both races could come together and discuss problems of mutual interest, it was always available. When it was for the benefit of her neighbors in Harlem, the "B" never hesitated to "use her color" to open doors, purses, mouths, or ears which are closed to a Negro, but open for a white person.

On the spiritual side, association with the Friendship House staff and volunteers offered many of us the sanctuary of a social life based on Christian principles. To the defeated men and women who came to the store-front clubrooms on 135th Street for help, Friendship House was a haven where some few of them found their way back to God.

With all it gave, Friendship House never won the complete confidence of Harlem because Harlem never understood the reasons behind Friendship House's existence. Knowing why she had come to Harlem, the "B" saw no need to explain her reason for being among us. Rather, she depended upon her good works to speak for her. However, as Friendship House and all it represented was built around her, the organization was often viewed with the same suspicion which the "B's" presence had aroused in our midst. Though she knew that a white woman of Russian birth, noble or otherwise, living in Harlem would cause talk, it was difficult for the "B" to understand how the Negroes she had come to serve could question her motives. When she did realize it, it was usually too late to smooth ruffled feelings or undo some offending act. Once, when she was very weary, the "B" told me that working with the Negro was like walking on eggshells. As the years rolled by she came to understand the background which had bred so much suspicion.

Although the "B" and other Friendship House workers met upper-class Negroes at meetings and conferences, invitations to visit the better homes were few. Where they seldom had the opportunity to see how the privileged few lived, the "B" and her workers were exposed daily to the poverty and overcrowded conditions in which the many lived. The "B" was appalled at the rents Negroes were forced to pay for inferior quarters and indignant over the manner in which unscrupulous merchants overcharged for second-rate foodstuffs, or shoddy merchandise. And, in the late thirties, most of the landlords and merchants in Harlem were white.

In my little St. Nicholas Avenue apartment the "B" met brilliant Negroes who had become brittle and bitter because they had not had the opportunity to display their talents properly and felt they had been cheated out of a better way of life. She taunted them for having accepted defeat and urged them to pick up broken threads, often finding outside help to revive old interests. She talked with Negroes from the South who hated anybody white and who almost convinced her, after she had heard their experiences, that they were justified in their hatred. We talked about Shorty, Edna, and the countless other Negroes who suffered at the hands of southern whites without any law to protect them. There were times when the "B" said she was ashamed of the white race. Then she wrote and lectured about all of this, and through her, many Catholics to whom the Negro represented an unknown quantity, heard the story of the Negro for the first time. She warned them that if they did not act, if they did not extend the hand of brotherhood to the Negro, the Communists would. Her critics said she relied too heavily upon dramatics, but few of her critics ever had lived in Harlem.

The long, happy hours at Friendship House fitted into my school work and gave me access to many of the books I needed for my research. The "B" encouraged me to start a "story hour" for the children of the neighborhood. This gave me an excellent chance to try out my stories as well as the work of other members of the Writers' Lab on the audience for whom the stories were written.

Voluntary poverty is not attractive or practical for the average trained Negro, and the first staff members of Friendship House were all white. Soon after one of them arrived, the "B" would suggest that I drill them on what not to do or say when among Negroes. Many nights after one of these informal orientation courses the workers would follow me home and crowd my tiny apartment while we read poetry and talked until the stars were almost ready to go out.

Although I thought all the look of Sugar Hill was gone, some of it must have stuck to me. One night when a member of the "Black Cabinet," as President Roosevelt's unofficial Negro advisors were called, came up from Washington to talk to us on housing, he walked over to me before the meeting started and whispered: "What are *you* doing in the midst of so much sweetness and light?"

The Baroness started sending me out to talk to small groups; then she concluded that America should hear what I had to say through the Catholic press. Our good friend Father Gillis, editor of *The Catholic World,* accepted my first article and a new venture was launched.

It was about this time that a shy, slender brown boy who worked on the Federal Writers' Project wrote a book which stunned the American reading public with its realistic portrayal of a rebellious, poverty-stricken Negro named Bigger Thomas. Richard Wright already had a collection of short stories, *Uncle Tom's Children,* to his credit. And though Claude had to admit that the young author was gifted, he slyly suggested that "the Party" had helped Wright to get his first book published. However, when *Native Son* became a best seller, Claude was not the only one who discussed Richard Wright's political affiliations.

When Wright first came on the Project he was so shy that the men in my group had told me to find out if he could talk. I did, and had several interesting conversations with him. The thirteen-year-olds at the Little Red Schoolhouse were anxious to meet him and he went down with me one day and talked to them at length. Richard Wright was from Mississippi and I was from Alabama, but the difference between us was that the Catholic Church had extended open arms to me and only the Communist Party had offered Wright the opportunity at that time to fight the injustices heaped upon his people. But for the Sisters of the Blessed Sacrament, I too might have become a Communist after Edna was killed. These thoughts were put on paper and the "B" sent the manuscript to another good Friendship House friend, Ed Skillin, editor of *Commonweal.*

The article, which appeared under the title "Native Daughter," drew a great deal of fan mail. The letters came to Friendship House and more and more the "B" assigned me to lecture duty. As I talked to well-meaning white men and women, zealous interracial groups, and sometimes to hostile listeners from both races, I came to realize that Negro and white Americans must first come to know one another before they can be expected to understand or respect each others' problems. It was also while lecturing for Friendship House of Harlem that I adopted the habit of prefacing most speeches with "As a Negro..." to avoid the possibility of having some uninformed white woman say, "Is it really true that all Negroes smell?" or have to face the stock question, "What would you do if your daughter married a Negro?" The organizations I spoke for sent the "B" a check for Friendship House, but their members taught me a great deal about race relations in America. The most important of these lessons was that constant separation of the races is the greatest barrier to mutual understanding.

With Franklin Delano Roosevelt in the White House, Negroes began to feel that they would get a fair share of the prosperity which was just around the corner. The need for a Federal Writers' Project was diminishing. The fortunes of all my friends were improving: Claude got a contract for his new book; Arnold de Mille went into photography and advertising; Ted Poston was writing for the New York *Post* and the Pittsburgh *Courier;* Ted Yates was doing publicity for a theatrical agent. As the school year closed I had finished two juvenile manuscripts and Myrtle Sheldon, an artist, dummied a picture book so I could peddle it.

The summer passed uneventfully and on a brisk, gray day in September Ted Poston took me to the office of Jim, a friend of his who was a senior editor for a large midtown publishing concern. Ted had to hold my arm to keep me from turning back, but once we were inside Jim's private office I forgot how nervous I was.

"That corn bread and collard greens talk," Jim said after the introduction, "it's Alabama, isn't it?"

"How did you know?" I asked.

"Someday I'll tell you," he laughed, then told us to come with him to the office of the juvenile editor.

Myrtle Sheldon had done charming illustrations for the

dummy of the book *Janie Belle* and the juvenile editor was encouraging. Jim, who had blue eyes and red-gold hair, not quite
as red as Mama's, was a pleasant conversationalist and after the
conference in the juvenile department we sat in his office and
talked until his next appointment was announced. He insisted
on walking through the reception room with us.

"I should have told you," Jim smiled as he held the door for
me, "that I like corn bread and collard greens talk."

It was because of Jim's preference for a southern accent that
I learned a valuable lesson in tolerance. It all began very casually.
Each day at four o'clock my phone rang. Jim, he said, was calling
to "hear some corn bread and collard greens talk." We had long
conversations about what was happening in the publishing
world, what the readers were saying about my manuscripts, and
sometimes just about a funny story that happened to be going
the rounds. After Edna's death and my experience with Mr. X
I had been wary of white men, and though I was well aware that
Jim was a substantial-looking man who wore his tweeds well, my
sole interest, I thought, was in getting a first book published.
After the long-distance romance with Arthur waned, I had
boasted of my immunity to men. The friend of Johnny and Ted
Yates who acted as my escort understood my literary ambition
and was eager to see me succeed. The telephone bell was the only
signal I recognized each day about five minutes of four when I
glanced at my watch and waited for the ring.

Jim and I were sitting in the Old Colony on Lenox Avenue
the night I saw the first danger signal. We were waiting for Ted
Poston and another newspaperman who had been Jim's roommate in college. Jim had told me he was almost positive that my
picture book would be accepted but he was not sure about the
other manuscript. This depressed me and I must have dropped
my eyes.

"Ellen," Jim twirled the bottom of a glass and spoke as casually
as if he was ordering a drink of water: "I want you to look at me.
You know that I'd like to make a home for you, don't you?"

"I'd like to have a home, too," I said as if there was nothing
unusual about the idea.

Jim was on one side of a table and I was on the other, but there was a world between us and we were silent before the knowledge. We sat and looked at each other until we heard Ted Poston's Kentucky drawl and he and Jim's friend joined us, with a young woman I had never seen before. Hours later they took me home and I went to sleep that night saying, "He wants to make a home for me, he wants to make a home for me."

The next day I went to Jim's office to tell him that I did not think I should see him again, but I lost my courage the moment I was in his presence.

"You were unusually quiet last night after the others joined us," he said. "Were you displeased about what I had told you?"

"No. I didn't like that girl who was with us," I said. "She was common!"

Jim was quiet a moment as he ran his fingers through the unruly lock of hair which insisted on dropping down on his forehead. "Ellen," he asked softly, "did you ever hear what Abraham Lincoln said about common people?"

"No," I admitted. "What did he say?"

"Abraham Lincoln said God must have loved the common people because he made so many of them. Always remember that, will you?"

"Always," I said, and I always have.

The lesson in tolerance far outweighed the differences, other than racial background, which introduced discordant notes in this friendship. Jim opposed formal religion and said the Church insulted his intelligence. We argued until he admitted that he had been born and raised as a Catholic and that there was an estranged wife in the background. The more I withdrew, the more Jim pursued. Whenever it rained I knew he was coming to Harlem to remind me of that home he wanted to make for me. He'd phone my house, then go to every place he had ever known me to frequent. Once he found me, I knew he would lash out at the small corner of reserve I refused to surrender.

Despite occasional quarrels, he remained a loyal friend. He was the first to tell me that my first book had been accepted and, atheist though he said he was, he taught me to love the common people too "because God made so many of them." May his soul rest in peace.

When the next blow fell I was grateful that God had given me the strength to disregard Jim's pleading and hold my emotions in check.

chapter 11

SIGNS OF THE TIMES

On Easter Sunday, 1939, Marian Anderson sang at the Lincoln Memorial in Washington and the hopes of Negro America soared with each note of her golden song. Harold Ickes, Secretary of the Interior, introduced Miss Anderson and as I listened to his tribute to this Negro girl I knew the pendulum was swinging.

All of the ugliness of that earlier incident, when the Daughters of the American Revolution had refused to allow Miss Anderson to sing in Constitution Hall because she was a Negro, was canceled out for me as I turned on my radio and listened to Marian Anderson sing "Ave Maria" under the ceiling of God's sky in the shadow of the statue of Abraham Lincoln—but for whom she might have still been a slave. I was heartened by the righteous indignation which had swept the country, by the manner in which the First Lady of America and many others had resigned from the D.A.R. Slowly the circle was expanding. Four years later the D.A.R. itself was to add another inch and drop the ban on Negro artists.

New York spruced up and put on her gayest clothes in anticipation of the 1939 World's Fair. I was as excited as I had been during my childhood when Ringling Brothers' Circus came to Smith Park. Advance publicity on the Fair was stimulating, but what was more important, Mama had agreed to visit New York for the first time.

I smiled knowingly, the morning the telegram came. "Once

my parent makes up her mind," I said to myself, "she doesn't waste any time. I'll bet she's telling me to meet her at Penn Station."

Instead, the message informed me that my aunt, Annie Hutchinson, had been killed in an automobile accident outside Montgomery, Alabama, where she had gone to work as a matron at Alabama State College after her son, Doctor Edward, returned to Birmingham with his young family.

The pain of bereavement was greater when I learned that she might have lived if the precious moments which can spell the difference between life and death had not been used up in shifting my blonde, blue-eyed aunt from the white hospital where she had been taken (with a fractured skull and broken neck) to a Negro hospital after a visitor established her racial identity. The circumstances of Aunt Annie's death overshadowed the remainder of my cousin Edward's life and his career as a physician. A few unhappy years later he was found dead. He died in his sleep and it was only in death that he escaped from the harrowing conviction that discrimination had cost his mother's life.

The constant stream of visitors that poured in and out of my apartment that summer kept Mama and me busy every minute. Each day when I returned from work I found another friend who had come to visit the World's Fair.

After working hours I visited museums, theaters, and historical sites with the out-of-towners. I made so many trips to the Fair that I soon had a "going home" feeling when I entered the gate. Days when it was physically impossible for me to go on one of these tours, Mama went. Although at first she had been reluctant to travel by subway, she soon became an expert at guiding visitors around the Fair Grounds. To my surprise, one of the city sights which the visitors enjoyed most was the Automat cafeterias. Putting a coin in a slot and having the desired food slide out was new and exciting to them.

War clouds were hanging lower and lower over Europe and the "B" was still somewhere on the Continent. All of the Friend-

ship Housers were worried but we knew she would not come
back until she was forced to do so.

The day I took Mama to Friendship House for the first time
I explained why the center was in the slums.

"I hope you don't feel badly," she said, "but all of Harlem
looks like a slum to me."

When we walked up Lenox Avenue to 138th Street and
stopped in to see Father Mulvoy at St. Mark's, Mama seemed so
happy to be off the streets that I became concerned. On the way
back home, when we had to step to the edge of the curb several
times to avoid animal filth on the sidewalks, she became irritated.

"Why," my mother asked, "don't these people take their dogs
to their back yards?"

It was then that I remembered that the dirty sidewalks were
among the things which had offended me most when I first came
to Harlem. I also realized that the ways of Harlem were almost
as foreign to my mother as they would have been to a resident
of Vermont.

The apartment seemed lonely after Mama and all the visitors
left. I was behind in my writing as well as in the correspondence
which had developed as a result of articles carrying my by-line
appearing in Catholic magazines and Negro newspapers. Among
the most cherished of the many who wrote at that time were the
Reverend James A. Hyland, C.S.Sp., then stationed at Chippewa
Falls, Wisconsin, and a Dr. Smith, who was the father of one of
America's most distinguished Catholic poets, Sister Maris Stella.
Writing from his lodge on Lake Okaboji, in Wisconsin, Dr.
Smith began his first letter to me: "Dear Miss Tarry, I am an
old man. I saw Abraham Lincoln on his way back to Illinois. . . ."

An amateur photographer, the retired physician began sending
me photographs which covered a span of years from my birth up
to the early forties when we lost contact. Through the lens of his
camera I learned about life in Iowa and Wisconsin as lived by
white American families like Dr. Smith and his children, in
considerable contrast to life in Harlem or in my native South.

My new friend, Father Hyland, had spent twenty-five years
in Negro parishes throughout Louisiana and was writing a novel

based on some of his experiences. He wrote to ask me to read and criticize his script. "Father Jim," as many called him, followed his letters with a visit, and I acquired an understanding spiritual adviser. Still another bit of good fortune was in store for me: I had the opportunity to see the venerable scientist, Dr. George Washington Carver, for the first and last time.

Dr. Carver had come to New York from Tuskegee, Alabama, to appear on John Hix's "Strange As It Seems" radio program. He had been confined to a hospital for fourteen months prior to making the trip and reached New York in a state of exhaustion. Though Dr. Carver's assistant had made reservations at one of New York's largest midtown hotels two weeks prior to the visit and received a confirmation by mail, when the two Negro men arrived at the hostelry they were told that there was no reservation in Dr. Carver's name. The assistant produced the letter of confirmation, but the clerk insisted that it must have been a mistake and turned him away with: "Maybe later—if you care to wait."

The lobby was crowded and Dr. Carver's assistant, who was A. W. Curtis, Jr., an able young scientist in his own right, knew the seventy-six-year-old man was in no condition to sit there for any length of time. Curtis explained Dr. Carver's condition and asked if there was any place beside the crowded lobby where they might wait. From 11:30 on the morning of his arrival until 5:25 that afternoon Dr. Carver was forced to sit in a smoking room. Curtis telephoned the offices of Doubleday Doran, the publishers who were negotiating for a book based on the scientist's life. When one of the editors failed in his efforts to get a room at the hotel for Dr. Carver, he sent another white employee to the hotel. The white man went to the desk, asked for a room, and was told: "Sure, glad to accommodate you."

The man then asked why Dr. Carver's reservation had not been honored. An excuse was given, but newspapermen had already picked up the scent of a story. The local editor of one of the Negro weeklies called me and I went to the hotel with a photographer.

Not knowing the facts in the case, I made the mistake of asking for Dr. Carver at the desk. The clerk lost no time in telling me that no guest by that name was registered. I knew something was amiss and I prowled around the main floor looking everywhere for a trace of Dr. Carver. After I spent about a half hour running into dead ends, the photographer became impatient and left me. I was more determined than ever to get the story. Floor by floor I walked up and down the halls, listened at doors, and ducked around corners when I heard footsteps. On the third floor I heard a familiar laugh. I followed the sound to a smoking room at the opposite end of the hall. Through a partly opened door I saw Ted Poston and a group of reporters standing around Dr. Carver.

An attendant blocked my path when I attempted to enter. "You can't go in there," he said. "No ladies allowed."

"I'm no lady," I said without thinking, "I'm the press!" and the horrified man stepped aside.

Ted heard me and came to my rescue. He brought me up to date on what had happened and shared his notes with me. We both felt a little humble when he told me how a few minutes earlier Dr. Carver had looked up at the editor who had come to help him and said: "Just think, Mr. Woodburn, I haven't had an address since eleven o'clock this morning."

When the reporters questioned Dr. Carver about having been denied quarters, he started talking about America's rich natural resources in relation to the war which was shaping up in Europe. Dr. Carver was a firm believer in the theory that God's good earth can supply most of man's needs. Reading over the notes I made that day his words still carry a message. He told the reporters: ". . . We are a nation of copycats. We keep our minds so shackled that our creative spirit is stifled before it is born. If we would only stop dealing in glittering generalities and study the commonplace things about us, we would enrich our lives so easily. In a national emergency, America's needs in food, clothing, and industry could be easily supplied through development of synthetic products, if laboratory workers would only probe the latent qualities of ordinary plants and farm produce."

The aged scientist talked about the method he was trying

to perfect of oil therapy for muscular disorders, and he pointed to the progress of his experiments with peanut oils, which had been used for massage on infantile paralysis sufferers. The reporters questioned Dr. Carver about the many useful products he had extracted from the lowly peanut until he asked them to let the subject rest and added: "I'm all used up, too."

It was only after the hotel had been threatened with a civil suit that Doctor Carver's reservation was honored and quarters were made available for him and his assistant.

I had gone to a telephone booth to try to locate my photographer when the porter came to the smoking room for Dr. Carver's luggage. As I started back down the hall I saw Austin Curtis on one side and John Woodburn, from Doubleday Doran, on the other side, leading the elderly scientist out of the lounge. He was still smiling though, and the boutonniere of field flowers which he had picked the day before was still fresh.

We thought the story had ended. Besides Ted and me, there were reporters from the dailies who had been incensed over the manner in which the gifted scientist had been humiliated because of his race. Now that it was all over we felt the need for refreshment and went to one of the many dining rooms in the hotel. The other newsmen led the way. Ted and I followed. I had been seated when I saw that he was not with me. In the doorway Ted was talking to the headwaiter, who had stopped him with: "I'm sorry, sir, but we are not permitted to serve colored."

The other reporters rushed to Ted's side and stood with him as he explained to the waiter that the hotel had just righted a similar occurrence, but that both incidents would be aired if he was barred. After a conference with the management, the waiter allowed Ted to enter the dining room. In a few moments Austin Curtis came downstairs and nobody attempted to stop him when he joined us.

Despite this small victory, I was disappointed because I had not gotten a picture of Dr. Carver to go with my story. One of the photographers offered to swap the promise of a glossy print for my telephone number. He kept his word and the picture arrived in time for me to turn it in with my story. Ironically, the only comment from the editor was: "Huh! Whoever took this picture must not have been a photographer long or he wouldn't have used such a light background."

Walking home from the newspaper office I thought about the children I had taught down in Alabama and how I had told them that George Washington Carver was one example of a Negro who had risen about the handicap of race and been acclaimed by the world.

The Baroness was still in Europe. Although we worried about her, I knew in my heart that she was enjoying the excitement of impending war. I chuckled when a letter came from Warsaw, Poland, in which she said: "It is the chance of a lifetime to be at the focal point. . . . And yet I would give my last penny, zloty, gulden, or pfennig to be in Harlem."

It was not until Hitler's troops declared war on Poland that the "B" started home to Harlem. Skilled in the art of escaping the enemy, Catherine de Hueck boarded one of the last trains to leave Poland. With her usual flair for the dramatic, she came back to Friendship House with the gas mask and knapsack she had worn for weeks, and prepared us for the fact that it was only a matter of time before we, too, would be a nation at war. She told us how she had crouched in the ladies room as the train raced across Poland with German planes circling overhead and prayed: "Please, dear God, let me get back to Harlem."

On Christmas Eve I received my first check for *Janie Belle,* the foundling story that became my first book. It was scheduled for a late summer publication date. Janie Belle had come through just in time to play Santa Claus to a group of my most cherished story-hour children and I fought my way in and out of Macy's toy department that day to be sure that my boys and girls would be happy on the next.

As Hitler's war machine continued to roll across Europe talk of the approaching conflict dominated most of the conversations. It was around February, 1940, when Harlem pushed aside the alarming news of the world and wept over her own loss. News leaked out that Father Mulvoy was being moved. At Friendship House we refused to believe it until the "B" went to him and he confirmed the rumor.

A member of the Holy Ghost Fathers, our priest had been stationed at St. Mark's longer than the order usually permits. It was difficult to explain the rules of a religious order to the non-Catholic people of Harlem. Father Mulvoy had won their confidence, he had found them jobs, gotten the indigent on relief, and brought doctors and nurses to the ailing. The thought of losing him was terrifying. To me it was almost like Papa dying all over again.

The Race Relations Bureau established by Michael Mulvoy had succeeded in placing many Negro girls in the utilities companies. And Father Mulvoy had made it a point to send non-Catholic girls as well as Catholics to fill these jobs as they became available.

"I'm not interested in Catholic Negroes alone," he often said. "I'm interested in Negroes."

The Negroes Father Mulvoy had been interested in held meetings and formed committees to protest his removal at a time when many of the projects he had supported were just beginning to bear fruit. We all might have saved our time and energy because there was no one to whom we could appeal who understood Harlem's problems at that time. I was one of the few who were personally assured that the work Father Mulvoy had started at the Race Relations Bureau would be continued. If this promise was kept, neither I nor anyone I know has heard about it.

Father Mulvoy was sent to a parish in Tuscaloosa, Alabama, where he also became chaplain to Catholic students at the University of Alabama, an all-white group. Michael Mulvoy championed the cause of the Negro at a time when ours was not a popular cause and his name is still revered in Harlem today.

Though I was friendly with all of the Friendship House workers, I spent the most time with Olga La Plante, Jane O'Donnell, and Charlie Ward. It was through Jane that I met the talented artist-sculptor, Reverend Thomas McGlynn, O.P., and his sisters, Virginia and Helen. Their father, Frank McGlynn, had been a character actor in the early days of Hollywood, and the girls were part of a singing trio when I first met them. Virginia became a volunteer at Friendship House and we all came to know a great deal about the work her brother, "Father Tom," was doing on the West Side of Chicago where he had founded the Blessed Martin de Porres Center. Father Tom had executed an interesting statue of Martin and also done extensive research on the life of this South American Negro who had become a Dominican lay brother in Lima, Peru.

The McGlynn statue of Martin de Porres was and always has been my favorite, though not of most of my people. Father Tom high-lighted the slightly Negroid features of Martin, who was the child of a Negro woman and a Spanish nobleman. He also put a broom in Martin's hand, as a symbol of the humility with which Martin chose the duties of a lay brother, though he was highly skilled at curing diseases and letting blood according to the practice of the early seventeenth century. Many Negroes took exception to these realistic touches and most churches use a statue of Martin de Porres which depicts him as a brown man with Caucasian features wearing conventional black robes.

The hours I had spent in research while working on the Federal Writers' Project had left me a renewed interest in folk tales. In retrospect, I examined the stories I had heard from my mother and my grandmother and I knew that through many of these anecdotes they had passed along to me a part of the history of my people. It was in this manner that I first learned that among my ancestors had been "rebs, slaves, and Cherokee Indians." It was disturbing to realize that much of the unwritten history of the Negro in America would be lost when "the old heads" died, and I felt the urge to start southward and talk with some of these old people. Concord, North Carolina, was my first stop.

Concord, which is in the heart of the textile district, was different from most of the Southern towns I had visited before but it was hard for me to put the difference into words. I knew that there was less hostility between the races than in Alabama, but it crept out in odd places. There was less pretense at sophistication among the Negroes I had met and caste lines were not as evident as in towns farther south where mulattoes dominated the social picture. In Concord, mulattoes were conspicuous by their absence.

One hot June afternoon I went shopping with a friend and our last purchases were made at a white drugstore across from the courthouse. I was thirsty, but remembering what had happened at the five-and-ten in Birmingham, I thought it would be wise to wait. The clerk, who was perspiring profusely, complained of the heat and stopped counting up our purchases to wipe his face. I knew he knew how hot it was and I took a long chance on his understanding.

"Would you be kind enough," I smiled at the white man as I walked a few steps to the fountain, "to serve us with two large cokes?"

The clerk and my brown friend looked at me as if they both thought I had lost my mind, but the surprise strategy worked. In a few moments we had been refreshed, had gone on our way, and the store had made a few cents profit. Though I stayed in Concord two months I never met any other Negro who had been served in that drugstore. Nor did I meet another Negro who had ever asked to be served.

My friend, Marion, was a teacher. She held a supervisory position in Cabarrus County at that time and she drove me to many towns and villages I might never have reached otherwise. Some of the tales to which we listened were variations of stories I had heard during my childhood in Alabama. There was a different story pattern thread in many of them, however, because most of the elderly Negroes I talked with in North Carolina were descended from what sociologists call "field Negroes," whereas most of the ex-slaves or children of slaves I had talked with in Alabama had been "house Negroes."

A story I first picked up in North Carolina which points up the difference was the tale of the "backlog" and how it had been used by slaves to prolong the celebration of Christmas on the southern plantations. I had never heard before that yuletide festivities usually lasted as long as the backlog burned in the open fireplace of the "big house." The slaves charged with the task of selecting the log would choose the tree with the hardest bark and greenest wood, cut it to size, and soak it in a secluded stream. On Christmas Eve the soaked log was placed against the back of the grate and fat pine was fed to the flames which had to be kindled to light up the drawing room or parlor. If it took as long as six weeks for the backlog to burn to ash, that meant six weeks of rest for the enslaved field hands.

Marion and I were returning from one of these story hunts the day we saw a car on the highway bearing a Louisiana license plate. I had received a letter earlier telling me that my friend Arthur from New Orleans would be passing through Concord enroute to a professional meeting in Baltimore. We hailed the traveler and within a few hours Arthur and I had quarreled over the reasons I advanced for my stay in Concord, and we parted in anger once more. Perhaps it was difficult for a practical businessman to understand how much I enjoyed roaming the countryside, listening to stories which seemed to serve no greater purpose than to furnish material for a magazine article and to give me a greater appreciation of the long, stony road my people have traveled.

If there was a Catholic church within the city limits of Concord in 1940 I never found it. The Bruners, whose family comprised a considerable part of the Negro population and occupied a number of the houses up and down Chestnut Street, were my hosts and they introduced me to most of the people connected with the civic life of the Negro community. But nobody I met could direct me to a Catholic church.

One day Marion passed a little church out in the country and turned off the road to investigate. It was a Catholic church which had been dedicated many years before by the famous Cardinal Gibbons of Baltimore.

Chestnut Street was excited over the trip Marion and I were to make to the Catholic church out in the country. It was a beautiful Sunday morning when we set out and we were both in high spirits. I had missed Mass for a couple of Sundays and was eager to kneel before my Prisoner of Love once more. As we drove off the highway I saw that a number of cars were parked in the grove beside the little white church which sat at the top of a hillock, almost obscured by lush foliage. A child of seven or eight years who was standing beside an old jalopy scampered like a frightened fawn when we parked. As Marion locked the doors of her car I noticed that a sudden agitation seemed to run through the group of pale, lean men and women with children of various ages who were standing under the trees in front of the church. They stared at us with open mouths. I was pleased that Marion was well groomed and thought the people were staring at us because they were unaccustomed to seeing city folk.

As we walked toward the church, the men and women stepped aside and looked in the opposite direction; the children clung to their mother's skirts as if in great danger. Nearest the steps, I saw two nuns who smiled. It seemed an eternity since I had heard Mass and I was impatient to get as close to the altar as possible. I walked up the aisle of the sparsely furnished church to the second or third pew, said my prayers, and looked around to hand my friend the simplified missal I had brought along so she would have some idea of what she was witnessing. Marion was not beside me.

The pews behind, which had been empty when I first knelt, were now occupied, but my friend was not there, either. A sickening thought came to me when I remembered how the child ran away as we first drove up, how the men and women stepped aside as we neared them.

Crossing myself, I hurried down the aisle searching for a brown face on either side. In the last pew, just inside the door, I found Marion. She was in a half-kneeling, half-sitting position and though she smiled at me I could see that her hands were trembling.

"What's wrong?" I whispered as I knelt beside her. "Are you ill?"

She shook her head.

"Then what is it?" I insisted. "Why didn't you follow me?"

"I did," she said. "I was behind you when the usher stopped me. He said *I* was supposed to sit back here—in this last row."

We had found Jim Crow in a Catholic church.

I looked from the intelligent brown girl crouching beside me to the ill-behaved white people in front of us who swapped recipes and local gossip when they should have been praying. From these conversations I learned that the Bishop of the diocese was expected to say Mass and later confirm a class of children. The surrounding county was dry, but flasks of whisky protruded from the pockets of most of the younger men and the older ones seemed ill at ease in their Sunday suits. It was my turn to stare with an open mouth when I saw mothers unbutton their dresses and nurse babies without making the slightest effort to cover their breasts. That Marion should have been relegated to what was considered an inferior place in the house of God seemed incredible and my anger mounted as Mass began and the ceremonies unfolded.

As soon as the last child was confirmed I rose to leave and Marion followed. The red-faced usher, standing by the door, smiled at us.

"I want to speak with the Bishop," I told the man without returning his smile.

"Wait outside," he said pleasantly enough. "The Bishop will be out as soon as he has changed his clothes."

The segregation pattern was repeated as we stood outside and the others again stared at us, once they had attained a safe distance. Fortunately, we did not have long to wait before the Bishop appeared and the two nuns rushed over to get his blessing. As the others approached him awkwardly, I told my friend that I wanted to present her to the Bishop. I did not tell her that I also intended to protest the manner in which we had been segregated.

Marion hesitated. "Are you sure it will be all right this time?"

I bluffed: "This time I'm sure." I reached for her hand and pulled her along with me.

We could hear our fellow worshipers gasp when I knelt and kissed the Bishop's ring before I introduced myself.

"You're from Friendship House in Harlem, aren't you?" the clergyman asked.

"Yes, Your Excellency," I replied. "But how did you know?"

"I recognized your name," he laughed. "I'm the Baroness' 'poor bishop.' I'm sure you know that she sends me magazines and clothing to be distributed among my people."

"Of course I know about you," I smiled as I remembered how 'poor bishop' sounded when pronounced with the Baroness' Russian accent. "But I never knew your name before."

The pleasant conversation reassured my friend, and she was behaving quite naturally by the time I presented her.

When the parish priest joined us, the Bishop introduced me and referred to "Native Daughter," the *Commonweal* article, which the priest said he remembered. At the time, I had the feeling that remembering the article gave the priest the necessary clue to my racial identity which was puzzling him. But it was difficult to smile when the usher who had stopped Marion came up and accepted an introduction without extending his hand.

The nuns chose the first pause in the conversation between the Bishop and me to tell him that Marion was a teacher and had promised to come back and help them with summer school. The priest, too, invited us to return. I was about to lodge a complaint about the treatment accorded my friend when the usher spoke up.

"Yes," he said, "you must come back every Sunday. I'll save the last pew for you."

As we drove back to Concord, Marion respected my feelings enough not to speak of what had happened. Both of us knew the sin had been one of ignorance rather than of malicious intent.

When Father Hyland, who was hard at work on his novel, heard that I was going to Birmingham from Concord he suggested a trip through the Teche country of Louisiana. He knew I would find the folkways of this Cajun stronghold interesting and he thought it would also give me a more critical eye for the script he was sending me to read from time to time.

A few days after my arrival in Birmingham I found myself on the wrong side of the color-conscious caste line. Arthur wrote from Baltimore to tell me that he would like to stop in Birmingham on the return trip to New Orleans so that he might talk over the Concord incident with me and possibly make amends.

When Arthur and his friends arrived, a round of pleasant social activities began. I introduced him to all my relatives, and as there were two other young men in his party, he met most of my female friends. Tall tales enliven most "closed parties" in Negro social circles and Arthur and his friends had an interesting collection, among which were several jokes about Catholic priests. I resented the jokes and, in the end, became indignant. Arthur in turn accused me of being a prude. In parting he expressed the resentment I had suspected he felt for years.

"*You* can't understand my problems, anyway." His words cut like a knife. "I'm *black!* And each of your relatives you introduce me to is whiter than the others."

The thrill of having a first book accepted is a personal reaction, but my entire family was elated the day in August, 1940, when a faithful mailman left a bulky package at our house containing the author's complimentary copies of *Janie Belle*. The Negro press carried reviews and pictures and one of my newspaper friends, Ollie Stewart, who had returned from South America after I left New York, stopped off in Birmingham to offer his congratulations.

A few days after Ollie Stewart left Birmingham, Nannie asked me to be her guest when the Congregational Missionary Society met at her house. I wondered about the invitation. Though nobody in the family ever alluded to the time Nannie stopped speaking to me because I had become a Catholic, many of the members of the Missionary Society had been equally critical and I felt awkward in their midst.

After the business of the day was completed, the minister introduced me as the "guest of honor." Nannie was standing outside the door while he spoke of Papa and how I grew up in the church. As he talked about my newspaper work in Birmingham and New York, the magazine articles, and my new *Janie Belle*, the intensity of Nannie's gaze made me look up at her. I saw the same proud love in her eyes that used to shine out when Ida Mae, Little Sister, and I were children and someone complimented her on our appearance. I was sorry that I had ever doubted her love. This was my first lesson in the virtue of patience. It was also my first conception of life as a circle which sometimes comes around full.

On my way to visit the Louisiana Teche I stopped off in Montgomery to see the City of St. Jude, a small Negro community which had been founded by Father Harold Purcell, former editor of *The Sign*.

Before Father Purcell came South he had read a great deal about the needs of the Negro in this area. After making a study of conditions affecting my people throughout the southern states he decided that the need, both spiritual and material, was greatest among the Negroes of Montgomery. Father Purcell mingled with the Negroes I had never known in Montgomery and found the neighborhoods where they lived overcrowded, the houses dilapidated, and the sanitation facilities inadequate. The priest was moved to take action after he learned that there was no city hospital for Negroes and saw places like Shuffle Alley, where twenty one-and-a-half-room shacks housed about one hundred Negroes. There was only one water tap and one toilet for the use of the entire alley.

In 1934, Father Purcell had rented a small frame house, at Holt and Mill Streets, which served as a chapel, with an improvised altar, an office, and a clinic. Quietly, Father Purcell went about the business of ministering to the Negroes of Montgomery and preaching the Word of God. At the same time, through letters, lecture tours, and the press he was telling Northern Catholics about the needs of their colored brethren. The priest's pleas were not in vain; in 1936 he was able to purchase forty acres on

the outskirts of Alabama's capital, adjacent to a Negro neighborhood. He placed the project under the patronage of St. Jude
Thaddeus, relative and apostle of Our Lord and "helper in cases
despaired of."

At the time of my visit, the building nearest the highway was
a church and school. One of the Sisters of the Holy Family, who
conducted the school, welcomed me to City of St. Jude and took
me inside the church. I have seen many beautiful places of worship but the one I saw that day was different from any of them.
I gazed up at thick overhead beams of white oak, tinted in blue
and gold, upon which the Ten Commandments had been carved.
I read the Apostles' Creed from the stained glass windows on one
side of the church. On the windows of the opposite side the seven
sacraments of the church were explained with pictures and text.

Highly polished floors glistened on either side of the blue car-
pet runner, which like the altar cloths, honored Our Lady with
their color. The altar gates were of marble adorned with gold
plating. The Last Supper was carved upon the base of the altar.

"Those altar gates have an odd history," said the smiling Sister
who was acting as my guide. "Father went to New York while
he was building, and while he was poking around in the basement
of a very large church, looking for anything he could find which
might be used here, he found those gates. They had been discarded, but Father had them polished up and there they are."

In the choir loft I listened to a hymn to Our Lady played on
an Everett Organtron and examined the well-bound hymnals
which were nearby. Every detail which adds to the effectiveness
and solemnity of worship had been taken into account.

As we walked through the large, airy classroom, I commented
upon the fact that the desks and other equipment showed none
of the signs of abuse usually seen in schools. After showing me
through the showers, locker and rest rooms, Sister explained that
with the exception of a few technical experts it was the men of
the community who had built the church and school. It was theirs
and any abuse of it was their own. Father Purcell had injected
subtle character-building into every phase of his work. He had
divined a secret which too few white people who work with

Negroes ever guess: the inner man as well as the outer man must be nursed back to health.

In the social center we walked through a kitchen, where two hundred children were fed daily, to the dispensary. Sister showed me rows and rows of shelves stacked with medicines which had been donated by Father Purcell's friends, then took me to the spotless clinic where medical care had been given to thousands of Negroes. Dr. R. T. Adair, a Negro physician I had met years before, had donated his services. With the aid of one of the Sisters, who was a registered nurse, he cared for the sick and performed minor operations. Obstetrical and major surgery cases were sent to St. Margaret's in Montgomery.

Upstairs in the social center I met the man who had dreamed this little city and already seen a part of his dream come true. Father Purcell shared with me the parts of his dream still to come and talked of his desires to build a hospital where expectant mothers and sick children could be cared for. He told me of his plans to build a high school and a college—if there was enough time left. Already he was showing signs of having sacrificed his physical self almost beyond endurance to achieve his goal.

I learned about the subsistence gardens which had been cultivated on a portion of City of St. Jude's acreage. Small plots were lent to large or needy families so that they might raise vegetables for the table. No rent was paid, but those who raised good crops were given the plots for another year. If crops failed because of neglect, the plot reverted to the community.

I told Father Purcell that many people in the North felt that his project was another experiment in segregating the Negro.

"If bringing Negroes out of Shuffle Alley to the City of St. Jude is segregation," Father declared, "then we want to segregate them!"

Father Purcell's teaching church and experiments in social rehabilitation made an impression on me which later found expression.

May Gagne, the little Creole girl I found in the Baroness's apartment the first night I went there, was waiting for me at the station in New Orleans. May had made arrangements for a friend to drive us to St. Martinville, which is in the heart of the Teche and at the end of the Evangeline Trail. Here Longfellow's heroine, Evangeline, is supposed to be buried under an oak tree which bears her name. It was in this locale Father Hyland had set his novel and I was eager to see it.

I saw Arthur briefly while we were waiting to start out for the Teche. He was still beset by resentments, though he enjoyed the distinction of being one of New Orleans most eligible bachelors. It was hard to believe my ears when he told me I had become so "professional," that I had lost my "femininity." My laughter infuriated Arthur because he thought it was directed at him. Remembering how Ted and Johnny had coached me on developing a professional attitude as a measure of protection, I knew I was laughing at myself.

We drove past the church built by Father Hyland for Negroes, and I remembered how Father had arrived in this little town twenty-five years before to find the whites worshiping on the first floor of the local church, the mulattoes in the balcony, and the blacks in a gallery. Always an ardent foe of segregation, James A. Hyland withstood the warnings and threats of the Ku Klux Klan and built a school and then a church, so the Negroes in this little town could worship God in dignity. I saw evidences of his labor and spoke with people who remembered this kindly priest. I met many people who were prototypes of the characters in his book. The seasonal rains beat us to Lafayette and we could not go on to St. Martinville because the roads were closed. I was grieved to miss the opportunity of seeing the scarred old oak where Evangeline was supposed to have met her beloved Gabriel and which later served as her last resting place.

We were anxious to get out of the flood area and Alice drove as fast as the speed laws allowed. In the little towns along the way we saw crowds of people who had been driven from their homes by high water. They were milling about emergency shelters erected by local chapters of the Red Cross. We were relieved when nightfall caught us only a short distance from Baton Rouge, where May and Alice had many friends, and we sang as the speedometer clicked off the miles.

Our song ended abruptly with a blowout. The roads were almost deserted because of the flood warnings which had been posted and we were resigned to the task of changing a tire when we saw two tiny specks of light cutting through the foggy night. We hailed the motorist and he sent help from the nearest filling station. I was interested to note that the motorist and the mechanic were white, but treated us with utmost courtesy. I mentioned this to May, who laughed.

"It's hard to tell who's who in Louisiana," she said, "so we won't look a gift horse in the mouth."

Alice telephoned the president of Southern University, whose son was a friend of hers, and he sent a student to show us the way to the campus. My fatigue vanished before the beauty of the moonlit lagoons and moss-laden willows overhanging rustic bridges. We spent the night in the new women's dormitory which was opened to the students when school resumed. We reached New Orleans in safety the next day and I prepared for the long trip back to New York.

In looking over the scribbled notes which recalled many of the high lights of this trip, I was impressed by the number of "Brown Bomber" cafés, bars, and theaters I saw in Negro communities. Joe Louis had brought a new sense of dignity to his downtrodden people. The pride on the faces of little boys who played boxing games and shouted: "I'm Joe Louis, the heavyweight champion of the world!" was something to remember.

There were signs of preparation for war all about us, and it was on this trip in 1940 from New York to New Orleans that I first became aware of how war affected human lives. Perhaps it was because I talked with so many servicemen in transit and listened to the bits of information they seemed eager to share about their families, their training and future ambitions and plans. At the time, I did not know how fortunate I was to possess this ability to listen.

Back at Friendship House I met Eddie Doherty. Eddie was a newspaper man and the "B" said he and Helen Worden, another writer, were gathering material for a series of articles on Harlem. Up to the time Eddie came to Friendship House, he and Miss

Worden had gathered most of their material on our community
on routine tours with the plain-clothes officers charged with ar-
resting the prostitutes who prowl the streets of lower Harlem.
They both knew, however, that there must be another side to
the community. That was why Eddie came to the "B."

The "B" waved us out of the library as she was anxious to get
to the papers piled high on her desk: "Tarry, you take Mr.
Doherty out and show him the *real* Harlem."

Eddie and his journalist-partner visited social agencies,
churches, schools, and all kinds of places of amusement. They
talked with average men and women as well as the outstanding
members of our community. Eddie did most of the leg work, and
when he had finished he knew both sides of Harlem well. He
also had a consuming interest in and devotion to Martin de
Porres, who was the patron of our Friendship House library. It
seemed only natural that Eddie would "adopt" Friendship House
and we accepted him as another member of our growing family.

Eddie touched my life with a wand which produced a story
for my second book and an introduction to a great American
whom future historians will record as one of the most courageous
men of our time. We all like to remember the way the book
happened because it was a happy bit of Harlem living.

In return for the help we had given with his story, Eddie gave
a party at his home in Westchester and invited the Friendship
House workers. He was to call for us in his new car and it was
agreed that I would join the group in front of Madonna Flat. As
soon as I crossed Lenox Avenue walking east I saw the crowd
farther up 135th Street and wondered what the commotion was
all about. The instant I saw tall, blond Eddie standing alongside
a shiny red convertible full of wriggling, giggling brown urchins
my story was started. As I drew closer I saw that Eddie was pushing a button on the dashboard which made the tan canvas top
of the car go up and down. Each time it went up or down the
boys squealed with delight and their eyes got bigger and bigger.

At the party we met Eddie's mother and his sons. The elder
one worked for an airline company. Jack, the younger boy, was

still in college and none of us guessed he would one day be a journalist like his father. There was a lot of brilliant talk and music and good eats, but my mind was busy with the tall, blond "Mister Ed" and his beautiful red automobile which had been full of little wriggling, giggling colored boys who squealed each time he made the tan canvas top go up and down. That night when I got home I made the first notes for *Hezekiah Horton,* as I called the little boy through whose eyes I saw the red car.

Harlem is always restless but there was an added air of rebellious discontent hanging over the community in the latter part of 1940. Hiring was going on in the plants which manufactured materials necessary to the war efforts of our friends across the sea. Prices were rising with the higher wages Harlem read about. Negroes felt that they were being left out of the war effort and they were angry. Wherever there was a gathering of Negroes there was bound to be hostile talk, which they considered righteous indignation. Too often I heard hate, too, and it frightened me. It was not unusual to see a couple of Negroes beating a white man who had come to Harlem to enjoy wine, women, or song and instead had gotten drunk and called somebody a "nigger."

What was happening in Harlem was happening all over the country. The Negro had not been integrated with the industrial effort to prepare for a war which we would inevitably enter. Tension rose in areas where money was slow to trickle in and it was obvious that some steps would have to be taken.

There was much talk of the need for a "leader," and A. Philip Randolph of the Brotherhood of Sleeping Car Porters was being mentioned as a man about whom Negro America might rally. In our Monday night meetings at Friendship House this general unrest was one of the frequent topics of discussion.

It was February of 1941 when a call to organize resounded. A. Philip Randolph, who had publicly expressed the belief that "nothing short of organized and dramatic mass protest and pressure could place the cause of the Negro in the mainstream of public opinion," proposed a "March on Washington Movement," with chapters in every major city. Participation in the war effort through employment was the objective. If the Negro was not integrated, a march on the nation's capital was to take place.

The March on Washington Movement captured the imagination of the Negro masses. During my lifetime I have read or heard talk of only one other mass movement among my people which reached national proportions—the Marcus Garvey movement with its back-to-Africa plan which was disintegrating around the time I came to New York. Garvey, who was deported to his native Jamaica, was said to have possessed many of the same qualities of leadership which were winning support among Negroes for A. Philip Randolph.

Unlike Walter White of the NAACP and Adam Clayton Powell, Jr., who had become a New York City Councilman, Randolph looked like a Negro. And in spite of a Harvard accent, he told the Negroes what they wanted to hear; namely, that they were Americans and entitled to all the rights guaranteed by the Constitution. Furthermore, Randolph promised to lead his people to the doors of Congress if steps were not taken to curb racial discrimination in industry.

The Negro press carried stories weekly of instances in which factory doors were closed in the faces of qualified Negroes. Pleas for fair play fell on ears that refused to hear. "Get ready to march" was the word passed along and July 1, 1941, was the deadline. Motor pools were set up and cars were canvassed as master plans for the line of march were projected. With each passing day the Movement gained momentum but there was still no word from the White House or Congress.

By June of 1941 the whole country knew that the Negroes were planning to march on Washington. President Roosevelt called A. Philip Randolph and Walter White to Washington for a conference. Layle Lane, a New York teacher, and a labor leader, Frank Crosswaith, accompanied Randolph and White. It is reported that the President sought desperately to persuade Randolph to call off the march. He pointed to the need for unity in a time of war and suggested that the conference method, rather than mass pressure, was the American way of dealing with minority problems. The Negro committee would not relent. Randolph realized, however, that the President was inclined to admit that the demands he was making for the Negroes of America were just and Randolph proposed an executive order forbidding discrimination in industry.

Pending any developments which might have resulted from the conference with the President, plans for the March moved ahead. It is rumored that there was a second conference in New York City with Mrs. Roosevelt and Mayor Fiorello La Guardia urging Randolph to call a halt to the proposed March on July 1. Randolph is said to have repeated his demand for an executive order and expressed his determination to march if the order was not forthcoming.

On June 25, 1941, Franklin D. Roosevelt issued Executive Order 8802, which stated:

" . . . I do hereby reaffirm the policy of the United States that there shall be no discrimination in the employment of workers in defense industries or Government because of race, creed, color, or national origin and I do hereby declare that it is the duty of employers and of labor organizations, in furtherance of said policy and of this order, to provide for the full and equitable participation of all workers in defense industries, without discrimination because of race, creed, color or national origin. . . . "

There was no justification for the March after the order was given, and Randolph canceled the mass protest. His followers received both the President's declaration and Randolph's "no march" order with mixed emotions. Negroes were skeptical that industry would comply with Executive Order 8802 and the machinery of the march had been put in such high gear that it was difficult to stop it. Many Negroes were so emotional they could not see the wisdom of their leader's strategy and insisted that Randolph should not have canceled the mass protest.

On June 28th, 1941, two days before the proposed march, a major network donated air time for A. Philip Randolph to make a radio speech explaining the reasons for his action and urging the Negroes of America to contribute their brain and brawn to the war effort. He reaffirmed the determination of the March on Washington Movement to fight until "full participation" was a reality.

President Roosevelt created the first Fair Employment Practices Committee, composed of seven consultants, two of whom were Negroes, to oversee the enforcement of his executive order. The order and the FEPC served to rekindle the Negroes' faith in their government.

It was not unusual for a member of the Friendship House staff to announce intention to leave the organization and embrace the life of a religious order. All of us knew that Jane O'Donnell was interested in the Ladies of the Grail and had visited their headquarters outside Chicago. But we had not expected her to become a "Lady," and we grieved when she announced her intention. I postponed the parting with Jane and accepted an invitation to go to Chicago with her. Eddie Doherty offered the use of his "beautiful red automobile" and donated his services as chauffeur. Neither Jane nor I regarded this mode of travel as an unusual way for a beautiful young girl to go to the convent of her choice. And Jane, with deep-set violet eyes and ash-blond hair that formed a wispy halo around her madonna face, was the most beautiful of all the girls who came to Friendship House to work.

We agreed to travel by easy stages and stop whenever we felt the urge because the three of us knew this would be our last trip together. Jane wanted to make a last visit with a friend who had become a Carmelite nun and we drove through the city in West Virginia where her friend was stationed. It was the first time I had ever been inside a convent of a cloistered order and it was hard for me to reconcile the description Jane had given me of her friend as a jolly fun-loving girl with the shadowy face of the nuns we saw. The "Sisters' part" of the convent at Rock Castle was noisy compared with the stillness which engulfed Jane, Eddie, and me as we stood in the vestibule of the Carmelite convent and rang a bell, then waited for the Mother Superior, whose face appeared behind a screen. Jane did not see her friend, but was told that she was well and happy. It was my first glimpse into the contemplative world where saintly souls turn their backs upon the secular life and live out their days in prayer and good works in order to atone in part for the sins of the world.

I had another new experience on this trip to Chicago. All the way Eddie insisted that we eat in the best hotels and restaurants. It was wonderful until one night at a mountain inn I remembered Claude McKay and thought of the things he had told me about the unpleasant experiences he had had when his white friends had attempted to take him to fashionable eating places. I felt ill when I remembered that I would not have been served either—if I had been black.

We also slept wherever accommodations looked good. Jane and I had great fun mailing our friends postcards of the hotels or lodges where we stopped. However, we were sufficiently aware of conventions to put an "x" beside our room and another by Eddie's.

On arriving in Chicago I found a message from Father Hyland. He had come to Chicago to talk over some criticisms I had made of his manuscript and joined us when we drove Jane out to the Grail. I left Jane at the convent, and I also met Bernard J. Sheil, Auxiliary Bishop of Chicago, who was one of Eddie's heroes.

Eddie often had told us about how Bishop Sheil had founded the Catholic Youth Organization and that he was beloved by the Negroes of Chicago. It was on a warm Fourth of July when I met Bishop Sheil at the Grail. All the time he was officiating at Benediction of the Blessed Sacrament I was torn between adoring the Prisoner of Love and feeling sorry that such a wonderful man as the Bishop was weighted down in that heat by so many robes and vestments.

Jane and I cried when we parted. She was so pretty and we had had such a gay time on our trip out to Chicago; I knew she was going to face days or weeks of strict discipline. So I felt sad, when I knew the parting which I had delayed was at hand.

Eddie drove back to Chicago as fast as holiday traffic permitted.

A party was in progress when we arrived. Eddie soon started

talking about the life of Martin de Porres, and everybody looked at us if they thought we were a little crazy. Later, I learned that interracial friendships were not as common in Chicago, at that time, as in New York. The fact that Eddie was white and I was a Negro had set us apart, to say the least. I was still to learn much more about Chicago. And Eddie and the "B" were to be part of it all.

chapter 12

ANGRY HARLEM

In spite of Executive Order 8802 and the FEPC, Negroes had not been integrated with America's war effort by the fall of 1941. There was grumbling and unrest everywhere, but particularly in Harlem, where so many of my people were concentrated. The Monday night meetings at Friendship House became more heated as reports of street brawls, riots, police brutality, and lynchings poured in from all parts of the country. Catherine de Hueck had seen these same signs of unrest in her native Russia during the regime of the late Czar Nicholas and she recognized the forerunners of uprising. She had learned from Eddie that Bishop Sheil was friendly with President Roosevelt and after listening to a series of complaints from Negroes who had felt the sting of discrimination, the "B" flew to Chicago to talk with Bishop Sheil. When she returned from this conference we knew we had a powerful friend in Bishop Sheil.

Father Hyland had asked me to show his manuscript to a number of publishers with whom he had been corresponding and each of them suggested that the manuscript be rewritten from a more subjective point of view. James Hyland was a mission priest and much of his time was spent in travel. To undertake the task of rewriting a manuscript on which he had worked for years would have been tremendous. As a compromise he hit upon a three-way mode of operation, which included my services. He was to write rough drafts, I would criticize and polish, then mail them to a friend of his in Chicago for the final typing. My trip through the Teche had given me a "feel" for the story, but we both agreed that New York offered distractions and Father Hyland asked me to go back to Alabama while I was assisting him so that my work would not be hampered by civic or social responsibilities.

As always, I dreaded the thought of leaving my adopted home. Though Friendship House was the focal point of my activities at that time, I had met many interesting people in the literary world and was reluctant to remain away from the scene. Through Roberta Bosley and Augusta Baker I had met the wife of James Weldon Johnson. A widow since the accident in 1938 which had snuffed out the life of this distinguished Negro poet and statesman, Grace Nail Johnson carried the image and memory of her "Jim" in her heart with a compelling and regal grace. I met her at a tea which Roberta had arranged at the 135th Street library, and was immediately impressed by the interest she expressed in the young and unknown writers of our race. This trait, she explained, was an extension of her husband's interest in the work of fledgling authors who so often sent their manuscripts to him for criticism. Mrs. Johnson told us James Weldon Johnson had contended that one never knew where genius might turn up and he had never returned a manuscript without reading it.

Before we left the library, Grace Nail Johnson had suggested that I show some of my manuscripts for children to the editor in the Junior Books department at Viking Press, publishers of many of her husband's works.

Following Mrs. Johnson's advice, I went to Viking, where I met May Massee, who had a wide reputation for publishing worthwhile juvenile books. So I became a Viking author. May Massee also understood my desire to have a Negro illustrate the little story of Hezekiah and the red automobile and was patient with my search for an artist whose sketches would meet her approval. We were both happy to select Oliver Harrington, whose cartoon, Bootsie, appearing in the Negro press, is an all-time favorite. My book was in the making when I went off to Alabama to help Father Hyland finish his manuscript. It was as if Fate were pushing me back to my original starting point.

I said good-by to New York once more. About a month after I arrived in Birmingham, the Second Regional Congress of the Confraternity of Christian Doctrine (Province of New Orleans) was held there. The high light of the Congress was a lecture by Monsignor Fulton J. Sheen, who later became a bishop and one of America's outstanding television personalities. To see this famed orator, Mama and I had to climb the steep steps of segregation and sit in a Jim Crow gallery, but we later agreed that the speech we heard was almost worth the humiliation. The other item in connection with this confraternity which I best remember was an article which appeared in the publication issued by the sponsoring organization under the caption: "Colored Catholics Have Own Day at Regional Session." I attended the evening meeting of the colored Catholics' "own day" and the entire session was devoted to protests from Negroes who resented being Jim-Crowed by a Catholic organization.

Each mail brought a fat batch of manuscript from Father Hyland, which I polished and sent on to Chicago for the final typing, but the weekends afforded me the first opportunity in years to enjoy college football and I attended every game within motoring distance. One of the last games of the 1941 football season was played in Columbus, Georgia, and I drove over with a party of friends. The draft had put many of the young men we knew into uniform and the day after the game we drove out to Fort Benning. We made a tour of the post and our last stop was a recreation center for Negroes. Most of the soldiers looked so young and the women who were visiting them looked either old or dissipated. When our party appeared some of the boys acted as if they were ashamed of the women with them.

There were six of us, three men and three young women. As we drove away from the recreation hall toward the gate I made a mental note of the fact that all of us were healthy, gainfully employed, and reasonably happy. It was Sunday, December 7, 1941, and the war was still thousands of miles away. Our team had won the day before and listening to the waltz music coming from a radio on the dashboard of the red convertible in which we were riding, all of us felt as safe and secure as any Negro can feel in Georgia. The music stopped abruptly and an announcer told us to stand by for a news bulletin. The Japanese had struck at Pearl Harbor!

The details of the attack were being given as we pulled alongside the soldiers guarding the gate. Nobody moved until the announcer finished and the music was resumed; then, in silence, we drove away from Fort Benning. Pearl Harbor meant war and we knew the lives of all of us would be touched by it.

Army camps throughout the state of Alabama were quickly activated. The number of uniformed men on the downtown streets of Birmingham increased and jokes about the "draft board blues" became grimly popular. Christmas and New Year's passed and in early 1942 Eddie's article on Harlem appeared in *Liberty* magazine. The last chapter of Father Hyland's book was sent to the typist and I bought a railroad ticket to New York.

One has only to understand rhythms to appreciate the difference between the slow, leisurely beat of life in a southern town and the quick pounding staccato—sometimes bass and sometimes treble—of life in New York. I feel it as soon as the train enters the tunnel leading to Pennsylvania Station and the passengers line up in the aisle with their baggage, eager to be swallowed up by the Big City. It is like receiving a challenge at the precise moment one sips from a glass of champagne.

Up in Harlem, where I went to live at the YWCA, I found the unrest among my people more pronounced than ever. Everywhere I went I heard resentment expressed over the second-class citizenship of the Negro at a time when America needed the strength of unified effort. Tensions continued to increase as incidents piled up. There was a riot in Hempstead, Long Island, a stone's throw from New York, when a white policeman was alleged to have clubbed the head of a Negro soldier he was attempting to arrest. Eight hundred Negroes were said to have gathered and in the struggle three policemen and one civilian were injured. A police car was wrecked and four Negroes were arrested, one of them a woman.

The day after the outbreak in Hempstead there was a race riot in Detroit when a Negro boy was shot by a white restaurant-owner's son. This was not the first clash between the races in Detroit, and I was especially concerned because my sister Ida Mae lived there. My fears were well founded.

My sister, we learned, had been on her way home from work when the fighting broke out. Her husband, who because of her lack of racial markings, feared for her safety in the Negro section she would pass through, enlisted the aid of several friends. They stationed themselves along the route of the street car line she usually rode and waited.

In the meantime, the car Ida Mae was riding reached the Negro community. Hoodlums started mauling the white passengers, but Ida Mae convinced them that she was a Negro. When they attempted to manhandle the elderly white woman sitting beside her, Ida Mae refused to relinquish her hold on the woman. They attempted to use force, but my sister shielded the old woman until her husband and his friends boarded the car and led the two women to safety.

Tensions were spreading like the flames of a forest fire. There is less solid neighborhood spirit in Harlem than in other Negro communities and there the clashes between the races remained minor, though disturbing. A theater on 116th Street was the scene of an outbreak when a white employee was said to have been heard using the despised word "nigger." A Negro mental patient was reported to have been shot by a policeman and a crowd stormed Harlem Hospital. Each week the Negro press carried stories of racial discrimination in local aircraft factories and defense plants.

That someone in the War Department exercised poor judgement in sending Northern Negroes to southern training centers has long since been conceded. The friction and bloodshed that resulted is factual history. As early as March of 1941, a Negro soldier named Felix Hall was found hanging from a tree near

Fort Benning, Georgia. At Camp Robinson, Arkansas, Negro troops were driven from the roads by whites. There were riots and brawls at Alexandria, Louisiana; Fort Bragg, North Carolina; and at Camp Dix, New Jersey. As the call to arms was being sounded in every town and hamlet of the United States a Negro was lynched at Sikeston, Missouri; the shores of Bataan were dripping with the blood of Americans when a white policeman in Birmingham pumped five bullets into the back of a Negro named Henry Matthews for some alleged minor infraction of the law.

The Baroness knew Harlem was due for a riot. Like the rest of us she had no idea when or how it was coming. We warned white audiences to whom we lectured and begged them to use their influence before it was too late to correct many of the situations which were building up hostile resentments in Negroes. The "B" drew great strength from the letters she exchanged with Bishop Sheil, who she knew had conferred with President Roosevelt, and we kept hoping for a declaration of social justice from a ranking member of the Catholic hierarchy. Once more the "B" went to Chicago and I received an urgent message from her which instructed me to call together a group of Negroes whose names she listed. She asked us to set down the most common grievances of the Negro. Though it was difficult to digest the indignities our people had known from 1619 to 1942, we managed to list the most pertinent complaints, covering racial discrimination in education, employment, and housing. On a copy of one of the drafts we made for this letter there is a notation in my handwriting: "Mr. Stevens, you take over from here." We relied upon a brilliant young attorney, Harold A. Stevens, now a judge in the Court of Special Sessions, to outline the legal aspects of the manner in which the civil rights of the American Negro were daily violated. We did not question the "B" as to what use she was to make of this letter, but as soon as it was in her hands she notified us that she was leaving Chicago on a trip which would take her all the way to New Orleans and that she intended to talk with every Catholic bishop who would listen to her. Those of us who guessed more about her mission than she wrote prayed that the Holy Ghost would direct her words.

My friend, Claude McKay, had been missing from his usual haunts for some time. When I found him he was alone and ill in a rented room. Claude needed medical attention and nursing care and I had no one to appeal to but my friends at Friendship House. Claude was fiercely proud and it was not easy, but the girls took turns nursing him and Olga prepared nourishing broth and other dishes which we hoped would strengthen him. Claude took his bad moods out on me, but I was grateful that he showed his charming side to the others. He had done so much for me it was a privilege to be of small service. Dr. Edward Best, who looked after the health of the members of the Friendship House staff, and seldom sent a bill, told me that Claude would never be well again. But Claude refused to stay in bed and after a few weeks he looked like the old McKay.

"I guess I'll have to go up to Friendship House and read some of my poems one night," was as close as Claude ever came to admitting he was sorry for the many unkind things he had said about "you Catholics." He came to Friendship House, read his poems, and met the "B" and Eddie. All who heard him were impressed, and I was relieved that Claude never treated his Friendship House audiences to one of the dramatic exits in the middle of a reading for which he was famous throughout Harlem's literary circles.

One morning on the corner of 125th Street and Eighth Avenue I met Dan Burley, then managing editor of the New York *Amsterdam News*. We had a pleasant talk and Dan asked me to work with him on the paper. It was like a dream come true for me to have the opportunity to write all day and get paid for it, too, and I knew I could trust Dan because his wife was a friend of mine.

My flair for attracting complicated situations was demonstrated the first morning I went to the newspaper office. Dan put a batch of assignments on my typewriter and the first one I picked up was on birth control. My story was to be built around a news release sent out by one of the advocating agencies, but knowing the attitude of the Church on this practice I did not want the story on my conscience or under my by-line. I saved the first assignment for last and then solved the problem by putting it in the waste basket. That was one of my lucky days. Dan never asked for the story on birth control.

The following months were a time of ferment and decision, but I was happy in my work. Dan was a considerate "boss" and an expert at waving the scent of a story under my nose. He knew I would never come back to the office until I had all of the facts, and he became resigned to the knowledge that regardless of the assignment he gave me it would be a feature with pictures attached by the time I put it in the wire basket on his desk.

Julius Adams, one of the editors, was on the desk one morning when an unidentified voice called and asked him to send a reporter to Pennsylvania Station to meet a woman who was coming up from New Orleans. The informant said the woman, who would be wearing a green dress, would have an interesting story to tell. Julius and the others laughed because I too was wearing a green dress that day and the labor editor, J. Robert Smith, who had met my friend, Arthur, in New Orleans made a suggestion.

"Send Tarry on that one," he laughed. "The lady from New Orleans may have a message for her."

There was more laughter but nobody said anything else about the tip. I watched the clock and as soon as it was time for me to take a break for lunch I left the office. I did not meet the lady in the green dress at Pennsylvania Station, but I met a man who took me on a merry chase which ended at this woman's house. When I came back to the office I had the first of a series of ship stories.

The lady in green was a stewardess on a ship which ran between New York, New Orleans, and the Caribbean. A Negro girl entrusted to her care for the voyage back to the States had been molested by a white man and the Negro crew members had threatened violence when the captain of the ship had refused to take action against the child's molester. It was an ugly story but one the reading public was entitled to know. The NAACP made an investigation and the paper carried an account of the follow-up.

At the seamen's halls I made friends who telephoned me as soon as a ship came in with a crew that might have a story to tell. German bombers and mined waters were taking a terrific toll of the ships and the men who manned the ships which carried our soldiers and war materials. Almost every merchant seaman who was fortunate enough to return to home port could relate harrowing experiences. These new friends passed my name and the telephone numbers of the paper and the Y, where I lived, from ship to ship. Sometimes they called early in the morning, sometimes late at night. Once or twice, when I had doubts about the tip, my old friend Arnold de Mille accompanied me but my fears were always unfounded.

There came a night when an anonymous caller instructed me to go to a hotel on West 23rd Street and ask for a certain name if I wanted a good story. I could not find Arnold or anyone else so I set out alone. On the subway ride to 23rd Street I reprimanded myself for taking a needless risk, but the temptation was too great. At the hotel I asked for the name I had been given and went upstairs to the room with shaking knees.

Instead of facing danger, once I was inside the room I faced three young Negro boys, two of whom were still bedridden from exposure. They had been through a dramatic experience, were grateful to be alive, and wanted to tell someone about it.

The boys were shipmates and they had made the voyage to Murmansk without incident. Each of them, however, commented upon the favorable change which seemed to take place in their white mates' attitudes toward them as soon as they reached a foreign port. One of them told me in a half-proud, half-ashamed way about visiting a house of pleasure in Murmansk with a white mate from Florida.

"As we walked out of the house," he recalled, "the white boy put his arms about my shoulders and said: 'Folks down in Florida wouldn't believe a white boy and a colored boy could have so much fun together, would they?' "

All three of the boys described their first moments of terror and then the determination to live when their ship first "got it," as they referred to a bombing. The lad who had told me about the vodka spree which ended in a Murmansk house of ill fame sat up in bed and pulled the blankets high about his chin as he concluded: "When those bombs began to fall out there in that water there were no white men or black men. We were just human beings struggling for existence."

It was a good story they gave me and the only request they made in return was to say: "The boys told us you would get our picture in the paper."

As the Negro soldiers began stopping in the Stage Door Canteen, the need for Negro hostesses became apparent. Osceola Archer, the talented Negro character actress, who had been one of the moving spirits behind the organization of the Canteen, visited me at the Y and asked me to talk to some of the girls who lived in the building about becoming hostesses, since many of the Negro actresses were on the road most of the time. The first night I had to go to the Stage Door alone because most of the girls I knew were either busy or had previous dates. With the exception of one or two boys from the 372nd Regiment, which was quartered in barracks on 110th Street, all of the Negro boys who came in that night were sailors and after I introduced myself they seldom gave me a chance to sit down. Several times white servicemen cut in and asked me why I was dancing with Negroes, but when the colored boys saw what was happening they started cutting in on the white boys and it all passed off in a spirit of fun. The Negro sailors were experts at the Lindy Hop, and when the Canteen closed I had to do a bit of acting to walk instead of crawl.

The next night I went to the Stage Door Canteen I took two girls from the Y, one of whom was several years my junior. As soon as the sailors came in I introduced her around. At closing time we had to help my young friend up the steps leading to the street, then put her in a cab and take her back to the Y. Later, when the cream of Negro society was flocking to the Stage Door Canteen to work as hostesses and hosts, I remembered those nights when there were only three or four of us to provide our boys with dancing partners. Later, the white hostesses made friends among the colored servicemen and the Stage Door Canteen developed into a grand experiment. It broadened my base of operations, and between Army paydays I was never surprised when I found one of the soldiers from 110th Street waiting outside the *Amsterdam News* for me in the hope of obtaining a small loan. I have often wondered what happened to the ones who came most often. I called them my "regulars," and not one of them ever defaulted.

Every agency concerned with the welfare of the Negro was protesting the treatment being accorded him. The NAACP was fighting on all fronts, at home and abroad. The Reverend John LaFarge, S.J., editor of *America* and organizer of the Catholic Interracial Councils was talking and writing the cause of inter-racial justice for all Catholic America. Under the supervision of George K. Hunton, executive secretary, the Councils' Vesey Street headquarters served as a meeting place and clearinghouse for information concerning race relations. This work was implemented by the *Interracial Review,* which won many friends for the cause to which it was dedicated. Few dramatic measures, other than Executive Order 8802 and the FEPC, had been taken, but America was no longer pretending to be unaware of the fact that one tenth of her population was being denied full citizenship. Though the March on Washington Movement had been the deciding factor in the battle of wits which forced President Roosevelt to follow his own inclinations and issue 8802, the Negro was still in a despised position, and he was clamoring to be heard. A. Philip Randolph and his lieutenants knew this and called a meeting for June 16, 1942, at Madison Square Garden. MOWM units throughout the country planned to hold similar demonstrations. Up to the night of the meeting, there was little doubt that A. Philip Randolph was in the most strategic position as far as leadership of the Negro was concerned. He had the support of the masses and it was assumed that all who were in the category of Negro leaders were also behind Randolph.

Between the hours of 7 P.M. and midnight on June 16, 1942, Harlem was like a deserted village. Every man, woman, and child who had carfare was packed into Madison Square Garden. Dan had instructed me to cover the woman's angle and I had to confine myself to the fact that Muriel Rahn, concert soprano, opened the meeting with "The Star-Spangled Banner," after which one of Harlem's outstanding civic leaders, Mrs. Bessye Bearden, introduced Negro America's First Lady, Dr. Mary McLeod Bethune.

On the printed program of the June 16 March on Washington Movement meeting which rests on my desk there is a notation beside Mrs. Bethune's name which reads: "The audience stood when she took the speaker's stand," but that does not adequately describe the way the people rose to their feet when Mary McLeod Bethune strode across the stage of Madison Square Garden, nor how they applauded until she had to beg them to stop. This elderly Negro woman had endeared herself to the hearts of her people by her struggle to found and maintain Bethune-Cookman College at Daytona Beach, Florida, and it was also common knowledge that she had the ear of Eleanor Roosevelt. They knew that Mrs. Roosevelt was said to listen to Mrs. Bethune on all matters concerning the Negro and it was also said that Franklin Delano Roosevelt listened to the advice of his energetic wife. Mary McLeod Bethune was the Negro's friend at court and the crowd wanted her to know that they were proud of her.

Heads nodded and murmurs of approval ran through the crowd when Mrs. Bethune concluded her speech by declaring:

" . . . We have grown tired of turning the other cheek. Both our cheeks are now so blistered that they are too sensitive for further blows. But regardless of our trials and tribulations at home, we must not for one moment lose sight of the fact that we must give all-out, unreserved effort to winning this war. . . . At the same time we want our flag to protect us: at home, in our right to produce and live; abroad, in our willingness to sacrifice and to die."

Amanda Randolph, of radio and TV fame, sang "Brown Sol-

dier Boy," written especially for this occasion and dedicated to
Joe Louis. Many of Harlem's most prominent women served as
ushers and guides and several outstanding Negro actresses were
featured in Dick Campbell's play, "The Watchword Is Forward."

It was assumed that a common cause had brought the outstanding Negro speakers of the day to Madison Square Garden, but
according to the men who "make book," everybody tried to get
into the act. If the speakers had condensed their remarks, once
it had been made clear that the meeting was running behind
schedule, the course of events might not have been changed.
But with thousands of Negroes listening, there is strong suspicion
that the stage of Madison Square Garden became a sounding
board for personal ambitions. Speaker after speaker read prepared speeches and in the end there was not time enough for
A. Philip Randolph to make the principal address. By contrast,
Adam Clayton Powell, Jr., then a New York City Councilman,
aroused the responsive audience to cheers when he announced
his intention to run for Congress in the approaching elections.

The June 16 meeting represented the most unified mass dem-
onstration I have ever witnessed. The MOWM had reached a
peak; from that time on its strength either seeped away or was
funneled in different directions. Mr. Randolph gave his speech
at a later meeting which was held uptown in the Golden Gate
Ballroom, but the shining moment had passed. Veteran newspapermen and students of Negro politics claim that some of the
other Negro leaders became fearful of Randolph's power and
by indirection and subterfuge withdrew their support. Perhaps
it is enough to say that the March on Washington Movement
served its purpose by winning Executive Order 8802 and though
Mr. Randolph's over-all leadership was brief, it was nevertheless
brilliant. Future historians will properly assess his role and record a detailed account of the March on Washington which
never took place. It is thrilling for a mere reporter to recall the
drama of the moment, fleeting though it was.

The "B" was in high spirits. After she had returned from the
trip on which she had spoken with most of the Southern prelates
she wore a smile of expectancy which we did not understand until

the fall of 1943 when the Roman Catholic bishops of America held their annual conference at Washington, D. C. Both secular and Catholic newspapers carried excerpts from a letter the bishops addressed to the American heirarchy which read in part:

"In the Providence of God there are among us millions of fellow citizens of the Negro race. We owe to these fellow citizens, who have contributed so largely to the development of our country, and for whose welfare history imposes on us a special obligation of justice, to see that they have in fact the rights which are given them in our Constitution. This means not only political equality, but also fair economic and educational opportunities, a just share in public welfare projects, good housing without exploitation, and a full chance for the social advancement of their race. When given their rights in fact as in law, they will prize with us our national heritage and not lend ear to agitators whose real objective is not to improve but to destroy our way of living.

"In many of our great industrial centers acute racial tensions exist. It is the duty of every good citizen to do everything in his power to relieve them. To create a neighborhood spirit of justice and conciliation will be particularly helpful to this end. We hope that our priests and people will seek opportunity to promote better understanding of the many factors in this complex problem and strive for its solution in a genuine Catholic spirit."

One success always led the "B" to try for another, but none of us had expected her next move. One day she casually told us that Bishop Sheil had expressed the need for a Friendship House on the South Side of Chicago to be co-directed by a Negro and a white woman. The "B," we learned, had promised to send "Tarry" and "Harrigan" before she bothered to tell Ann Harrigan or myself about it.

The last thing I wanted to do, at that time, was leave New York. Writing satisfied me, as jewels and fine clothes satisfy many women. Writing for a newspaper gave me the opportunity to project many of my interests and quieted that old urge to do something about the plight of my people. I felt as if I had found my niche in life at last.

The "B" thought differently. She was convinced that I would be in a position to render even greater service to interracial justice in my position as co-director of Chicago's Friendship House, whose local patron was to be Bishop Sheil. Ann Harrigan got a leave of absence from the Board of Education and the "B" had everything set for the Chicago center except the Negro half of the directorship.

While I was spending sleepless nights trying to make a decision, a Negro sharecropper, Odell Waller, killed a white landlord who had abused him and his aged mother, and was electrocuted in Virginia. There was little doubt that Waller had killed in self-defense and his execution aroused tremendous protest from Negro communities. For months prior to the execution the Negro press carried stories about the case. The day of the funeral, Pauli Murray, a brilliant young woman who was working for one of the organizations that had raised funds to defend Waller, telephoned me an eyewitness account of the ceremonies and faithfully relayed the mutterings and outbursts she had heard among the crowds of angry Negroes who had followed Odell Waller to his grave. When I turned in the story on the Waller funeral, I felt as if I had buried Shorty. I made up my mind to stick to my journalistic career and let some social worker co-direct Chicago's Friendship House. The Baroness lulled me into a false sense of security by saying she understood my position.

A few days later one of the priests from the Bishop's office came to New York and talked with me. Father reminded me that I was the only Negro woman with certain qualifications who was also familiar with Friendship House objectives and policies. So flattering a compliment, coupled with the fact that he told me my people needed me for this job, melted my resistance. Knowing the "B" had strong feelings about Friendship House workers accepting salaries, my last feeble effort to avoid going to Chicago was to demand a salary. The "B" made an exception to the rule which insisted upon staff members embracing voluntary poverty and working for food, clothing, and shelter alone. In a few weeks my agreement to go to Chicago was signed and sealed.

Viking Press had published *Hezekiah Horton,* and the James Weldon Johnson Literary Guild held an autographing party at the Hotel Theresa before I left for Chicago in September. My friend and teacher, Lucy Sprague Mitchell, May Massee from Viking, and many of the other publishing people I had grown to love came up to Harlem and I stored away happy memories to take to Chicago. My loyal friend Marguerite Cartwright, who is one of the most colorful Negro educators on the national scene, gave a delightful party afterward in her lower Fifth Avenue apartment and my uptown friends went downtown.

chapter 13

MEMORIES OF CHICAGO!

Ann Harrigan preceded me to our Chicago post.
I was in the midst of packing when her letter arrived. She was
safe and happy, but she hinted at some slight difficulty about
finding an apartment. I did not attach much significance to it
at the time because the Baroness had assured me that Chicago
was waiting for us with open arms and I had never yet come to
grips with a housing shortage. Ann also wrote that she had found
an excellent secretary who had, in turn, introduced her to a Mrs.
Sunshine Edwards, in whose *funeral home* Ann said she was staying—temporarily.

" 'Temporarily' is right," I laughed as I tossed Ann's letter
on the bed in my cozy Harlem YWCA room. "Nobody will ever
catch me staying in a funeral home!"

That night after the last bag had been packed, I read Ann's
letter again. This time I noted that most of the letter was about
Mrs. Edwards, the funeral director, who was well-to-do, had a
cook, two cars, a chauffeur, and was generous with both cars and
the chauffeur. In a postscript Ann said it might be wise to wait
a while before I shipped anything for the apartment we had an-
ticipated. Already I had sent dishes, silver, linens and blankets.
There was nothing left to send but the furniture I had put in
storage when I left the St. Nicholas Avenue apartment.

"Once I get to Chicago," I thought, "I'll find an apartment.
There'll be no funeral home for me yet awhile."

It was a gray September morning when Ann met me at the

La Salle Street Station. After the usual greetings she guided me to a long black limousine. A liveried chauffeur held the door open until we were seated. As we drove away I was sure Ann was avoiding my questioning eyes.

"Whose car is this?" I demanded. "The Bishop's?"

"No. This is Mrs. Edwards' car," she answered. "Ellen, I've looked all over Chicago and I can't find a vacant apartment anywhere. I can't even find rooms—except at Mrs. Edwards'. So that's where we will have to stay for the time being."

"You mean that's where you *stayed*," I corrected. "We agreed to live together and work together. But I never agreed to stay in anybody's funeral home!"

"Oh!" Ann laughed, "I never suspected that you were superstitious."

"I am not superstitious!" I fought back. "But I am not going to live in an undertaking establishment. It's too depressing!"

The crooked smile on the chauffeur's face, when he held the door for us to get out in front of the gray-stone mansion on South Michigan Boulevard which housed Mrs. Edwards' establishment, only added to my irritation and reminded me that he would probably tell his employer all I had said.

The instant we entered the house my nostrils twitched and itched from the heavy odor and the scent from flowers. The carpets on the floors were so thick I could barely hear our footsteps. As from a great distance, I heard soft—very soft—organ music. Ann tried to pull me up the stairway, but I stared at the ornate casket surrounded by flowers which dominated the front parlor.

"I wish you would hurry," Ann begged. "We will have our meals over at St. Elizabeth's Rectory. We're late already."

I took a deep breath and followed Ann to a huge room on the floor directly above the front parlor. There were two beds in the room.

"Mrs. Edwards thought you might prefer to sleep in here with me—until you get used to the place," my partner explained.

Ann hurried me through a change of clothes, then walked me a block or so to the Rectory where I was introduced to a cook who was actually named Mrs. Cook and to pretty caramel-brown

Mildred Wiley, who was to act as our secretary. We were joined by another worker from Mobile, Alabama, and in a few moments we had discovered many mutual friends. In the midst of this pleasant meal there entered the Reverend Vincent Smith, S.V.D., who was the only Negro priest in Chicago at that time. Though I did not realize it, I met one of the great spiritual men of my time. Father Smith was so gay and full of good humor that none of us would have ever guessed or suspected the austerity which would attend his future.

After lunch, Father Smith offered to drive us to the stores. As we rode along 43rd Street, Mildred spoke when she was spoken to, but Ann was so gay I became suspicious.

When Father Smith opened the door of the first store, which had formerly housed a cheap dry goods business, I understood Ann's agitation. I also understood how hard she must have had to fight her conscience before she wrote that letter urging me to hurry to Chicago. If she had made one slip of her pen and described the trash on the floor or the nails which stuck in my shoes at every other step, the filthy walls, leaking faucets, and non-flushing toilet bowl, I would never have left the Harlem YWCA.

The other store, where I was expected to set up a Children's Room, was no better. From the sign out front, I saw that this had been the Jones Brothers' Chicken Market and there were a number of ancient chicken coops sitting around to bear odorous testimony. We put newspapers on top of wooden crates and sat down to make plans for converting what confronted us into a two-room store-front community center. By the time *they* had finished we had to return to the Rectory for an evening meal. I had been little help because all I could envision was littered floors, smelly chicken coops, and a funeral home, with thoughts of the Harlem YWCA and the *Amsterdam News* stabbing my heart.

I ate in a daze. I kept remembering the warnings my friends in New York had given me and how I had told them that the trouble with most New Yorkers is that they think everybody is camping out the minute they leave Manhattan. Ann led me back to our residence and I was only aware of the fact that I walked a block or two, then climbed steps and entered a door. Once we were in the hallway opposite the front parlor I noticed that something seemed to be missing. Then I remembered. It was the casket I had seen earlier. It was gone. My sense of desolation mounted as I realized it was either in a cemetery or in transit. I stood trembling. I was not going up the steps. Ann knew I was disturbed and braced herself.

"Miss Harrigan," a voice called from the rear office, "I have a message for you."

Ann pulled me along as she went to the office and I met "Sunny," as Mrs. Edwards' friends called her, and the other members of her staff.

Though I was prepared not to like my landlady, I was attracted by the laugh lines around her piercing black eyes, which twinkled from suppressed humor. Sunny looked more like an Indian squaw than a Negro. Ample proportions and touches of gray hair at her temples added to the dignity of her appearance. She greeted me warmly and her secretary handed Ann a message which, she said, had come from the Bishop's office.

After we had gone upstairs to our room I saw Ann frown as she read the message. Then she handed the slip of paper to me and asked what I thought it meant. At the top of the message sheet I saw a woman's name which was wholly unfamiliar. Underneath the name was written: "Curls on top—roll on side."

Neither of us could imagine how such a message could come from the Bishop's office or what it meant. As I examined the other side of the paper I saw a notation which said our appointment was set for two days hence. I explained to Ann that whoever had taken the message had written it on the back of a message sheet which had already been used, and the mystery was solved.

We devoted the next day to going from one real estate office to another in search of an apartment which did not materialize.

Later in the day as we were returning to Mrs. Edwards', we saw a carload of people in front of the house. At the foot of the stairway there were two caskets visible. One was flush against the side of the stairway.

An attendant rushed past us and answered the door. I heard a man's voice call a name which sounded familiar.

"Ann," I whispered, "that was the name written on that slip of paper we had yesterday."

We had started up the steps. Neither of us was able to control our eyes, and we looked down upon the remains of an attractive brown-skinned woman. With a gasp, I noted that her hair was *curled on top* and *rolled on the side,* just as the instructions had read. We understood, then, that our message from the Bishop had been written on the back of the instruction for arranging the hair of the corpse. Maybe, I facetiously suggested to Ann, that had been a first step toward correlating our work with community interests.

Cleaning the stores that were to be Friendship House was like nothing I had ever known before. And trying to find help for this task was our first Chicago failure. The Army had tapped the manpower of the South Side and everybody else was working at the defense plants. I, too, longed to get a job at a defense plant where the hours would have been shorter. As Ann and I made appearances in the various parishes, a thin stream of volunteers joined us, and we invoked the help of Blessed Martin who, we are told, gloried in such humble chores. So much equipment was needed and we had so little money we despaired of ever making the place presentable. This problem was solved when a religious from a nearby seminary, who was a cabinet maker, came to our rescue. Then the Bishop gave us permission to purchase from the Catholic Salvage Bureau.

Eddie Doherty had left *Liberty* magazine soon after he turned in the article on Harlem which he had co-authored with Helen Worden. Though he never said so, we suspected that Eddie had broken with his editor when he refused to write a sordid story on Harlem. Eddie went to Chicago to work on Marshall Field's *Chicago Sun* and he was one of the few bright spots on our horizon during this period. When the Baroness came to Chicago, he now and then took all of us downtown to enjoy a good meal and sometimes a show. Ann and I seldom went out during the week, because our twelve- and fourteen-hour shifts left little time or energy. But Eddie's treats always came on the weekend and we were glad when the Baroness came to town because we knew he would show up.

Ann never ceased to marvel at the number of people in Chicago from Birmingham. There was seldom a time when we were out walking that someone from my hometown did not stop us and ask what I was doing in Chicago. It was not unusual for a member of the audience to get up in a meeting where we had been introduced and pointing to me, say: "I've known this child all of her life. I knew her mother and father before she was born." One day, as we walked across 43rd Street, we had been hailed three times by people from home when Ann made an interesting observation:

"I never knew before that Chicago was a suburb of Birmingham, Alabama."

The South Side of Chicago, with its strong racial pride bordering on nationalism, was so different from Harlem it was difficult at first for Ann and the "B" to understand that our techniques also had to be different. Too often, I yielded ground because there was so much love and unity of purpose among the three of us. Yet I was the only one of the three who knew how adept my people have become at saying one thing and meaning another, or why they adopted this defense mechanism. I remembered having the fury of rebellion overwhelm me without warning merely because my face suggested the face of the oppressor. Groping for words to express this, I felt disloyal to my own kind and equally disloyal to these two friends who had joined hands with me to launch this interracial venture. I could never tell Ann how many times I found living quarters for us and was told "Oh, that's different" when I explained that my roommate was white. If the position had been reversed, and there must have been times when it was, she wouldn't have told me, either.

Whether or not there would be a clothing room at the Chicago Friendship House was one of the first issues to give us grave concern. In Toronto and Harlem the "B" began giving clothes to the poor soon after she opened the doors of both houses. I had always contended that stark charity is a mixed blessing, a relief to some and a push down the ladder for others. I was firm in my contention that the least fortunate of my people need an opportunity to help themselves instead of an angel of mercy to dole out food and clothing. I had listened to Father Harold Purcell talk about his auction sales at City of St. Jude and heard him say: "Nothing here is free. A man leaves an IOU or a promise of a day's labor for each pair of shoes or every handkerchief he takes out of this clothing room. We want to teach our people to help themselves—not to make them dependent. We must bolster the dignity of the human person."

The "B" was adamant and I was convinced that my stand was sound. So I prayed for a small miracle and it came in the form of a memorandum from the Bishop, informing us that the distribution of clothing to needy fell within the province of the Catholic Salvage Bureau.

With the help of God, His Saints, and loyal volunteers, numerous matters of policy were ironed out, the nails and tacks were pulled out of the floor, old chicken coops were thrown out, walls were painted, cabinets and book shelves put in place, and shining new linoleum laid and waxed. Chicago Friendship House opened its doors to a friendly public, with the blessing of our benefactor, Bishop Sheil, and assurances of co-operation from local social agencies and the civic leaders of the community. I was happiest, perhaps, that we had a good press; both the white dailies and the Negro weeklies carried generous coverage. That night, after the opening, Eddie Doherty, the Baroness, Ann, and I sat and marveled at how the stores had been transformed and how it had all started in a little one-room apartment back on West 138th Street in Harlem.

Soon after we first arrived in Chicago, various residents had told us that Chicago's most powerful Negro weekly had a record for attacking Catholic ventures on the South Side. We held a conference with the publisher and, although he was skeptical, after we told him why the Bishop had asked us to come to Chicago and outlined the purposes of the center, he seemed impressed.

"If you say the Bishop is all right," the Negro publisher smiled, "we will take your word for it and the paper will go along with you."

Ann and I were grateful for this pledge of co-operation and interested in the fact that we were put in the position of vouching for the good intentions of a Prince of the Church. The publisher kept his pledge and the paper backed us in whatever we did. Recently, this same publisher's paper conferred an award upon Bishop Sheil for his outstanding contributions to interracial justice. Friendship House had played a small part in bringing two important forces in contact with one another.

Soon after we arrived in Chicago, Bishop Sheil made a speech at Kansas City, Missouri, before the Annual Conference of Catholic Charities on "Delinquency and Racial Minority Groups." There are many who insist that the Most Reverend Bernard J. Sheil was the first ranking member of the Catholic hierarchy to sound the call to arms on a national scale in defense of the principle of the Brotherhood of Man under the Fatherhood of God when he said, in part, at the Kansas City conference in 1942:

" . . . I shall restrict my remarks to one contributing factor, and as applied to one such minority group, namely the Negro in America.

"The Negro has been selected not because he represents the largest single minority group in the country but rather because in the case of these twelve million Americans it is fairly obvious that delinquency is a practical protest against a discrimination that is ethically indefensible, socially unjustifiable, and radically un-Christian.

" . . . These people (Negroes) are no longer satisfied with weasel words and insincere promises. Their demands are most reasonable. They are simply asking that they be given their rights as American citizens, rights guaranteed to them by the Constitution of this country. The opportunity to progress, to better themselves economically, to share in the industrial, social, political, and cultural life of America—these are the things that the American Negro seeks—and he can no longer be denied them. If the Negro is worthy to die with the white man, then he is worthy to live with him on terms of honest, objective equality. It is the most dangerous kind of hypocrisy to wage a war for democracy and at the same time to deny the basic benefits of democracy to any group of citizens. Democracy is not divisible. We cannot be part free and part slave any more in 1942 than we could in 1862. . . ."

The Bishop flung an added challenge in the face of Christian America when he said: ". . . Nor can the churches be absolved from all blame for that social injustice, economic inequality, and racial discrimination which have been such firmly entrenched obstacles to the full development of American democracy. The Fatherhood of God and the Brotherhood of Man are the basic dogmas of the Christian faith; they are the expression of the creation and the Incarnation with all the relationship that these imply. . . . Failure to understand this is failure to grasp the very core of the Christian religion.

". . . History gives overwhelming evidence of this one fact: that when the Church loses sight of her first duty to Christ's poor, to the masses . . . then does the Church begin to decline, to become infected with wordliness, to lose the love and the loyalty of small people, the little ones of Christ, whom the Church must not only teach and guide but also protect.

"Let us make no mistake. The strength of the Church lies not in real estate holdings, not in institutions, but in the mass of the common people. It is their rights that the Church must vindicate before the world.

". . . If the Church takes her rightful place in the very forefront of the fight for social justice, for the vindication of the rights of the common man, she need have no fear of communism . . . because she proposes to men a religion that is far more revolutionary since it seeks literally to renovate the face of the earth. . . . What philosophy, what economic system, could offer such a challenging doctrine? We have the truth, we have the means, we have the personnel. Let us, for the love of God, use them."

In 1942, these were brave words for an American white man to utter, words far stronger than we were accustomed to and more prophetic than any of us dared hope.

Young John H. Johnson, who had published only one or two issues of the *Negro Digest,* reprinted this powerful speech and it was in connection with this venture that I first met the Negro who was destined to build up a strong publishing empire.

Humor continued to mingle with drama and pathos. When we held a small "thank-you" supper for the press, Eddie Doherty concluded his remarks, as usual, with a talk on Martin de Porres. Eddie is one of God's most unaffected children and his speech expresses his moods as well as his thoughts. On this particular night he was the Chicago newspaperman—one hundred per cent. He shared with us the praises and the defamatory remarks he had heard various people utter concerning Blessed Martin. His language was lusty, but it was graphic, and I already had the broad grin on my face which comes from surveying a job well done. However, I complimented myself too soon.

I was scribbling notes for a release when I heard Eddie use the word which sums up illegitimate parentage in the most despicable manner and precede it by quoting a person who had, at the same time, referred to Martin's color. It was like a thread of electricity running through the air. Eddie loved Martin and had no way of knowing he had dug his heel hard on one of the Negro's sensitive spots. Ann knew and said "I'm sorry" with her eyes. I could not rebuke Eddie and yet I knew somebody had to appease the wounded feelings of the Negroes present. As I sat quivering inside, Lucius Harper from the Chicago *Defender* editorial staff rose.

"When I was a boy in knee pants," he said, "I got a job at the old Chicago Press Club. It was a real thrill to a youngster to rub elbows with men like Eddie Doherty, who just spoke, Ben Hecht, and many other men who have and still are writing for newspapers. The language they used excited me and I tried to talk the way they talked. Sometimes they used big words and sometimes they used rough words. But always they used expressive words. I have often wondered about these men—whether they have changed much—if their habits are the same. Tonight I had a partial answer. Judging by that word my good friend Eddie Doherty just used—he hasn't changed one bit."

Laughter and applause rocked the table where I was writing. Lucius made an excellent talk—I was told. I tiptoed out of the room while the audience was still laughing at Eddie's expense. Later that night when Eddie sat with the staff in one of our post-sessions, we all agreed that Lucius had saved the day. Lucius handed in his last assignment some years ago, but if spirits can read copy I am sure he will chuckle over this reminiscence.

Father Hyland's book was accepted by a western publisher, but many changes had to be made in the script and he came to Chicago to ask my advice. He was pleased with what he heard about the new center and came to one of our meetings the night Frayser Lane, an Urban League official, was guest speaker. Father brought with him a young woman who had expressed great interest in the Negro and his problems, but had not had any contact with my people. The audience was interracial, and after Mr. Lane's speech a spirited question and answer period followed. Most of the questions came from the whites, who had much less awareness of life in Negro communities than any comparable group in New York City might have.

Frayser Lane, a portly brown man with a rare combination of intelligence and common sense, handled himself with credit and dignity, although some of the questions he had to answer must have irked him. In a whisper, Father Hyland's friend commented on Mr. Lane's poise and his ability to parry words, then told me that she had a question she had always wanted to ask a Negro.

"Now's the time," I assured her. "These youngsters will keep him talking all night and I'm going to close the meeting in a few minutes."

"Mr. Lane," I heard her say a few seconds later, "I have always wondered why the American Negro did not fight like the Indian?

Why didn't your forebears band together and resist the indignities which were heaped upon them?"

"Madame," Frayser Lane took a deep breath and cocked his head to one side, "there is a saying which goes as follows: The American Indian fought and fought and died. The American Negro laughed and laughed and multiplied!"

Thus it was that another Friendship House meeting disbanded amid laughter.

There were meetings, though, which were broken up by hecklers. Bishop Sheil was not beloved by the followers of the controversial Father Coughlin and the Coughlinites, who were very strong in Chicago, loosed their wrath on us. The "B" was their pet whipping boy and when they failed to find her, Ann and I had to substitute. Fortunately, good sense prevailed because these people were all white and there were times when they would have deserved what they might have gotten if Ann or I had attempted to fight back by bringing our Negro supporters into the battle.

Though authors were a penny a dozen in New York, it was different in Chicago. In 1942, this was especially true of Negro authors, and I had many requests to visit libraries and schools. Children who had read *Hezekiah Horton* always wanted to know about "Mr. Ed and his beautiful red automobile." When I was asked to speak at the Lincoln Center the librarian asked if I could bring Eddie along and he consented. The night before we were scheduled to speak at Lincoln Center there was a supper at Friendship House to which many of the civic leaders were invited. In the middle of the meal, Mildred Wiley brought me a telegram which read: "CANNOT JOIN YOU TOMORROW. AM OUT HUNTING AN ELEPHANT." The wire was signed: "EDDIE."

Sometime during the day I had heard that an elephant named Modoc had escaped from a circus in a nearby town and had wrought havoc wherever it wandered. There was great concern for property in the rural area where the big animal was roaming and even more concern for the elephant's life, as frost had already fallen. Eddie, I reasoned, had drawn an assignment to cover the elephant hunt.

"I've got it," I waved the telegram before the astonished group. "Mr. Ed and Hezekiah are going to hunt an elephant in the beautiful red car!"

Ann, who had gotten used to my outbursts when a story idea was born, read the telegram to the gathering and explained that they had just witnessed the beginning of a new book for children. We all agreed that hunting an elephant in a red convertible should be an exciting literary adventure. It took eight years for my Hezekiah and "Mister Ed" to finish their adventure, but that, too, started at the Chicago Friendship House.

As time went by, visitors drifted in and out of the Center. Father Vincent Smith came one pleasant day and brought a young man who had an interesting story to tell. Joseph J. Robichaux, Jr., was one of the first Negroes to join the staff of club directors for National Catholic Community Service, member agency of the United Service Organizations. Joe was in charge of a club for servicemen in the Newport News-Norfolk area of Virginia and he spent the morning telling us about his work. I was secretly envious of my male friends, most of whom were in the Army or serving as war correspondents. Listening to Joe talk I had the feeling that USO offered an excellent opportunity for service to one's country. I was to remember this later.

There were many days at the Chicago Friendship House when I felt like a lone voice crying in the middle of the Loop. The worst part of our venture was past history. Never again would we have to pull tacks, scrub floors, or throw out dirty chicken coops. I wanted desperately to enjoy the fruits of our labor, but that little voice which speaks so loudly kept telling me that the South Side had taken Friendship House into its big heart and I was no longer needed. I felt I had served my purpose and that it was time for me to move on.

Ann, who was not consciously aware of my misgivings, gave many lectures to white organizations. If she was out at night without me I usually stayed up until she was safe inside our extraordinary place of residence. One of the few nights she was out alone I came home from the Center so exhausted my only thought was of a bath and bed. I was almost asleep when I first heard the downstairs doorbell. Mrs. Edwards seldom left the office unattended when business was good, and I wondered why nobody answered after the bell rang the second time. It was only when the ringing came at minute intervals that I decided Ann had forgotten her key.

I ran down the steps and switched on the porch lights and the lamps in the hall and parlor. Then my heart gave a wild thump! There was a crowd of scowling, angry-looking people standing on the porch.

"What have I done now?" I asked myself as I remembered pictures I had seen of lynch mobs and thought back over all the people who had come in the Center that day. I measured the patience I had tried to call into play alongside the irritation I always felt when loafers or the idle curious took up time which need not have been spared.

One of the men motioned impatiently to me to open the door, and no Southern sheriff ever complied more quickly. "We want to see Mrs. K——," he demanded as his friends pushed me out of the way and stepped briskly inside.

"You must have the wrong address," I said. "No Mrs. K—— lives here. " 'This is the Edwards'—" I realized I was addressing thin air. The gentleman had joined his friends in the parlor where they stood before the bier of a woman, who I saw by the register, was Mrs. K——.

I had been wrong. Mrs. K—— was a lodger for the night.

I found myself laughing. I understood at last what Sunny had meant when I first moved in. I had gotten "used to it."

The bond of friendship which developed between my landlady and me weathered a few storms. Sunny's immeasurable generosity coupled with her desire to make everybody happy created unusual situations. Her secretary and the embalmer were well aware of the fact that Sunny was considered a soft touch and she never liked them to know when she had made an unwise loan or overplayed a hand of bridge. That was how I became her silent partner.

On her way to the casket factory, Sunny invariably stopped at some friend's house where a bridge game was in session. Sometimes the ante in these games ran so high or Sunny's luck ran so low that she emerged without the money to purchase the necessary casket. That was when she came to the Center and paid a visit to her silent partner. Loans were repaid soon after the funeral, but this practice gave rise to the question: "Which body is yours and which is mine?"

The feeling that I had served my purpose at Friendship House grew with each passing day. It would have been humanly impossible for anyone to try harder to understand a people and their habits than did Ann. I knew, however, that she would never have the understanding necessary to the smooth functioning of the center as long as I stood like a buffer between her and our Negro members. Also, I felt myself drifting along with the tide of parties and dances which enliven the Chicago social scene and that was certainly not why I had forsaken New York.

The score was different with the "B." I was constantly making suggestions which I felt were sound, but they did not coincide with her views on how the center should be run. Yet we loved each other. She had taught me so much—or perhaps it was that she had taught me so much of what not to do—that made me feel so grateful. She had written:

"Dearest Ellen: . . . May I ask you to also get an idea into your head? . . . Criticisms of the 'B' are the most welcome things ever . . . especially when they are made by a person whom I consider one of my few *real friends* . . . and when they are (as they usually are from you) constructive . . . for to me also you have been part and parcel of FH ever since you walked into the flat . . . one of the bricks that go to make up its strange structure and foundation. No matter what happened or will happen, that will always be. . . . Because it is of God . . . your coming to us and my coming to Harlem and the two are fused in the eternal designs of the Lord of Hosts. . . .

"Darling . . . I grant you that I will perhaps never 'understand' the Negro as for instance you will never understand the Russian in me or the Russians in general. That is what all this war is about . . . peoples not understanding other peoples. . . ."

This seemed a friendship I could ill afford to lose, but neither could I afford to lose the respect of my people, and certain habits, customs, and policies had to be taken into consideration and the awareness thereof incorporated in the foundation on which we hoped to build a strong community center.

It was the middle of December when I told Sunny Edwards that I had decided to leave Chicago and return to New York. She gave me two weeks' free rent and started inviting guests to a New Year's party. She also chose this occasion to honor Etta Moten, the charming Negro actress of *Porgy and Bess* fame.

The entire first floor of the old mansion was decorated in festive style. In the chapel, the pulpit and the casket stand were pushed back to make room for dancing. Sunny engaged a caterer who set up a lavish buffet and a bar in the office. A friend who played at one of Chicago's swank night clubs officiated at the organ. People from all walks of life crowded in. I was flattered to share honors with so gracious a woman as Etta Moten. There was dancing, brilliant conversation, food, drink, exquisitely dressed women, and important-looking men.

When Eddie Doherty came, Sunny asked Julia Kennedy, who once toured with the Williams Jubilee Singers, to entertain. That brought back sad memories. I never told Sunny that Julia had sung at Papa's funeral.

I was glad that a friend with a delightful sense of humor called me away from Eddie during the last solo. I reminded my friend that each time I had seen her she had a fresh cocktail in her hand.

"It's like this," she said, "every time I think of another person whose funeral was held here I go and get another drink. I'm just trying to forget where I am."

"Don't let it worry you," I grinned. "You'll get used to it."

The next day I left for New York.

chapter 14

USO DIARY

As the train pulled into Grand Central Station I dreaded leaving my roomette. This, I reminded myself, was the first time I had come to New York without looking forward to seeing a friendly face when I left the train. I was feeling very sorry for myself when the porter handed my bags to a redcap and I walked up the ramp.

In the distance I saw a crowd at one end of the cab stand. When flash bulbs went off I reasoned that newspapermen had snared a personality.

"It must be a movie star," I thought. "They usually come into Grand Central."

"Try to avoid that crowd," I told the redcap. "I'd like to get a cab as soon as posible."

A tall man in a black chesterfield coat and a homburg hat was walking toward me. He looked vaguely familiar—no doubt someone connected with my Chicago sojourn. Then I heard his voice.

"Ellen, here's a friend of yours."

It was Father Meegan, Bishop Sheil's secretary. He told me that he and the Bishop had just come to New York, too. When the priest led me through the crowd of reporters standing around the Bishop I opened my mouth to say "Your Excellency," but nothing came out. I must have looked funny because Bishop Sheil threw back his head and gave one of the hearty laughs which always made me feel so comfortable. Then Father Meegan, who had been holding the door of a cab, tipped the redcap and gave me a push which landed me on the back seat of the car.

"Welcome to New York, Ellen," the Bishop called. "But don't forget to come back home."

"Just think," I told the cabbie as he drove away, "the Bishop himself welcomed me to New York."

"Yeah," the man said dryly, "but he told you not to forget to come back home. Where's that?"

"Come to think of it, I'm beginning to wonder myself!"

The Y was crowded and I could not get my old room, but in a few days I was comfortably situated in another part of the building. It was great to be back in New York, though everything seemed more congested than when I left. There were more men in uniform in the Y cafeteria, too, and it was always crowded. The housing shortage we had felt in Chicago had come to New York as the defense plants in Long Island and New Jersey expanded and workers from distant towns and states jammed the city and suburbs. Many of my friends were working at the Office of Dependency Benefits, a government agency located in Newark. Several of the girls I knew at the Y were making handsome salaries at the Western Electric plant, also in Jersey. The tempo of everyday living in New York City was faster than ever and few lives were untouched by the conflict which engulfed the world.

I went down to the Stage Door Canteen and it was a joy to see so many Negro hostesses. There was also a lounge for the servicemen at the Y and I offered my services there. Nights after we had visited the lounge a bunch of the girls would sit in my room and talk. They claimed that most of the men in uniform were "on the make" and they said that "I can't give you anything but love, baby" was the soldier's theme song. The girls compared notes and laughed about the boys all having the same "line" without realizing that we were being initiated in to one form of war psychology.

One of the big surprises awaiting my return was the news that Claude McKay was a frequent visitor at Friendship House. Though Claude's moods could change at a moment's notice, he seemed much less bitter than in previous years. His health was not good, but he was not confined to bed.

I was finishing the first of a half dozen drafts of Hezekiah Horton's elephant hunt in the red automobile when Joe Robichaux, Father Smith's friend who was with National Catholic Community Service-USO, telephoned to say he would like to come to the Y to visit and wanted to bring a friend along.

In one of the "beau-parlors" where we received our guests, Joe introduced me to Ralph Metcalfe, the former Olympic star, who was a field consultant for NCCS. Joe had come to the Metropolitan area to open up a club at Orangeburg, New York, for the benefit of Negro soldiers at Camp Shanks. Ralph, he explained, acted as a national supervisor of Negro installations and was interested in recruiting workers. Ralph explained that NCCS, unlike YW or YMCA, had not had a backlog of trained personnel at the outbreak of war and it was necessary to make every effort to attract qualified workers. I promised to introduce them to the young women in the building who I thought might be likely prospects. I resisted their suggestion that I myself might be a candidate.

News about men travels fast in a women's dormitory and I did not have to leave the parlor to introduce my friends to Joe and Ralph. Most of them just "happened" to walk past the parlor. Later they said there was too much of a man shortage in New York for me to monopolize the attentions of one as important-looking as Joe or one as handsome as Ralph. It was fun, though, and the visit Joe and Ralph made to the Y produced several prospects, even though the final outcome was unexpected.

One night Joe was talking with me in one of the parlors when there passed by a pretty olive-colored girl I had not seen before.

"That's Hilda Sims," he said. "What's she doing here?" And he ran up the hallway to get the answer to his question.

Joe brought Hilda back to the parlor, and though she said she had come to New York looking for a job, after listening to her a few moments, I knew she was in New York because she wanted to go on the stage. Joe tried to persuade her to work for NCCS and she promised to think it over.

Dan Burley had asked me to come back to the *Amsterdam News* so it was chiefly to humor Joe that I filled out the application for a position as a director of women's activities. With Hilda and another friend I went down to the New York office of National Catholic Community Service and was interviewed.

When Hilda could not get the assurance that she would be employed in the Metropolitan area she discarded the idea of working with NCCS. She was planning to study dramatics during the year and she stuck by her decision. Less than two years later she was starring in the play *Anna Lucasta*.

One of the reporters left the *Amsterdam News* and I went to work with Dan once more. Just as I was settling down again Joe called to tell me that he was reasonably sure I was going to be assigned to a NCCS-USO club at Anniston, Alabama, adjacent to Fort McClellan. He wanted me to do my field work at his Orangeburg Club. When I objected to leaving the paper, he told me that Bishop Sheil was eager to have more Negroes join the NCCS staff. Joe knew that would impress me; besides, the salary he offered was much more than what the paper was paying. Once more I smothered my journalistic ambition and turned toward a more practical career.

The USO Inter-Agency Orientation Course was given at Columbia University and I moved over to International House. The time passed quickly and by the end of May I was a USO worker-in-training at the Orangeburg Club serving Camp Shanks, which had just been designated a Port of Embarkation.

My USO career started off with the best part coming first. When Joe drove me across the George Washington bridge for my initial training period, the countryside was so beautiful I felt like a bird on the wing. It was late afternoon of that first Monday when the soldiers started drifting in. As darkness fell and the lights went out it made me think about Chicago Friendship House, where a fuse always blew out as we prepared for our Monday night forums.

A private named Bob White was the first soldier from Camp Shanks whose name was entered in my diary. I looked up from the work on my desk as he came in the door. He approached a group of hostesses and I heard them laughing. This happened a second time with the same result. It was then that Bob White delivered a speech which expressed my sentiments when I first came to New York.

"You-you know what?" the soldier stammered with a southern accent. "You folks sho do talk funny up here. I-I can't understand what you sayin' halft the time."

Bob White was from Birmingham, Alabama.

The second day at the Orangeburg Club was pretty much a forecast of what my life was to be like for years to come. Tuesday night was "dance night." I left the Y on Tuesday morning and it was Wednesday morning when I got back. I saw soldiers in training for the first time that second morning when Joe drove me to a conference at the Pearl River Club. Every road we took was cluttered with marching troops and we crawled along beside them. This was also the first time I noticed that a frisky dog or two usually followed the soldiers.

"I don't see any Negroes," I told Joe. "Where are our boys?"

"You'll see them later when I take you on the post to get your pass."

After the conference we came back to Shanks and went to the Provost Marshal's office and I saw the Negro soldiers. They were digging ditches and doing construction work. White soldiers manned all of the offices we visited, and though we drove around the post I did not even see Negro soldiers drilling. Before we left, Joe found a group of our boys and he introduced me to those I had not met. When white troops marched by I commented on the white boys' red faces and their sweat-soaked shirts.

"Let 'em sweat!" one of the Negro soldiers said. "We do all of the dirty work. I don't care if all of them burn up."

I heard a new kind of lauguage and a different slang. I met "C. C. Rider," who said "hold the phone" each time he wanted to punctuate a joke or attract attention. I met "Corporal Rhode Island," "Boo," and the 224th MP's. And I met Chaplain Arthur Miller, who was a shining example of what a conscientious chaplain can mean to his men. I was impressed by the way the Negro men looked to him for guidance in matters both temporal and spiritual. "We can depend on the Chap to look out for us," was what they told me.

The chaplain invited us to the officer's mess hall for dinner and there I saw Negroes cooking, waiting tables, and washing dishes. I must add that they did their work with proficiency. And I was struck by the enormous amount of food I saw.

I talked with the hostesses and found that most of their experiences with the boys were similar to the experiences I had had at the Stage Door Canteen and the Service Lounge at the YWCA.

I met one girl who worked at the Camp Shanks PX and she told me how the boys usually drank beer and tore up the place the night before they were shipped out.

"A person with a soft heart couldn't work on this post," she said. "The boys are not supposed to write letters while they are waiting to be shipped. But they beg you so hard it's tough to say no."

"Never say *no* to a soldier," her hostess companion laughed, and continued to powder her nose.

I told Joe that the more intelligent boys claimed that the Army setup was like a vicious circle, with "crackers" on top who were determined to keep the Negro soldier down. Joe warned me not to let myself get upset as, said he, "most soldiers gripe."

Little Sister wrote to tell me that a mutual friend had found a place for me to live in Anniston. I had bought the ticket and made all my plans to leave when one of the area supervisors came to the Orangeburg Club and told me that Joe and Chaplain Miller had put in a request for me to stay in New York. By declining their offer I changed the pattern of my life.

A few days before I left I received a letter from Lieutenant Charles Ward who had been "Mister Charlie" to the 135th Street following at Friendship House. Charlie was stationed at a camp in southern Georgia where he was over a company of Negro soldiers. For the first time he met Negro men who were neither intellectuals nor pathetically poor. What he saw and heard was new and strange to him, and when he thought of me going to an Army camp to provide recreation for Negro soldiers, he became alarmed and begged me to reconsider. I was pleased at Charlie's concern for my welfare, but saddened to know that his first contact with the masses of my people had been so shocking.

My last night at the Orangeburg Club was pleasant and I took a bus back to New York, then got a subway. I noticed a familiar-looking Negro man sitting with two white girls, but thought no more about it until I looked up and saw that the man was smiling at me. It was Canada Lee, the actor, and he walked half the length of the car to ask me to come with him and meet his friends. That was the last time I spoke with Canada Lee. Soon after the completion of the film *Cry the Beloved Country,* Canada Lee died. But I shall always remember the friendliness of our last meeting.

I left New York June 8, 1943. According to my diary, everybody I met during the morning was talking about a rally, spearheaded by Adam Powell, which had been held at Madison Square Garden the night before. It was reported that 5,000 had been turned away from the Garden.

Two of Mama's friends helped me to pack and waved tearful good-bys as I boarded the train and turned my back on Manhattan once more. This time, we all realized that my absence would only be temporary and that as soon as the war was over I would be back in New York once more.

I discovered among my fellow travelers two women whose trail-blazing activities with the Negro Nurses' Association had always commanded my respect, Mabel Staupers and Estelle Massey Riddle. They were en route to a North Carolina State Nurses' Convention at Winston-Salem and we talked until the porter prepared our berths.

The next day the train was crowded to capacity. There were soldiers everywhere, although most of them seemed to be standing in the lines leading into the dining car. I was served a meal after 300 white servicemen had finished eating. These boys in uniform were as hungry for companionship as for food, and each one who started a conversation had a story to tell. One of them asked me if I would make up a foursome for a bridge game. After we started the game I heard the grouchy Negro Pullman porter when he asked the officer in charge of the soldiers: "Is it all right for them to play with *her*?"

"Sure!" the officer answered. "Only too glad for the boys to find something to do. It's a long trip."

I was amused because the porter had heard me talking with the redcap who brought my bags aboard the train and he was trying to tell the white officer that I was a Negro.

I had to leave the Pullman coach at Atlanta to get a train to Anniston. I was carrying my typewriter and a heavy bag and it was difficult to find a porter to help me. The one I found led me to a white coach and I was sorely tempted to stay there. But I knew I would get off to a bad start in the community where I was to work if word was passed along that I came in town "passing for white." The Jim Crow coach I rode was one of the smallest, dirtiest, and most crowded I had ever seen. In describing my reaction I wrote: "What a temptation it was, just to sit down like a human being. I'm in Dixie now, but it's hell. . . . I can offer this up for my past sins and maybe things will be different some day. It's hard to hope, though, in a Jim Crow dinky."

Robert Jones, who had been one of the two little altar boys at Immaculate Conception in Birmingham the first time I went to Mass, met me at Anniston. Bobby, as his intimates insisted on calling him, was assistant director of the "Colored USO" and he introduced me to McDougald, the director, who was also from New York. Within a short time after my arrival I had seen all there was to see of the Club and met the Funderburgs with whom I was to live.

Bobby, who like my sisters called me "Sister Ellen," had done a terrific job of advance press agentry and I immediately found myself confronted with all kinds of jobs—especially those which called for cooking. Luncheons and dinners had been scheduled against my arrival and I could not let Bobby down. I met Ralph Metcalfe's wife, who had supervised the Club until Bobby and McDougald arrived, but Ralph was going into the Army and they left soon afterward. My first days in Anniston left me with a sharp memory of heat, sweat, and nausea.

The Negro trainees finished the orientation courses, and as

soon as they were given passes to come into town, the lines outside my office door lengthened. The first question they asked was:
"Lady, can you get me a room?" All of them looked forward to
having their wives, sweethearts, or mothers visit them.

One day at the Anniston Bus Terminal when I was going to
visit my family, I watched two coaches load up with white soldiers as the Negro servicemen looked on hopefully. When the
third bus pulled in I decided not to wait any longer. The white
driver stopped me.

"Sorry, ma'am," he said. "We're all filled up. Just saving a few
seats for Negroes in the back there."

The conductor motioned to two Negro soldiers and some
others that they might board the bus. I pushed past him and sat
beside them on the long seat in the rear. There were seven of
us on the seat—the two soldiers, a woman and two children, a
blind man with his guitar and tin cup, and I. The heat was almost
unbearable, and it took us more than three hours to cover the
fifty-nine miles to Birmingham. I wondered about the other
Negro soldiers we had left waiting for a bus and whether or not
they ever got a chance to use their weekend passes.

Birmingham was booming. All the plants and steel mills were
going full blast. The soldiers from Camp Sibert, the Tuskegee
Air Base, and McClellan came up for the weekends, and the
money they spent for recreation made business good. The chronic
"male shortage," of which Birmingham females always complain, was no more. The girls were having difficulty keeping their
dates from conflicting. Our house was a meeting place, since
Little Sister and my Cousin Lucy had friends in all three of the
Army installations.

Mama and Mama Ida were glad to see me. I noticed that my
grandmother seemed less active than in years past and I was glad
I had come to Alabama to work. On Sunday I went to Mass at
Ensley, a suburb of Birmingham. Holy Family, a new Catholic
church for Negroes, had been built since my last visit.

One of the consolations of these days of sweat and labor was
the hostesses, both junior and senior. They were my responsi-

bility. The young girls all became like daughters to me. When I think of the women who sacrificed time and energy to spend hours "on the door," who served more coffee and doughnuts than I had ever known could exist, and spent night after night planning programs for the boys who came in and out of the USO, I am grateful for having had the privilege of working with each and every one of them. It must have been a mutual admiration society because they never missed an opportunity to say, "We love you, too."

The junior hostesses were given charm courses which stressed behavior and appearance. Many of the girls' mothers were senior hostesses and this created a wholesome atmosphere for the boys. The nights were warm and young love blossomed while the moon hung low in star-clustered skies. Watching the couples around the Club must have reminded me of my own youth, which had gotten lost in a depression. An entry in the diary made around this time reads: "Bobby showed an old picture, First Love, tonight. Afterward I sat on the stoop outside the kitchen door and felt lonesome. I'm homesick and I don't know where home is."

It would be unfair to mention the role which volunteers played in USO clubs without pointing to the contributions made by soldiers' wives. Many of these women left comfortable homes to follow their men and often found themselves in homes which lacked the conveniences to which they were accustomed.

Two of the service wives who worked side by side with us in Anniston were Ruby, from Detroit, and Ernestine, from Kansas City. They referred to themselves as "old soldiers" and had a language of their own. They "policed" up on anything they wished to acquire and "subdued" anything or anyone that offered resistance. Once a program was "in the bag" they spent their spare time playing cards with the boys or whichever staff member was available. Whenever I showed disappointment over not turning a card trick, Ruby always reminded me that, "You can't do business with Hitler!"

I played ping-pong and prepared luncheons and dinners during the week. On Sunday it was breakfast for the staff and Catholic boys who came to the Club after Mass. I played shuffleboard and bridge, served doughnuts and coffee, found rooms for visiting wives, sweethearts, and other females who said they were, then listened to the gripes of trainees and the stories of the cadre and officers. Nights when I walked down the dirt roads, stopping every so often to shake the rocks out of my shoes, I was comforted by the knowledge that I was making a contribution to the war effort.

With McDougald to supervise the maintenance and upkeep of the Club, Bobby to push over-all programs, and my junior and senior hostesses to welcome the boys and cater to their entertainment needs, it was not long before the Colored USO in Anniston became the most popular place in town, for both military personnel and civilians.

The Northern boys had the most gripes. They referred to their conflicts with Jim Crow as "the battle of Alabama." Many of them developed a hatred of the Southern states which still exists. I suffered along with them and often had to put a professional smile in my voice when I felt more like cursing. At other times, I thought about the incident at the little country church near Concord.

Bona fide wives seemed to make it a point to surprise their husbands and arrive in towns adjacent to Army camps unannounced and without living quarters. One Sunday afternoon a young woman from New Orleans came to the Club looking for her soldier husband. I learned his battalion and serial number from a letter she produced and called headquarters. The white officer in charge was most co-operative.

"I'll call down there," he said, "and tell the nigger in charge to tell him to go in town to his wife right away."

The Club was located on the fringe of a white neighborhood. Although civilians, other than hostesses, members of the Business and Professional Men's Club or the Young Men's Development Club, were not supposed to use any of the facilities, the priest who served as our moderator had instructed us to allow the whites in our neighborhood to come in and out of the club for the purpose of purchasing Coca-Colas, in order to insure their good will. Because of these instructions, we felt helpless when white women in various stages of dress and undress walked in and out of the club. The Negro soldiers resented it, too.

One Sunday afternoon, a white woman wearing a smock over a long dirty nightgown came in the club, walked over to the coke machine, got what she wanted, and walked out. When we went to the next staff conference, which was composed of personnel from all member agencies in the city, colored and white, we presented this problem. The other workers insisted that we should refuse to allow the white neighbors to enter the club since they had abused the privilege. After McDougald, Bobby, and I got back to the Club we admitted to ourselves that we were helpless. The order to keep the whites out of our Club had to come from a white person and none of us was white.

The junior hostesses called themselves the "Patriotic Sweethearts." Our program included dancing whenever the jukebox was turned on, with a band on hand once each week, but the girls decided to *give* a dance. Bobby, who was a wizard with shears and crepe paper, decorated the club with red hearts and streamers of blue and white paper. We contracted for the dance orchestra which had been formed from the post band, and for days everybody looked forward to the Patriotic Sweethearts' Formal Dance. The girls bought evening dresses and gave me the money to order corsages.

The Special Services officer made arrangements to have the soldiers transported by Army trucks. When the girls began arriving, I was in my office. I could hear the senior hostess, who was on the door, demanding identification cards. As familiar voices answered, I wondered why it was so difficult to recognize the hostess. A phone call kept me at my desk and the Army trucks were in front of the door when I reached the lounge. I was as surprised as the boys when I saw the Patriotic Sweethearts. It was hard to believe that we were seeing the same girls who came to the Club daily. In the diary I labeled this dance "the miracle of the gowns."

The music was good and the boys danced until their shirts stuck to their backs. When the band played "Let Me Call You

Sweetheart," the girls formed a V for Victory and the boys were
proud to step up and claim a dance. Some of the couples sang
as they danced and we knew that the first formal was a social
success.

The band was heard weekly over a local station and that night
they broadcast from the Club. Soon after they signed off, I was
standing at the door talking with the hostess on duty. A taxi
drove up and a soldier ran up the steps.

"What's going on here?" he asked. "I was in my bunk—almost
asleep—listening to the radio when I heard Clifford Brantley singing 'Body and Soul.' The announcer said it was coming from
the Colored USO. What's happening?"

"Go inside and find out," I laughed, as the soldier swaggered
to the door of the recreation hall, then came back to me.

"You can see I ain't no square," he grinned. "I don't fool
around no USO's—they're too slow for me. But, lady, this joint
is jumpin' and I'm going in and get with it."

We had to flash the lights off and on a half-dozen times before
we could clear the hall that night. It was only after the truck
drivers pretended to drive off and leave the boys that we got
them all off the premises. They had seen the local girls with new
eyes. From that night on our constituency was assured.

One movie night we showed the picture, *Farmer Takes a Wife.*
When the scene was flashed on the screen showing Gloria Swan-
son and Adolph Menjou drinking a toast, one of the soldiers
yelled: "Drink one for me, buddy. Anniston is dry!"

We soon discovered that Anniston was not as dry as we had
thought and that the boys were personalizing their cokes within
the safety of the men's room. Thereafter, the senior hostesses paid
special attention to bulging hip pockets.

It was not unusual for soldiers who knew they were about to
be shipped out to ask me to prepare some favorite dish for them.
One such request led us to keep "going-away kits" on hand so
the boys would have some token by which they might remember
the Anniston USO. I have never forgotten the faces of the two
boys who were responsible. They knew they were due to go and
they came to the Club and asked me to broil a steak for each of

them the next night. I bought the steaks but the next night they were confined to the post. Two days later they drove up in a jeep, which they admitted had not been assigned to them. I lighted the oven of the stove and opened the ice box. As I opened the wax paper in which the steaks were wrapped, we knew that the Alabama sun had cheated the boys and the steaks had spoiled.

I stood in the doorway and watched them get in the jeep they had commandeered. One of them turned around and laughed. "If I get killed in action," he called, "you'll know I died thinking about that steak you never cooked for me."

Some of the senior hostesses said I wept over each shipment. There must have been some truth in what they said because one night when Bobby and McDougald were away and I was closing the building with the help of the janitor, I saw one of our regulars hanging around as if he had something to say. I had the keys to the front door in my hand when he made his speech.

"Miss Tarry, I can't tell you when, but I'll be leaving soon. If you get a tip on our time of departure will you come out to the Fort and cry the way you did when the last shipment pulled out?"

I was at the Fort when my friend's company marched down to the waiting troop trains. I waved good-by to him but each time I thought about his request for tears we both laughed.

There was only a handful of regular parishioners and an equal number of children attending Mass at All Saints' Church when I arrived in Anniston. Each Sunday morning we saw one or two new servicemen and their wives in the congregation. McDougald played the organ and Bobby and I sang. We drafted the Catholic boys who spent the night at the Club for extra choir members. Sometimes the organ was out of tune and the singers were off key, but when McDougald played "O Lord, I Am Not Worthy," the boys put a lot of feeling in their music.

The NCCS-USO staff members also acted as godparents at christenings and witnesses at weddings. For weeks we laughed about the sergeant from Louisiana who married a girl named Maggie. The priest told the bride to repeat after him as he said: "I, Margaret, take this man ..." The girl whispered, "Father, it's

Maggie, not Margaret." Then she said in a strong voice: "I, Maggie, take this man. . . ."

Though I enjoyed going to Birmingham to see Mama, Nannie, and Mama Ida, I came to dread riding the bus, and decided to use the train instead. The first train trip to Birmingham was uneventful. Returning to Anniston, I bought a ticket and was ready to board the train when I realized that the agent had sold me space in car S-2 and Negroes were supposed to ride only in car S-1. There was no time to go back to the ticket office so I rode to Anniston in the white coach. McDougald was waiting for me at the place where S-1 usually stopped. On the way home he gave me a subtle lecture on respecting community patterns and could not understand why I did not talk back.

After the train incident I decided to ask some of the soldiers to drive me to Birmingham. Each staff member had one free day in a work week but my off-days were spent answering questions by telephone, vouching for hostesses or defense workers who had lost their identification cards, and finding rooms for unexpected relatives. Ernestine, the president of the Soldiers' Wives Club who lived on the Post in quarters provided for the older non-commissioned officers, invited me to spend my days off at her home, where there was no telephone, so I could rest. Ernestine would call for me the night before my free day and though we tried to slip out of the Club unnoticed, some of the soldiers always managed to follow her home for a late snack. To discourage this, Ernestine tried serving peanut butter and crackers, but they still ate with relish.

The quarters provided for Negro noncoms reminded me of the shacks I had taught in at Slater School many years before. Beaverboard partitions divided off a bedroom, living room, kitchen, and bath. There was no ceiling and Ernestine kept the army cot, on which her guests slept, on the rafters. Climbing the ladder to get the cot always made me think about the story of Jesus telling the lame man to take up his bed and walk.

The first notes of reveille would awaken me and I would lie there and listen to Ernestine trying to arouse her husband, Pete, who was the band-master. The noncom quarters were at the top of a hill and the smell of coffee from the company kitchens used to drift up to make us hungry. But we always postponed breakfast as long as possible. It meant making a fire in an old coal stove and we dreaded the task. In a short while we would hear marching feet—"*Hut!* two-three-four—*Hut!* two-three-four" or variations of the cadence according to the sergeant's accent, brogue, or fancy. At noontime when the soldiers marched past to the mess halls, I always felt sorry for the white boys with their sweaty red faces. I am sure our boys were just as warm but they never looked as distressed.

There was an ordnance plant just outside Anniston and hundreds of young Negro men and women came to the area to work. The townspeople were sometimes critical of the girls and it became necessary for us to provide recreation for these defense workers as well as for soldiers and their families. Extra planning and additional skill and diplomacy were required to handle three groups simultaneously. I also became the Sunday school teacher for the handful of children who came to Mass.

Ralph Metcalfe went into the Army and Joe Robichaux became Field Consultant for NCCS. Then we heard that Joe, too, was a GI. Joe did not write, but after weeks of wondering where he was I received a long-distance call. His chief complaint about the Army was the fat man's diet they had him on:

"I've got to get out of here and get something to eat."

Whoever signed Joe's release from the Army was wise. It would have taken a great deal of training to turn so individualistic a recruit into a soldier. Joe, who is an excellent recreation man, and one of the coaches responsible for the outstanding sports records established by the Chicago CYO, came out of the Army and did a notable job with National Catholic Community Service in the supervision of Negro clubs. He is now the director of Sheil House, a community center in Chicago.

Early one morning the phone rang. It was a cousin from Lafayette. He was enroute home from Camp Stewart, Georgia. I was delighted to see a portly, blondish soldier in place of the little boy we had called "Toot." When my cousin found out it was my day off he suggested that I accompany him to Lafayette and in a short time we were on a bus bound for my mother's birthplace.

Mama's sister, Lucy Ida, was surprised to see me with her son. The house seemed strange without Mama Ida, but it was thrilling to see the same old walnut trees and remember the rich taste of the nuts at Christmas time, to find the pomegranate trees still standing and to look in the flower pit where Mama Ida used to store her potted plants for the winter. The white frame church was still standing on the top of the hill and the white college was still across the street. My aunt took me for a drive so I might see how the town had grown. I did not see much growth, but I found words to ask about something I had wondered about. I asked where my grandfather—her father—was buried.

In the family burial plot I had seen the graves of two great-grandmothers, Sarah and Chloe, and an uncle, too. But never had I seen a grave with a marker to tell me that it was the last resting place of the grandfather whose picture hung in Mama Ida's room.

The sun was setting by the time we drove to the white cemetery on the other side of town. My aunt took me to a little red brick mound with a Confederate flag on it and I read my grandfather's name on the headstone. I thought of all I had come to know of him through his yellowed letters which my grandmother had allowed me to read. I remembered how Mama Ida and I had laughed over the funny little note in which he said:

Dear Mama: I had one too many so I will stay at the office tonight. Be sure to tuck the babies in and cover the fire. I will see you tomorrow morning. Love. Papa

It was only in death that convention had succeeded in separating him from the ones he had loved and the thought was comforting to us as we stood looking at his grave.

When I returned to Anniston there was a soldier waiting for me at the Club. He claimed I had promised to go out to the Fort to see a picture with him the night before and took me to task for breaking the engagement. I explained my visit to Lafayette and he seemed surprised.

"Lafayette in Chambers County?" he asked.

"Yes. Have you ever been there?"

"I'm from Oklahoma," he said. "But all of my people are from Lafayette. I never heard anyone else mention the place."

I made a mental note of the fact that he was named Patton and said I would ask Mama Ida if she remembered the family. If I had forgotten the name I might have saved myself a lot of trouble.

Training cycles began and ended, soldiers came and went, but "Lady, can you help me to find a room?" was standard procedure for beginning and ending each day. Though I kept a room registry, it was impossible to house the steady stream of visitors who found their way into Anniston to visit their soldier kin. We kept a supply of cots at the Club and when I could not find any other place they slept there.

I asked one soldier whose wife had come in town with nothing but a suitcase and a desire to find him: "Why did you send for her before you found a place for her to live?"

"Send for her? I didn't. She just came."

As our regulars increased, few meals were eaten without a guest. The staff reluctantly agreed to pool resources and hire a cook. This was a great relief; now my cooking time could go into the program.

Traveling remained a problem even when I stayed in Anniston and my sister came to see me. Several of the boys looked forward to Little Sister's visits and they took turns entertaining her. The soldiers from New York spent a lot of their time at the Club talking with me about the "big city" and they were helpful with many chores. One New Yorker was Eddie, a handsome lad from the Bronx, who told me more about guns and how to break them down and put them back together than I could ever absorb.

Eddie drove us to the railroad station late one Sunday night after my sister had spent the weekend in Anniston. He stood with my sister at the ticket window in the colored waiting room. I watched his anger mount as the white agent ignored them and made up tickets for the white passengers on the other side of his cage who had appeared after Little Sister and Eddie. The train had pulled under the shed before the agent threw the ticket at them and picked up the money Little Sister put down.

We walked past a line of coaches with only a few white passengers in each to get to the half-coach behind the engine which was reserved for Negroes. The Negro passengers were standing in the aisle. Eddie put Little Sister on the train and came back in a rage. "I'm a man!" he reminded me. "Is this what I'm getting ready to risk my life for?"

Little Sister was standing, but we saw a man get up and offer her a seat as the train pulled out. Later, I made a notation in my diary:

"... That train was one reason race riots are born.... What I felt for the crackers who stared at us was hatred—not of or for the persons—but a hatred of the injustice which they symbolized. ... Eddie was so angry I was frightened."

I knew what would have happened to that white ticket agent in Harlem.

Bobby, McDougald, and I often attended dress reviews and receptions at the Fort. Only five or six Negro officers came to McClellan while we were in Anniston and there were never over three of them stationed there at one time. In talking with most of the older white officers of "top brass" rank we discovered that they thought of the Negro men serving under them as good-natured children. I can think only of two colonels—one I knew by name and reputation and one who befriended me on numerous occasions—that were exceptions. The younger white officers were different but they seldom stayed at Fort McClellan long. When Bobby and Mac left me and my lack of pigment lured these white men into a false sense of security, I listened to a number of choice stories about their "nigra" Mammies. We often wondered why some of our boys who were in their good graces did not tell them that intelligent Negroes resent "Mammy" stories.

Mama Ida's birthday was August 1. I was sitting in the lounge playing cards with a group of service wives, waiting for the soldier who was to drive me to Birmingham, when we heard the

announcement over the radio that a race riot had broken out in
Harlem. I had known that the area was like a keg of dynamite
waiting for a match and I could imagine the havoc the announc-
ers described. The outburst was said to have been caused by a
rumor that white policemen had shot a Negro soldier at the
Hotel Braddock on Eighth Avenue next door to the *Amsterdam
News*. As the rumor spread, the tensions of the past months
erupted and mobs roamed the streets wrecking every business
place in the shopping district known to be owned by whites.
Mayor La Guardia used loud-speakers as he rode through the
streets of Harlem with Walter White and other civic leaders who
begged the people to remain calm. The riot was suppressed before there was too much bloodshed, but thousands of dollars'
worth of damage was done and many Negroes laughed off the
looting which followed. They felt it was a just harvest for many
of the unscrupulous merchants. A few suffered for the many.

There were many times when I was compelled to go to the Fort
on official business. If the USO car was not handy, I called a cab.
In 1943 there were no Negro-owned cab companies in Anniston
and we were forced to ride with drivers who were not always
courteous. One day I had to go to headquarters to make special
arrangements for the band. The driver circled the post and
picked me up after the conference was over.

We laughed about the coincidence of my getting the same cab
back to town and he asked where I wanted to go.

"The Colored USO," I replied.

"No, you don't," he said. "Can't you send somebody else?"

"The Colored USO," I repeated.

"You colored?" he asked.

"Yes. I'm colored," I answered.

"Damn! Here I was thinking you was the colonel's wife and
you're just a nigger. Don't you want to sit up front with me?"

I declined the invitation, and when the driver stopped in front
of the Club he asked for sixty cents more than we had ever paid
for a one-way ride to or from the Fort. He refused to let me see
the meter, which he claimed he had already "flipped." After I
challenged him he ended the encounter with:

"Damn you, woman! Get out of this car. We don't want to haul your kind anyhow."

The white taxicab drivers must have marked me as a prime target as this was not the last insult I suffered.

The life of a USO worker was hard but there were many compensating factors. Most of us had rounded out our talents when our tour of duty ended. Servicemen's families increased, and wives with babies continued to surprise their husbands. Bobby became proficient at washing diapers as I sat at the telephone trying to locate missing husbands and scarce rooms.

A broken jukebox or coke machine could spell tragedy to a program and our jukebox always played well until a few hours before a jukebox dance or a record hour. The coke machine got out of order only on days when the thermometer soared into the higher nineties. It was at these times that we appreciated our regulars. The soldiers never hesitated to offer whatever talents they had. One of them, an artist, painted signs and assisted Bobby so much that the men in his outfit named him "Jimmy USO." Another boy from New York was a photographer. He set up our darkroom, then dared anyone to use it without his permission.

In early September, our staff felt the first note of sadness. Bobby went into the Army. Fortunately, we only had a week to grieve before he was deferred because of a foot injury. He came back to Anniston as soon as they let him out of Fort Benning.

On the last Sunday in September the hostesses and soldiers' wives were in the process of decorating the Club for a fall tea when McDougald asked me to go with him to the railroad station.

"More women," he complained, as I tried to think of where I might find more rooms.

When we reached the station I found Mama and Little Sister. It was my birthday and they had come down to surprise me. Back at the Club the ladies' tea emerged as a full-fledged birthday party, with gifts, ice cream, and a cake with sixteen candles. Our regulars were on maneuvers but news of the party reached them by grapevine. By the time refreshments were being served a group of them came in. They had walked from the maneuver area, fourteen miles away, and they came to the Club in their field shoes and jackets. Some of them had beards a week old, but all was forgotten in the sentiment of the occasion.

In late October a chill crept into the air and we initiated a series of coffee hours in our lounge which were made cheerful by an open fireplace with burning logs which the boys kept piled high. The sight of the open fireplace made me think of our old home on Sixth Avenue and the beautiful dreams which came to me while watching the dancing flames.

At Thanksgiving, Bobby transformed the lounge into a harvest scene with flowers, pumpkins, and a table dominated by a horn of plenty, from which all the autumn fruits spilled in profusion. The junior hostesses and the soldiers' wives visited the hospital at the Fort on holidays. On Thanksgiving Day we carried fruits, cigarettes, and magazines to the boys in baskets that Bobby had decorated with red, white, and blue crepe paper. A shipment was scheduled that day and the girls also carried along kits for the soldiers who were leaving.

The boys confined to the hospital were always grateful to visitors, but on holidays they were more expressive. We had stepped into one of the wards in answer to a call from one of our regulars when I saw that all of the other patients were white. It was contrary to local custom for the girls to enter the ward and they waited for my instructions. The boys looked so young and so lonely that I asked McDougald, who was with us, to take two of the baskets in to them. They called out their thanks and waved to the girls as we walked down the ramp to another ward.

It was not long before Bobby was assigned to a club near Fayetteville, North Carolina. My sister came down for the farewell party and the night she was ready to go back to Birmingham the Club was so crowded neither McDougald nor I had time to take her to the station. We enlisted the services of Charlie, the janitor, and when she walked out of the Club Little Sister laughingly said, "I've never left Anniston without kissing somebody so I guess I'll have to kiss Charlie."

Charlie remained unkissed that night. On his return he told us that when they got there the train was about to pull out of the station. The agent told Little Sister to buy her ticket on the train and the conductor pulled her aboard a white coach, which, we learned, she rode in to Birmingham. "Who can ever explain the South?" was all I could say.

I found a square package on my desk one morning, and when I opened it there were two copies of *The Dove Flies South*, Father Hyland's book. It was gratifying to see the successful culmination of so many years of Father's work and I knew that like me, he looked forward to the days when the Dove of Peace would really fly to our beloved but partially benighted Southland.

The only excitement between Thanksgiving and Christmas was the unexpected visit of our regional supervisor from New Orleans. A few minutes after we learned he was in town, someone telephoned from the Fort to tell us that most of the soldiers attached to the Infantry Replacement Training Center would be confined to camp. All of our regulars belonged to IRTC, as the Negro MP's and members of the Sanitation Company were older men with outside interests who only visited the USO on special occasions. McDougald was holding his head. A USO Club without soldiers was serving no purpose, he reasoned, and the supervisor might recommend that the Club be closed.

Ernestine was the only one I took into my confidence when I left in search of soldiers. She insisted on going with me and we walked in the direction of a "creep joint" I had overheard the boys talking about. They said it was across the street from the "pro" (prophylactic) station and that was where we went. We saw about two dozen soldiers standing around talking and we introduced ourselves and invited them to go over to the Club for a jukebox dance. Some were suspicious, but over half of them drifted in the direction I had suggested. We needed more of a crowd and Ernestine and I were trying to think of another point of soldier concentration when an MP truck drove up. We asked them to bring every Negro soldier they could find to the USO.

When we got back to the Club, four or five card games were going in the lounge and the jukebox was enticing couples to dance. We would not tell McDougald where we found the soldiers, but he was too happy to ask any questions. Ernestine was clucking like a mother hen and I was attempting to supervise the games and the dancers, glancing at the front door every few minutes. The MP's worked hard for us that night, and the Club was bursting with activity when the phone rang again. McDougald rushed to the office and came out laughing. Someone from the white USO had called to say that the supervisor had been detained and would not get to our club until the next morning. Some of the hostesses had been distressed to hear that I had been on the street in front of a questionable place begging "rough" soldiers to come to the USO. Several of these boys joined the ranks of our regulars, however, so our excursion was not in vain.

Christmas, 1943, marked the beginning of the story which might have been called "An Answer to a Mother's Prayer." The prayer was said in our NCCS-USO Club at Anniston, but it was answered in North Devon, England. Christmas Eve was as cold as any I have ever known in New York City and an epidemic of flu and head colds had deprived us of half our volunteers. A small group of soldiers' wives who had not gone home for the holidays, my friend Eddie, and two or three other servicemen worked with the staff until the 500 gifts we had begged from merchants and friends in Birmingham and Anniston were wrapped and close to 700 sandwiches were made. Everything was in readiness when it was time for midnight Mass, and we left our chores to celebrate the birth of the Infant King.

When we came out of church it was sleeting so hard that we had to scrape ice off the windshield of the old USO car. The boys were waiting for the sandwiches and urns of coffee which we had prepared. Watching the food disappear made me think of the machines which scoop up the snow from the city streets. It was 4 A.M. before we had everybody out except the soldiers who were to sleep in the Club so they could catch early trains the next morning. Rain and sleet were pelting the windowpanes as I started for the Club on Christmas Day. Cold winds from the north had embroidered the trees with icicles and the streets were puddled and slushy. Even the children remained indoors with the toys Santa had brought them.

Telephones were ringing and McDougald was running from

his office to mine when I reached the Club. Call by call, I learned that the epidemic had struck the home of each of the volunteers who had been assigned the task of preparing a turkey dinner for the soldiers. The men would have a midday meal in their mess halls and by evening they would be coming to us for the meal we had promised them. I knew, from previous experience, how the soldiers would suddenly appear in droves, walk in the Club, and look around for girls or food, then walk out in disgust if they saw neither.

I knew we needed a miracle—quick. With the help of the other staff members, I put the last two turkeys in the oven. Salads and side dishes were to be made and the wassail bowl was still empty. That would mean whipping up dozens of eggs, a gallon of milk, which had been substituted for cream, then opening a case of cider. The buffet table still had to be set up and decorated and bows tied on most of the wreaths. I went to the telephone to call the junior hostesses who had not reported. I was speaking to one of them when the front door opened and a soldier I had never seen walked in. He saw me and smiled, then walked over to my desk and waited until I had finished the telephone conversation.

"Smells mighty good in here," he said. "I know it's a little early, but my men haven't been in town long and they don't have anywhere else to go. Maybe you could find something for them to do—put them to work, I mean."

I told the young sergeant what had happened.

"I'm the man you're looking for," he said with a clipped northern accent. "My men are in the trucks outside. All you have to do is tell me what you want done and I'll see that they do it."

I had to wipe the steam away from the window over my desk and look out at the trucks before I could believe help was so near. A few minutes after the soldiers were in the club the sergeant had split them up in work details and I was grateful that so many of them must have had mothers who trained them well.

They brought in logs for the open fireplace in the lounge and tied the red ribbon bows on the wreaths throughout the Club. In the recreation hall they set up tables at the foot of the stage so as to form one long buffet, then spread white table cloths and placed holly leaves around the edges for a border. The boys wrapped red crepe paper around drinking cups and filled them with candy. They stacked plates, napkins, and silver on nearby serving tables and told me to notify the kitchen staff to bring on the food.

The food was ready, but preparation of the wassail bowl had taken precedence in the kitchen. Our staff secretary was in charge of the bowl and each time she thought it was finished one of her soldier-helpers would taste the wassail and tell her it needed more flavoring. I surprised one of them with his mouth to the bottle, draining the last drop of vanilla.

"Miss," he chuckled, "since you have to buy flavoring why don't you buy lemon extract? It has more of a kick to it."

The buffet looked beautiful with the turkeys, the huge wassail bowl, and the fruit cakes. It was still sleeting, and there was not a hostess in the Club. Soldiers were beginning to come in and a puddle of water had formed outside the checkroom. Then the gloom of the day disappeared. Two senior hostesses came in. Both of the women had illness in their families, but they also had sons in the service. One of them, Mrs. C., had three boys overseas. They said they came to serve in the hope that someone was doing the same for their boys. As the ladies took their places behind the table, another member of their group came in smelling of liniment and cough drops. She put on a Santa Claus outfit and the soldiers acted like little boys when she walked around with a sack on her back handing out the gifts we had wrapped.

Instead of the usual "Where are the girls?" the boys were asking: "When do we eat?" I dreaded the time when the food would be gone and the jukebox started. Many of the girls had called to say they had no means of transportation. There were no street cars; the bus service was paralyzed; taxicabs belonged to yesterday. I shared my problem with the young sergeant and he came to the rescue again. It was difficult to get his drivers to leave the food and the warmth of the Club, but he managed to send trucks for many of the girls who lived in distant neighborhoods.

By the time the food was gone there were enough junior hostesses to dance with the boys and I was grateful for their happy
feet. The band came late, but after the musicians ate they gave
the best they had in return.

Hundreds of soldiers ate Christmas dinner with us that day
and Mrs. C. carved each piece of turkey for each plate. Other
hostesses came later and when they tried to relieve Mrs. C., she
refused to relinquish her carving knife.

"I just pray someone is doing something for my three boys
today," was all she would say.

The music drove away all thoughts of the sleet and slush outside and the holiday spirit reigned. It was not until the soloist
began singing "White Christmas" that the boys were reminded
of home and loved ones. The happy feet were suddenly quiet
and the boys and girls sat or stood where they were. When their
longing for home reached its peak one of the soldiers joined the
soloist and without thinking much about it everybody else followed suit. The band played the chorus again and then broke
into a jazz arrangement that turned most of the couples into
Lindy Hoppers.

After the last soldier had left and the lights were out, the staff
members sat in front of the open fireplace and laughed over the
problems of the day. They had made a "home away from home"
for the boys on Christmas Day.

In February we celebrated USO's third birthday and our building's first with a week of daily activities. The closing event was
a Sunday tea. Most of our regulars had been shipped to embarkation centers and the few who were left knew they would soon be
gone. Though the boys never voiced any fear of the battlefield,
they often asked if we thought they would find "a club just like
this" at their next station or whether they would meet people
who would be friendly in the community closest their next camp.
Mrs. C., who had carved the turkey on Christmas Day, was late
coming to the birthday tea. She handed me a letter which bore
a postmark of South Molton, North Devon, England. When I fin-

ished the letter I asked her to share it with soldiers. I watched the faces of the ones closest to me as she read:

Dear Mrs. C——,
    You will no doubt be very surprised to receive a letter from someone who is a complete stranger to you, but as we have just started off another year and I have become acquainted with your son J——, I had a feeling that I would also like to know his people in the U.S.A.
    First of all I should explain that I am a Police Constable and have become friendly with J—— as a result of his unit being stationed here. I am married and have two sons and one daughter. We had J—— and a friend with us for the whole of Christmas Day and believe me we really enjoyed their company. . . .
    J—— has told us all about you and I feel that we have become friends across the sea. . . . Another thing which should please you is the fact that the whole town has taken to the boys and I believe it will do us all a lot of good in more ways than one. I can assure you that the boys have, without exception, proved themselves to at least be real gentlemen. . . .
    It will no doubt be some time before you receive this letter, but nevertheless on behalf of my wife and myself I should like to wish you all a very happy New Year and sincerely hope that you will have the pleasure of welcoming J—— home again before we ring in another New Year.
    I hope you will forgive me for taking the liberty of writing to you in this way, but now that I know J—— I felt I reasonably must get to know his people. My wife and I would like very much to hear from you so if you have time to write, please do. . . .
                                        I remain,
                                        Yours sincerely,
                                        W. J. D——

    The men who listened to this letter had also heard the rumor that white American soldiers had told the English people Negro soldiers were savages who had tails. They seemed to stand a little taller as Mrs. C. read . . . "the boys have, without exception, proved themselves to at least be real gentlemen."
    Our photographer caught a picture at the moment their pride was most evident. Mrs. C.'s prayer had been answered. She mailed a copy of the picture taken around the table to her English

friends. She also enclosed a clipping which appeared in Negro newspapers. When her English friend wrote again, he said his younger son, upon seeing the table, exclaimed, "My, what a lot of good things they have to eat!"

There were over 438,291 Mrs. C.'s serving in the hundred or more NCCS clubs throughout the country. I learned many a useful lesson from those whom it was my duty and pleasure to work with.

On February 14, after a Valentine Dance, we drove McDougald to the railroad station. He caught a train for New York. McDougald had been assigned to the Orangeburg Club where I had done my field work. I was the last of the original three and I felt lonely without my two friends.

Mama Ida and Mama both knew the Patton family that had migrated to Oklahoma from Lafayette. When I told them that one of the sons was at Fort McClellan they were very eager to meet him. Mama and her sister, Elon, had once kept company with the soldier's twin uncles and a bond of friendship was established. Patton was in charge of the officers' club and mess and we often found the opportunity to co-operate.

On one such night Patton phoned to say he had a larger party crowd than he had expected and asked me to bring out paper plates and napkins if I could find someone to drive after we closed. One of the hostesses who had a car agreed and to the Fort we went. It was near midnight when we made the delivery and Patton suggested that we should wait until he could ride back to town with us. There had been many instances where white MP's stationed at the gates to the Fort had been insulting to Negro women. But I usually showed my pass, explained that I was on official business, and went on my way. This night was different.

The soldier was at the wheel when the white guard pushed aside the hand I had put out of the window to show my official pass. The guard looked at us for awhile, then said: "Let me see that pass again. And what's *your* name?" he asked the hostess.

There was a sneer in his voice and a scowl on his face. We knew we were in for it and we knew too it was because he was not sure of my racial identity. Another guard came out and looked on contemptuously.

"Tarry," the first one said. "What's your address?"

"It's all there on the pass," I said. "And my name is Ellen Tarry, Miss Ellen Tarry the pass says."

"Miss?" he laughed. "Since when?"

"You get out of this car," the other guard ordered the soldier, who did as he was told and showed his credentials. More insults were thrown around and they took the soldier inside for questioning. We did not know what was going to happen until they brought him out again and told us to go on about our business.

There was no sleep for me that night. I kept remembering the way the white soldier had sneered when he said, "Miss? Since when?" I wondered if my grandfather, sleeping so peacefully in the well-kept white cemetery, knew about the legacy he had left behind. Then I remembered how Mama had told me her father used to bail Negroes out of jail when he discovered that they were in danger of being lynched. She said he would take them out in the country to "Uncle" Anthony Barrow's, as Mama referred to Joe Louis' paternal grandfather, until they could be smuggled across the state line and put on a train which would carry them to safety. I recalled the accounts she had given me of how he escaped from a Yankee prison during the war between the states with the help of a Northern soldier whose friendship he had made. In spite of having one leg, he managed to get home, though he had to borrow somebody's horse to do it. I was his grandchild and I did not intend to accept the humiliation without fighting back.

A new cycle had begun and we were getting additional requests for rooms, but I remained away from the Club a day and a night until I felt better and had been missed. When the soldiers asked where I had been, I told them what had happened at the Fort two nights before. I saw them pass the information along and by the end of the week I had been summoned to the Fort. The Special Services officer apologized for what had happened and gave me a pass which entitled me to come and go without question. After that I let my grandfather rest in peace for awhile.

New soldiers came to the Infantry Replacement Training Center, completed their cycles, and went on to Europe or the Pacific. They got younger and younger until only a handful of our regulars were left. Eddie and Patton were among the few. We continued to serve coffee and doughnuts, used all of our program skills, and begged the people of the community to share their homes with the soldiers' wives who kept coming. I missed Bobby and McDougald. Anniston seemed farther away from New York or Birmingham than ever before. The boys griped, the hostesses who had become engaged to soldiers who had been shipped out grumbled, and we all felt the gloom reflected in the war casualties.

By April I was ready to leave Anniston and I wrote Joe Robichaux and told him. He telephoned to tell me that I would soon receive a letter instructing me to go to New Orleans for a training course to prepare USO workers to serve the returning veterans. Joe also promised to recommend me for a job in the public relations department if I would stick with the organization.

At the Colored USO in New Orleans I was assigned to living quarters uptown. As the taxi driver carried me through the Negro business district I remembered some of the streets from my first visit to the Crescent City. We were on Dryades when the driver stopped suddenly and swerved to avoid a car which was backing out. The driver of the other car got out to see if any damage had been done, and I recognized an old friend. It was Arthur.

The next morning was Sunday, and Arthur drove me to Mass. I spent the day with May Gagne, and that evening Arthur drove me home again. I sensed that he had something to say, and we sat in front of the house and talked pleasantly for a few moments. Arthur seemed less brittle, and I decided he had changed for the better. I sat and listened as he talked about us and our friendship, but it was as if I were a third person suspended in space above the two people on the front seat of Arthur's car, while he said most of the things which would have made me happy if they had only been said eight years earlier.

Arthur paused and waited for me to answer. The right words would not come because all I could think of was the poem, "Maude Muller," the part which reads: ". . . For of all sad words of tongue or pen/ the saddest are these: / It might have been!" On the chain around my neck was a wedding ring. I had married the soldier named Patton in a secret civil ceremony. One week later I had discovered that the contract had not been made in good faith. No one shared my secret but Little Sister and the Funderburgs, with whom I lived, and I could not bring myself to tell Arthur. My silence perplexed and annoyed him. Without questioning he took me to the door and we parted with a curt "Good night."

Three other Negro women who were taking the USO course lived in the home where I was rooming. On social occasions when we saw Arthur they were impressed by his good looks and seeming stability. They chided me for what they thought was my indifference and there was nothing I could say in my defense. I was glad when the last session was over and actually looked forward to going back to Anniston.

The night before I left New Orleans Arthur drove me to the station so I could check my bags. I had always enjoyed the hot tamales peddled from pushcarts along the side streets of New Orleans and he drove through a section where we could get them. I knew he had more to say, and when he stopped the car in front of the house I kept wishing one of the other girls would come out. But I had used up my supply of quick miracles and I sat and listened to my friend as he told me about all the things I had done wrong over a period of eight years. There were many charges I might have made, too, but it was too late. So I said nothing but "Good-by."

The Club at Anniston was a welcome port after the emotional storm at New Orleans. The chain around my neck became heavier with each day, but there was so much to be done I had no time to worry about the muddle in which I found myself. Joe was working hard to get me out of Anniston and I told myself that that was the first step toward a solution of my problem.

Hectic weeks passed and I knew it was impossible to salvage anything from the Patton relationship. I wrote Father Hyland and told him what had happened. He advised me to return to New York as soon as possible and promised to meet me so we might discuss my plans for the future. There was so much to be done I had to forget personal considerations. We were losing volunteers steadily. The girls were marrying soldiers before they left for overseas assignments and the older service wives were returning to their homes after their husbands left McClellan. The younger soldiers' wives who came either had babies or were expecting them. It was hard to work up the enthusiasm which had sparked our earlier programs. My loneliness increased every time I heard a train whistle cut through the stillness of the night.

The month of May was saddened by the death of Aunt Lizzie, who had lived next door to us on Sixth Avenue. I went up to Birmingham for her funeral. That afternoon I stopped by the office of my cousin, Doctor Hutchinson, and he mentioned the fact that I was pale and had lost weight. He insisted upon making a quick examination. Then he began asking me questions. When I left his office I had told him my secret and he had told me that I was going to have a baby.

All my adult life I had prayed that I would one day become a mother, but it did seem then that the answer to my prayer was ill-timed.

The long hours at the Club became a blessing and kept me from thinking about my future. Ironically, most of the young service wives seemed to discover in my presence that they were pregnant. The Club was a favorite fainting place and they all came to me. I bathed their faces, held the ammonia bottle under their noses, and fetched salt water after attacks of nausea. When they cried I cried with them because I felt sorrier for myself than I did for them. And that was the only way I could afford the luxury of tears in public.

Eddie was one of the last of our regulars to leave. As much as I hated to see him go I was relieved because he had become suspicious and I did not want to discuss what had happened. At first, I went to bed each night thinking that I might wake up the next morning and discover that both my secrets were part of a dream. But slowly a change took place: I no longer thought about myself or what was going to happen to me. My thoughts were concerned with the welfare of the child God was going to give into my keeping.

One night I was sitting in the office bringing my diary up to date when I received an emergency call to come to the Fort. I rode out, attended to the matter at hand, and stopped by the noncoms' quarters to visit Ernestine and her husband. They insisted that I share a late supper with them and called a cab to take me back to town. The driver who answered the call was the most silent of the white men who drove the cabs we used. He had never spoken to me other than to repeat an address. That was why I was so surprised when he said:

"You're from New York, ain't you?"

When I said that I was, he fell silent for a few moments. Then he asked, "I'll bet you knew a lot of white people up there, didn't you?"

"I certainly did. Most of the girls I worked with were white."

"That ain't what I mean."

We were driving through a wooded section between the Fort and Anniston. I did not intend to let the man guess my fear. "I'm afraid I don't know what you mean," I stalled.

"Didn't you know no white men?"

"Of course," I laughed. "I'm a Catholic and my priest is white."

"Not like that," he said. "I mean real close. Like men and women. Like me and you're gonna be tonight. I been watching you a long time. This is the first chance I ever got with you."

There was no use to pretend any longer.

"I'm flattered that you had looked forward to being with me," I bluffed, as the man drove the car in the opposite direction from my home, "but it's too late and the people with whom I live have been expecting me for some time. They keep a light on the porch until I get home."

"You ain't going home tonight," he said. "You and me are gonna be together."

I stared at the back of his wrinkled red neck as I thought a prayer. He drove along, half-turning his head ever so often to leer at me, as if he was not sure I was convinced of his intentions. Nervously, he lifted the cap which sat at a half angle on his straight copper-red hair. In desperation, I remembered hearing Mother Funderburg tell about how she used to have to "hold" her boys "down" when they were young.

"I live with Ilon Funderburg," I told the driver. "His wife and mother know that I went to the Fort. If I'm not home in a short while, Ilon will go looking for me. And God help you if I'm harmed!"

He straightened his cap a few times and I knew I had made an impression. I followed up my advantage by telling him how Mother Funderburg never went to sleep until I was in the house. Then I resurrected every stray rumor I had heard about the expert marksmanship of the "Funderburg boys." He turned the car around and took a road that was familiar.

I sat on the edge of the seat. One hand was low on the door of the car. All I wanted was a chance to jump, but the man kept turning his head to make sure I was still there. It seemed as if we had been riding around for hours when he came to a rut in the road. He had to slow down. When he shifted gears, I jumped. The boys on Sixth Avenue used to say, "Ellen runs like a Injun, with her head down"—and that was how I ran that night. Rocks cut my feet and my breath cut at my chest. I heard the man yelling at me that he would "get" me, as his car started, then stalled. But I knew where I was and I remembered a ditch where we had surprised two lovers late one night. If I thought he was going to overtake me, I could hide in the ditch. Then the car started again and I kept running and praying until I saw a side street which led to the house where I lived. I turned quickly, and the car took the main road.

I could not find my key but Mother Funderburg heard me beating against the door and let me in. When I told her what had happened she wanted to shoot in the direction I told her the man had taken. Later, when reason returned, we realized that there was little we could do that would not subject me to possible criticism for being out alone so late at night. We decided not to tell Mother Funderburg's son and we just sat and talked until morning because there was not much else we could do. I was a Negro woman in the South and the cab driver was a white man. I did not tell my friend about the incident with the guard at the Fort or the aftermath, but I knew that that cab driver would never pick up another fare at the Colored USO as long as I was there.

When the city of Rome fell to the Allied Army on June 4, 1944, the hostesses were in the midst of a training course which we hoped would better prepare them for entertaining trainees as well as the soldiers who would be coming back to the Fort before too long. This was the last course I would give at Anniston and I was pleased when civic workers from the community, as well as from Gadsden and Birmingham, came to the Club to lecture to the girls. When the course was over I resigned and prepared to leave the little town where I had learned so much about personal and human relationships.

To think of the future would have been to collapse in defeat. I had to master the art of living from day to day. Mama came to Anniston, and when I told her my double secret I also told her I was going back to New York. Though she hated to see me face so much alone, she knew it would be useless to try to stop me. She worried less after I told her that Ted Yates had found a place for me to live.

It was hard to leave the many friends I had made, but the hardest part was leaving the family with whom I had lived. Nights when I was restless I would sit on a stool at Mother Funderburg's feet and she would brush my hair and repeat all the reasons why I should stay in Anniston with them. It was difficult to give up the comforting assurance of these kind friends' love but it was no longer I who mattered. I had to renounce the marriage I had made in secret and prepare a home for the child I had cheated before it was born. But I promised God and the baby that it would be born in a place where it would be free.

chapter 15

THE LAND OF THE FREE

In New York, where there were no doors marked "Colored" or "White," I felt like a human being again. The past year seemed like a book I had read and all of the characters were vague. When life stirred within me I thanked God that my child would be born a thousand miles away from the scene of the racial incidents I had known and recorded.

The apartment Ted Yates found for me was located in a section of lower Harlem where I had never lived before. I was isolated from most of the friends who might have helped to ward off the hours of desolation and fright which plagued my nights. I had returned at the height of the vacation season and it was difficult to locate old acquaintances. A business arrangement with a Negro magazine was canceled, and I lost the knack of thinking beyond the needs of the day. When courage was lowest Father Hyland rang my doorbell. I told him all the things I would have told my Papa if he had been living, and Father counseled me with the wisdom of a kind parent and a Godly priest.

"Miss Ellen," he said after we had talked for hours, "what is, is best!" And those were the words I repeated whenever I faltered.

Though my prayers were a feeble cry, someone must have been bombarding Heaven for me because Joe Robichaux brought Father Vincent Smith to my house before Father Hyland left New York. Father Smith had been made pastor of a New Jersey parish and seeing him was a pleasant surprise. He it was who guided me until the shadows had passed and the cleansing power of the Sacraments had led me back to the foot of the Cross. At the time, neither Joe nor I knew that Father Smith was even then weighing his determination to seek the sanctuary of a Trappist monastery.

Hope for my professional future was revived when May Massee of Viking Press wrote and asked me to meet with Marie Hall Ets, an author-illustrator who had suggested a juvenile which would depict the everyday lives of Negro boys and girls in an urban setting like Harlem. Marie and I met at the Viking offices on the same day New York was lashed by the August, 1944, hurricane and we made our first plans for the juvenile story which became *My Dog Rinty*.

Between planning sessions for the book came comforting letters from Mama's old friend John Wesley Patton, who offered me and his grandchild-to-be the security of his Oklahoma home. I had made my decision, however, and there was no turning back.

More surprising was the letter from Claude McKay. Claude was working for Bishop Sheil in Chicago. He was teaching in the Sheil School of Social Studies and wanted me to know that he was taking instructions and preparing for baptism. Afterward he wrote: "... I'm not a Catholic like the American Catholics. I'm more like the European Catholics—I still feel free. Guess I'll have to say I owe my conversion to you." I knew how hard it had been for Claude to become one of "you Catholics" and to admit that a mere female had anything to do with it. Later he wrote about this admission. Though he claimed to despise the word gratitude, when Claude learned that I was alone, awaiting the birth of my child, he asked a friend of his who made periodic business visits to New York to call on me so that he might be assured of my well-being from time to time.

The housing shortage in Chicago became insignificant in comparison with the living conditions I found when I returned to New York in 1944. The apartment I first occupied had been sublet from friends of Ted's. When the three months were up I had to sleep on the divan in the living room of the apartment on St. Nicholas Avenue which I had turned over to friends. Various friends joined me, and we walked the streets hoping to see a "for rent" sign. We went to real estate offices, we advertised and told everybody who would listen that I had to find a place to live before my baby was born. My doctor, who became disturbed over my anxiety, begged his patients to notify him if they heard of any vacancies. I thought about the rooms I had found for soldiers and their wives and the comfort of the home I had left in Anniston and Mama's big house sitting on the top of a hill. Half-frightened, I would slip out at night, telling myself that "God walks with those who walk alone," and look for empty apartments. Each time I see a woman walking a dark street alone I want to reach out my hand to her and say, "I, too, once walked alone in sorrow."

The anguish caused by the housing shortage was forgotten when the child I had expected for Christmas came in November. Instead of the son I had prayed for, God sent me a daughter and my mother arrived one day before the little girl. One of Mama's friends who had comforted me during the months of waiting summed up the boy vs. girl situation in a most practical manner: "God knows what He's doing. A little girl will be much cheaper. You can always sleep with her and save on room rent."

Another friend, who lived a few blocks up from the little apartment on St. Nicholas Avenue where I had waited, opened her home to me and I found quarters. It was a fourth floor walk-up, with few of the comforts I would have wanted for my child, but it was a home and I was with friends.

When the little girl we had named Elizabeth after my own Little Sister was a few weeks old, a telegram called Mama home to the bedside of Mama Ida. It was only after I was alone with the baby that I recognized the scope of the responsibility I had undertaken. Looking at the fat little girl wrapped in pink blankets as she slept in her bassinet, I questioned my right to condemn an innocent child to the heritage that comes to each Negro in America at birth.

One cold December night when our cubbyhole of a room was bright with the reflection of a new moon shining on Christmas snow, I remembered the wonderful words I used to whisper whenever a sliver of moon appeared in the sky over my Alabama home:

"Wish I will, wish I might;
New moon, I make this wish tonight."

Through the years, across the miles from Alabama to Louisiana and from New Orleans to New York, this childish habit had persisted. Sometimes it was after leaving a theater, sometimes outside a church, on a crowded city street or from a churning ferry, that my friend, the new moon, heard these words. A new coin, when I had one, was held high as assurance that my wish would come true.

During war years, nights are always long and lonely for womenfolk who are alone with their children, and I had ample time to remember the wishes I had made for myself that had not come true. Already a galaxy of prayers as countless as the stars had been offered up for the girl-child God had entrusted to my care. I smiled at my own childishness when I felt the familiar words form on my lips.

"Wish I will, wish I might;
New moon, I make this wish tonight!"

It was no new coin I showed my old friend this time. Proudly, I held high the young flesh of my flesh and blood of my blood. Silently, I asked the moon and its Creator that this new life might be useful, fruitful, and normal—in spite of the handicaps I knew lay in wait.

During the following months Elizabeth passed through various stages of change. Fair at birth, her skin tone deepened into a smooth brown—like caramel candy. The dark mass of curls took on a reddish-brown hue and coarsened in texture. This, I hoped, would make life less complicated for her than it had been for her mother.

Except for colic, brought on by my dogged insistence in following a fixed feeding schedule as I had been instructed, Elizabeth was a healthy, happy baby. Fortunately, her colic struck at night. During the day, after bottles were washed, formula mixed, and clothes were on the line, I was with Marie Ets working at all the business which goes into making a book. The story was written, but we had to find a "typical" family and get permission to take pictures. Though it was hard finding a family to fit our needs, getting permission to take pictures in homes, places of business, public service centers, and churches in Harlem was an enormous task. My people's understandable suspicion of the white man and anything connected with the white man's world created situations which would have defeated the purpose of the book if I had not presumed upon many friendships. By the time Alexander and Alexandra Alland had taken the last picture for the book, I was immune to insult.

To write of Harlem in 1945 without making mention of the great sorrow which blanketed the community on April 12 at the death of Franklin Delano Roosevelt would be a serious oversight. Regardless of the numerous controversies which have arisen over the role played by our wartime president, Roosevelt was the first chief executive since Lincoln who succeeded in creating a national atmosphere in which the Negro felt as if he were really free.

I was ironing the last of a pile of tiny dresses when the announcement was made over the radio that Roosevelt had died in Warm Springs, Georgia. At first I thought I had been mistaken, then as additional details filled in the death picture my first impulse was to call out to someone, to say: "Can it be true?" But I was alone except for the baby. I took her in my arms and said a prayer for the repose of the soul of this very human, physically handicapped man who, by being aware of the changing tides and nodding at the right times, had helped my people to walk taller, to dream and to hope.

When I went out to shop, the streets were crowded with little groups of Negroes standing aimlessly together looking as if they were lost. Some were crying. Others were asking: "What will happen now? What will become of us?" Franklin Delano Roosevelt succeeded in making many enemies, but none of them that I have known was black. He was our "Great White Father," the first since "Father Abraham," and we were bereft.

By devious methods many of the soldiers I served at Fort McClellan managed to get my New York addresses and letters from across the seas began arriving soon after my return. I had learned enough about combat psychology to appreciate the role of mother-wife-sister-sweetheart correspondent which was conferred upon me. There were, though, many letters which left me with a poignant understanding of the ravages of war. I wept over the one from "Jimmy USO" who wanted the baby to have a gift from him before he "moved up to the front line." Mama burned most of this correspondence, along with a packet of humorous notes from Claude, because, she said, "you have too many letters from men lying around here." I will ever remain grateful for those letters because they reflected history in the making and carried me close to the scene of the struggle.

Soon after V-E Day was celebrated, Joe Robichaux suggested that it might be well for me to start making plans to go back to work. I saw the wisdom of his suggestion, but pushed the idea as far away as I could. When school was out in Alabama, Little Sister came to New York to see her namesake and I was happy that I had a little family again.

In August I went to work for local National Catholic Community Service as supervisor of the Harlem Area. NCCS had offices in the Harlem Servicemen's Center and, for the first time, I had the opportunity of working with men from all branches of the Armed Forces. I was especially impressed by ths spirit of co-operation demonstrated by the Navy personnel. When I complimented one of the sailors on the manner in which they always assisted the staff, he said: "On the ship there's nowhere to go. So you learn how to pull together. That's all there is to it." The boys in blue were younger than most of the soldiers who came to the Center and much less sophisticated.

Talk of peace was in the air. The soldiers in the Pacific wrote "it will all be over soon" and others asked: "Did you read where we shot up Okinawa?" Servicemen returning from Europe came in the Center daily and my co-workers became accustomed to the loud and joyful greetings which were exchanged when one of the boys who had been at McClellan walked in the lobby. On August 12 we heard that peace had been declared and we were all disappointed when the rumor proved false. But everybody felt it was only a matter of days—maybe hours. Nobody believed that our enemies would risk another atom-blasted Hiroshima. The servicemen entertained us with wild versions of how they were going to celebrate when the good news came.

On August 14, I left the Center at a few minutes past six and went to the YWCA for dinner. I had eaten and was standing at the information desk talking with a friend when we heard cries of joy coming from all parts of the building. My friend turned on the nearest radio and we heard the last part of the announcement that our war with Japan had come to an end. It was 7:01 P.M. by the clock on the wall. V-J Day had come at last.

The Servicemen's Center, located near 137th Street on Seventh Avenue, was only a half block away, but by the time I ran to the corner of Seventh Avenue whistles were blowing, horns tooting, and people shouting. Soldiers and sailors were dancing in the street, throwing their hats away and letting everybody know they were glad their fighting days were over. I pushed my way through the crowd gathered outside the Center where the director was putting up loud-speakers and some of the servicemen were putting records on the machines. More civilians gathered to watch the boys celebrate and they, too, caught the spirit and joined in. Photographers and reporters came, Pathé News cameramen took pictures, and when the doors were finally closed the staff was battleworn. When I reached home they told me that my daughter of nine months stood at attention when the National Anthem was played following the announcement of peace.

One of the priests who had supported our efforts to recruit hostesses from the parishes of Harlem was Reverend Emil Kapusta, who with his social vision of Harlem often reminded me of Father Mulvoy. Father Kapusta was aware of most of the needs of Harlem, which he discussed with me from time to time. One of these needs was a Catholic Community Center, and in my diary, under the date of August 21, 1945, I made the following entry: "After I talked with Father K today I had vision of a new club after the war era. Maybe my old dream of a Catholic Community Center and Residence Club for working girls will come true." The entry further states that I went shopping earlier that morning for bubble pipes and that the clerks in the stores acted as if they thought I was crazy until I explained that we were having a bubble-blowing contest at the USO that night. Bubbles and dreams are sometimes made of the same stuff.

"The Boys Came" was my label for the months following V-J Day. I renewed friendships from the Stage Door Canteen, the Service Lounge at the YWCA, Camp Shanks, and Fort McClellan. The boys from McClellan all wanted to see the baby, regardless of the hour of the night, and she displayed a preference for males at an early age. Some of them, including "Jimmy USO" were hospitalized, but they telephoned from the separation center and promised to come to the city as soon as they were well. There was sadness, too, when they brought me news of the ones who would never come back.

Eddie, who had fought all over Europe, called my house soon after he reached Fort Dix. Days later when we met he told me about Benoit, a boy from Louisiana who had been at Fort Mc-Clellan. We remembered when Benoit had become engaged to a girl from his home and they were married in the Anniston church. Though Eddie and Benoit were assigned to different companies after they reached Europe, they often met and they were fighting in the same area the morning Benoit got a cable telling him that he was the father of a baby girl. Later that day, Benoit's outfit was on the side of a hill digging in for an attack. Suddenly someone yelled "Benoit!" and the proud new father raised his head to see who was calling. A bullet from the gun of a German sharpshooter perched in a nearby tree ended his life. His buddies shot up the tree and they told Eddie about it and

he told me. Eddie said the Germans used the names they overheard to lure our soldiers into death traps.

"Do you think things will be better for us now?" was one of
the questions the Negro servicemen asked when they spoke of
their experiences under fire. Some of them had served in a mixed
unit and they predicted that the Army would sooner or later see
the wisdom of integration, not so much from a sense of social
justice, they thought, as from expediency. One soldier told me
how he and his buddies had come in one day from the front lines
and found an overseas edition of an American newspaper which
carried an account of a statement made by a white American
from the South who had said that the Negro was "one-third pigment, one-third superstition, and one-third thief." He said they
felt as if they were fighting the wrong enemy.

"For the first time in my life I felt like a man!" was the way
the Negro soldiers expressed their reaction to the manner in
which the English, French, and Italian people had received them.
It was thoughts of the future which made them morose, and
many found the period of adjustment painful to them and their
loved ones.

I sometimes felt guilty, after an evening with these boys from
Europe, when a letter came from the Pacific. And there was hardly
a day I did not hear from one of my friends in the East who
was "sweating it out," begging me to petition the President, a
congressman, or a senator to let him come home. They counted
up their points for me and griped about everything in general.

At Christmastime gifts of appreciation came from far-off places
and I placed most of the V-mail letters and foreign currency
these homesick boys had sent me in an ebony chest inlaid with
mother of pearl which had come from Korea. To children of
another generation names like Pearl Harbor, Manila, Leyte,
Okinawa, and Iwo Jima will spell history and they will take an
interest in the thoughts and dreams of men who suffered there.

The year of 1946 gave much and took more away. My sister,
who had resigned her position as a teacher in Birmingham, ac-

cepted work in New York with one of the government agencies. She was thrilled at the return of a group of the soldiers she had known at Camp Sibert, and when they left New York, men were coming in from the Pacific Theater. By spring I had learned a great deal about jungle rot, battle fatigue, and the diseases and longings of men who fight and live in jungles.

The housing shortage became even more acute. There were strikes and shortages of fuel, food, and whatever human beings needed most. I was grateful from the training NCCS had given me. It was a pleasure to sit and talk with a veteran who, because of a leg wound, could only tap his foot to the rhythm and watch the others dance. I was glad that I knew better than to ask him if he wanted to use the elevator to reach the three floors above and had the good sense to invite him to ride with me when some routine duty required my presence on the upper floors. The art of listening became a joy and some of the tales I heard from the men who came back outranked those I had heard in the earlier years.

Attendance swelled at the Center and hostesses we had not seen for months reported for duty and helped us entertain the returning servicemen. We took the girls to hospitals and nearby camps and gave them showers when they came in to tell us that they were engaged.

My daughter, at eighteen months, was recovering from a nip-and-tuck battle with a streptococcic throat infection when a message came from Alabama. Mama Ida was dying. Though my grandmother was only three years away from ninety, we found it hard to think of life without her. I wanted her to see my baby and have her bestow her blessing upon this first great-granddaughter before it was too late. Elizabeth's physician advised against the trip to Alabama, but gave his consent—along with a warning—when I explained the nature of the journey.

There was a hint of spring in the air when we took off at twilight from LaGuardia Field for this half-sad, half-happy flight. It was too early for the moon, but a few brave stars came out for our leavetaking. Elizabeth rested her curly head on my shoulder and fell asleep soon after we flew over New York. Within a short time we landed at Pittsburgh and the lights of the city were only minutes behind us when I first heard the pelt of the rain against the wings of the plane. There were a few air pockets, then a bell rang and the sign at the front of the plane flashed: "Fasten seat belts."

After fastening the belt as tight as I dared, I looked down on the sleeping child and thought of the investment in prayers and wishes which she represented. Noting the even rise and fall of her breast, I closed my eyes and tried to close my ears to the sound of the rain. The hostess made her way up and down the aisle, her face frozen in a fixed, carefully rehearsed smile as she tried to calm the passengers and give the lie to our danger.

"Will we make it?" one of the passengers asked a crewman who emerged from the cockpit on his way to the washroom.

There was a pause.

"I think we will," was the terse reply.

Elizabeth slept and I prayed between lurches. The pilot was bringing the battered ship down for an emergency landing at Knoxville, Tennessee, when the child awoke. As the ship made the edge of the Knoxville field and touched ground I peered out of the window at the ambulance and stretcher bearers who were standing by.

None of the passengers minded the rain which baptised us as we emerged from the plane. The uncertain gait of the others was comforting; I knew their legs were as wobbly as mine. Inside the waiting room the men began joking about the danger which had been so real to us a few moments before and everyone's thoughts shifted to shelter for the night.

My seatmate, a young executive enroute to a conference in Birmingham, smiled at the baby while we waited for room assignments.

"She's a swell little traveler," he said.

Elizabeth, refreshed after her long sleep, answered the compliment with a curtsy. Sure of an interested audience she pulled all the tricks young ones use to attract attention and kept us amused as we waited. One by one the passengers received their hotel assignments and went outside to waiting taxicabs. My seatmate and the baby and I were the only ones left.

"Hotel Farragut," the young woman behind the desk told him. "That's the only room with a bath that's left. We'll call you as soon as we get a flight to Birmingham. From the looks of the weather that will be sometime tomorrow."

The young man, who had already been helpful with the baby, waited for the clerk to assign me to a room. There was an awkward pause when we both realized that she was giving no indication of being aware of my presence.

"Er, miss, if that's all you have," he said, "I'd rather give it to the lady and the baby. I can rough it."

"Just a minute," she answered. A flush covered her face when our eyes met. She hurried into an inner office, and we could see her talking animatedly with another woman and a man. Something like the shutter of a camera clicked in my mind.

A Negro porter joined the group inside the office, then came out in the lobby, looked around, and rejoined the clerks. In a few minutes a young man appeared at the counter, asked for my credentials again, and began shuffling through a batch of papers and file cards.

I was remembering my prayers and the wish that Elizabeth might have a normal life when he spoke.

"We don't have any hotel accommodations for Negroes in Knoxville," he said sarcastically, "but one of the Negro bellboys at a hotel in town is trying to find a room for you—and your baby." He said other things, too, but I barely heard him. I was too busy questioning God about the way He runs His world.

It had not been accidental that I was the last to be assigned to a room. My lack of pigmentation had made me just another passenger—but my caramel-colored baby made everything different. Yet the clerks would not have dared to make the charge unless they had been sure. The Negro porter had actually made the decision for them; he had said the words which meant "Yes, the baby is a Negro." I remembered the furtive look he gave Elizabeth and me when he came out of the office. For a fraction of a second, my faith in God and man hung in the balance. Then I remembered: "... And there was no room in the inn...."

The Birmingham-bound executive avoided my glance as he accepted the slip of paper entitling him to the room which had been denied my child and me because we were Negroes. As he went out to a waiting cab he pulled his collar high about his face.

Elizabeth squirmed and whined until I put her on the floor again. She would play a while, then pull my skirt and hold out her arms to be picked up. I recognized the signal. She was over-tired. The physician had warned me against undue fatigue which, he had said, would render her susceptible to another cold. In view of the recent strep infection, it would be dangerous.

I could not remember the name of a single Negro in Knoxville to whom I might appeal, despite the fact that Papa had gone to school in Knoxville and a prominent New York minister was then president of Knoxville College. There had also been two soldiers in Eddie's company at Fort McClellan who were from Knoxville. I thought about Dr. Carver when he had been refused a hotel room in New York. All I knew was that I was without a room and I had to find one for my child.

When the promised room finally came through, we had to face the problem of how I would cover the thirteen miles to town. One other flight had come in, and there were more passengers. But they were white, and whites and Negroes were not allowed to ride in the same taxicabs.

The problem of getting to town was solved a few hours later by two white men who brushed the local custom aside by telling the driver, "To hell with that, we want to get in town! We're on government business and we don't have any time to waste." And they got in the cab with the baby and me.

We were the last to get out because the driver had difficulty finding the Negro tourist home where we were to be quartered for the night. It was well past 3 A.M. when the woman who operated the place showed us to the only available space, her sleeping porch, and I dumped Elizabeth and my bag on the bed. She smiled up at me as I sat there in dejection, ready to let go of whatever was holding me together.

"Ride the horsy, Mummy?" she begged, holding out her arms for me to take her. "Let's ride the horsy."

Looking into the big brown eyes which were watching me I summoned strength from some secret reservoir to fight back the rage which had been piling up for hours. I held out a hand and in a little while I was playing horsy while Elizabeth rode.

After the child fell asleep, I spent the remaining dark hours thinking of all the speeches I might have made at the airport concerning my rights as a first-class passenger and the stupidity of the system which was responsible for the situation which we had all had to face. I waited impatiently for the dawn, which appeared reluctantly, then tip-toed through the hallway until I found a telephone.

A steady drizzle was falling and the skies were overcast when I called the airfield. Hours passed before I was told that a flight had been scheduled to Birmingham that afternoon and a taxi would call for me. Then the cab arrived. I saw the other passengers were white, but thinking someone had undergone a change of heart, I gathered up Elizabeth and my bags and started out. The driver met me at the steps of the porch. Stuttering and saying words which had no meaning, he asked if he could use the telephone. The woman who owned the place nodded and he went in the house. We stood on the porch and wondered what would come next.

The front door slammed.

"You'll have to wait for another cab. I'm full," the driver said. "Another one will be along after awhile."

I asked the proprietress to take care of Elizabeth for a few minutes. I went to the telephone and called the airfield again. Once more I gave my name, present address, and all particulars. After explaining that I was a Negro, I reminded the clerk that I expected the airline to honor the ticket I had been sold and before I could board a plane I would have to be provided with transportation. I mentioned the fact that my daughter's health had been endangered and threatened a civil suit.

The clerk explained that she had been on duty when we came came in the night before. A graduate of a well-known eastern university, she tried to apologize for what had happened.

"Last night," she said, "I didn't have the heart to tell you. I hope that the baby is all right. And if you'll just be calm and trust me—I'll promise to get you out here."

Unexpected kindness had broken the dam and I could not go to the baby until I regained a semblance of composure.

In spite of the proprietress' "Please, ma'am, don't go up in the air in all that rain with this sweet little baby," I was ready and waiting when the next car came and a Negro driver in blue denim overalls started us on our journey. When he insisted that we sit in the front seat with him, I was curious. As soon as the driver busied himself with starting the motor I looked in the back of the car. Then I understood.

On the floor of the car was another passenger: a huge sack of United States air mail.

"Uncle Sam's mail is so valuable," I said to the driver, "we should feel flattered to have the privilege of riding with such precious cargo."

"Lots of things happen down here just don't make no kinda sense," he grinned without taking his eyes off the ribbon of highway which stretched out before us. I looked at the huge black hands gripping the steering wheel and wondered how strong men of his breed were able to restrain themselves when "lots of things" happened.

Elizabeth and the driver made friends, and after the mail was delivered he offered to keep her while I checked my luggage and made sure I had a seat on the plane scheduled to leave for Birmingham. At the Western Union office I sent a telegram to a friend in Birmingham giving the flight number and expected time of arrival, but, for some strange reason, I also requested limousine service at the point of destination.

On my way to rejoin Elizabeth and the overalled driver I passed a mirror and noted that the orchid corsage I had received just before I left New York had miraculously survived. From the reflection in the mirror I could also tell that my one and only expensive outfit was none the worse for wear. Elizabeth and her friend had made a game of retrieving the melon-colored hat, matching her suit, which kept falling off her head. Baby laughter attracted the attention of other passengers and they gaped as we walked out to the plane. We were an odd-looking trio—Elizabeth, with soft brown curls framing her brown face, perched on the shoulders of the denim clad Negro, as I brought up the pale rear guard with my orchid corsage boasting that someone connected with me had money to spend on a frivolous luxury.

From Knoxville we went on to Chattanooga, then flew straight into another storm. Once again the bell rang, the signal flashed, we strapped ourselves in and the pilot began the battle to fly his plane in spite of stormy weather. Ten minutes away from the Birmingham airfield we could feel the plane coming down. Then suddenly the sun broke through the clouds and I thought of the first afternoon I saw sunshine burst through the stained-glass windows of an old church down in Greenwich Village. It was like feeling the glory of God all around you and being ashamed that you had ever feared. This feeling was short-lived.

There was no one to meet us at Birmingham, and we joined the passengers who went to the limousine. Elizabeth and I sat on the back seat, and I was talking with a pleasant young nurse who told me she worked at Jefferson Hospital when I happened to look up and see the chauffeur staring at me.

"Wonder what's holding us up now?" one of the men asked.

Without offering an explanation the driver got out of the car and walked over to a Negro porter. I listened to the nurse with one ear and cocked the other in the direction of the red-necked chauffeur.

"Boy," he said in a stage whisper, "is that a *nigger* baby that white woman's holding?"

The male passengers gave no indication that they had heard, but the nurse gasped. Instinctively, her training asserted itself and she continued to talk as if nothing had been said and I pretended to listen.

It was seven miles to town.

As the Negro porter hesitated, I braced myself for a repetition of events at Knoxville. Shrewdly, the Negro cloaked his face with the protective mask my people often use when in the presence of whites. I detected a tiny spark of recognition in his shifting eyes.

Perhaps, I thought, he is some boy I once taught. He might even be one of my sister's former pupils; the family resemblance is striking. Then I made the decision. I did not intend to move and God would have to help us all if the man called my baby that name again. Maybe Mama Ida would never see her great-grand-daughter after all.

Then the porter spoke. "Tell you the truth, Boss"—he scratched his head—"I just don't rightly know."

The driver spat in disgust and took his place behind the wheel. Nobody spoke as we rode toward town. We were a mile away from the field when a car carrying two of my friends passed. I was too exhausted to hail them.

Over and over I kept thinking: "He called my child a *'nigger* baby.' He called my child a *'nigger* baby.' "

I wondered if it was fair for Negro mothers to bring children into a world that would scorn them because of their color. I felt guilty and ashamed that I had brought Elizabeth to Alabama to be called a "nigger baby."

The limousine stopped in front of the "white" entrance to Terminal Station. We were the first to get out and a redcap took our bags. Elizabeth caught the excitement of the crowded terminal and I had to hold her hand tightly to keep her from dancing away from me.

I spoke softly to the porter: "Will you please take me to the colored waiting room?"

His eyes widened. "Oh, no, ma'am! I can't take *you* over there."

"Will you take me to that colored waiting room," I ordered, "so I can telephone my colored mother and get a taxicab to take my colored baby home."

When I spoke to my mother I learned that friends had been checking planes, trains, and buses since the night before. One of them had left the terminal minutes before the limousine drove up.

I scarcely noticed the driver of the cab I hailed at the entrance to the colored waiting room until he spoke.

"I didn't know you had a baby. She sure is cute! It's been a long time since you was home."

I looked in the mirror over the steering wheel and recognized the face of a boy I once had taught.

"That white man," I blurted, "the driver of the limousine— he called her a 'nigger baby.' I should never have brought her down here."

"That's too bad," the driver consoled. "You know how it is down here. You can't let those kind of things get you down."

How could this youngster understand? I asked myself. He did not see the contempt on the man's face or hear the sneer in his voice when he said: "Is that a nigger baby . . . ?"

Nobody at home understood, either. They said: "You are just tired and upset. You'll feel better after you have rested."

I could feel my lips repeating "Nigger baby . . . nigger baby . . ."

Maybe I am just upset, I thought. Maybe there isn't anything world-shaking about one little brown girl being called a "nigger baby." Other Negro mothers had had to watch their sons burned at the stake. Not their daughters, though—they had served a different purpose. That was how many unhappy mulattoes had been born. Knowing the history of my race, I thought, maybe it is silly of me to get so wrought up because some "poor white trash" had called my child a name.

In horror, I realized that not only was I indulging in the same kind of name calling, but I was also falling prey to the kind of reasoning which is a part of the Southern Negro's conditioning, the resignation which makes him "stay in his place" on the lowest rung of America's socio-economic ladder.

A call from Mama Ida's room reminded me of the reason for the trip. "How is she?" I asked.

Mama shook her head sadly and I knew that a long full life was nearing its close. With Elizabeth's fat little hand in mine I went to my grandmother.

"So you finally got here?" Mama Ida said as soon as I opened the door to her room. "Hand me that child and let me see how she looks."

Elizabeth would not leave me and I had to hold her up so my grandmother could see her. After a few moments Mama Ida spoke.

"She's a fine baby. She doesn't look like you, but she's a fine baby just the same. From what I can remember of her pa's people, she looks a little like them. I-I want you to know," her voice faltered for the first time, "I sure am glad you brought her to me. I'm so happy to get to see her."

The kiss my grandmother put on Elizabeth's forehead was the benediction I had prayed for.

Mama Ida slept away a few days afterward. The memory of her happiness at seeing Elizabeth softened the sorrow. Back in New York I tried to ease the pain of the humiliations we had known in Knoxville and Birmingham. The thing which had happened to my child and me was as old as our history in America. But the very personal nature of the pain made it sharper. Each time I told white friends about it I saw pity in their eyes and, more than once, stifled the impulse to say: "So you wonder how it feels to be a Negro? You wonder how you would have acted if you had been in my place—if someone had called your child a 'nigger baby.' "

In 1947 Jackie Robinson was signed to play with the Brooklyn Dodgers and became the first Negro to play on a major baseball team. We got an apartment in Riverton, a middle-income housing development opened by the Metropolitan Insurance Company, and for the first time I had a comfortable home for my daughter. That winter New York was blanketed by a series of snowstorms, but for the first time in years I was warm and did not have to keep Elizabeth wrapped in blankets and sweaters. My good friends, the Handmaids of Mary, accepted her in their nursery school and we both entered another phase of development. In the late spring of 1948, National Catholic Community

Service closed its Harlem office. Within a few weeks the Harlem
Servicemen's Center closed also.

During the years since I had first met Grace Nail Johnson she
had been one of the closely knit group of my loyal friends. We
had shared mutual dreams for our people and she had accorded
me the rare honor of allowing me to look back with her over the
years of her girlhood in New York long before there was a Negro
Harlem. She had allowed me to listen as she recalled the distinguished years with her gifted husband. She invited me to Great
Barrington, Massachusetts, where I visited at Five Acres and saw
the log cabin in a grove of hemlocks where James Weldon Johnson had written so brilliantly and so prophetically. One of our
mutual dreams had been concerned with opening up direct chan-
nels of book distribution to our people. When Mrs. Johnson
learned that the New American Library was preparing to bring
out a paper-back edition of her husband's *Autobiography of an
Ex-Colored Man,* she saw an opportunity to try out some of the
theories we had advanced and after a series of conferences I was
hired as a consultant by this publishing firm.

Publication date for the reprint of *Autobiography of an Ex-
Colored Man* was scheduled to coincide with the memorial cele-
brations which had been planned for Mr. Johnson's June 17
birthday. Knowing the great admiration Claude McKay had for
James Weldon Johnson, I invited Claude to come to New York
and speak at the New York ceremony which was to be held at the
135th Street library. Claude had been writing me regularly for
the past months, as he had collected what he considered the best
of his poems, old and new, and he wanted to have them published. He had sent them to me and I had, in turn, given them to
my friend Toni Strassman to place.

Two weeks before the time I expected Claude in New York, I
received a letter and he told me that beside being happy to talk
about his friend "Jim Johnson," he was glad to come to New
York because for the first time he would see his daughter. The
child, he said, had been born in the West Indies and reared by
his brother. I had never before heard of Claude having a child

and wrote back to ask for her address. I was amused when he answered and said he wanted to see his own child first, before anybody else saw her. The girl was grown and married and in New York to do graduate work at Columbia University—but I did not press the point as I knew Claude well enough to know he wanted to see how she looked before any of his close friends met her.

One morning I searched the mailbox to see if there was a letter from Claude telling me when he would arrive. As I went out to the Riverton playground to get Elizabeth, I saw a girl who had worked at Friendship House and she told me that someone from Bishop Sheil's office had called Friendship House to find out how to reach me. Claude McKay had died that morning and they wanted me to locate his daughter.

The workers at Friendship House were already trying to locate Claude's daughter, Hope, when I was notified. My friend, Tom Boylan, a police deputy inspector, sent a patrol car to the address I had and as a result of these combined efforts the young woman was soon on her way to my house. It was difficult for me to talk with her about the death of the father she had never seen and Claude's old friend, Harold Jackman, who had been so much a part of the Harlem Claude and the poet Countee Cullen had known and loved, joined me to help greet the daughter of our friend.

Harlem, the Black Metropolis about which Claude McKay had written so much, was saddened to learn of his death. Claude would have chuckled at the turn of events which resulted in his having a New York funeral after the solemn requiem Mass in Chicago at which Bishop Sheil presided and another Mass here at the Church of the Crucifixion. Boyish mischief would have played around the corners of his eyes and mouth and he would have sworn that "the Reds" were responsible for his mortal remains arriving in New York late—four hours after the Mass had been said *in absentia.*

Claude would have been the first one to laugh at the people who were aggrieved by his "new religion" as well as the ones who established themselves in the good graces of his grief-stricken child, and faltered at the funeral home where they had arranged "memorial services" with Protestant ministers only in attendance because, they said, "Ellen Tarry is sitting in there waiting to jump down our throats."

If Claude's poetic voice had not been stilled he would have expressed his appreciation for the manner in which Edward Perry read "If We Must Die" and the way a group of Frendship Housers rushed up to the casket as soon as Eddie finished and began a Rosary. I was consoled when I knelt at the bier and the beads I was telling Our Lady caught in the satin lining of Claude's casket. On the way to the cemetery I looked down and saw that the tiny pearl crucifix on my rosary was gone. Claude, who hated the word gratitude, had accepted a last gift from one whom he had befriended. It was comforting to know that the angry, bitter McKay of past years was at peace when God called him home to that part of Heaven where weary, battle-scarred writers go.

The incidents at Knoxville and Birmingham were still fresh in my memory when a friend walked in my living room waving a New York evening paper.

"They've bombed two Negro homes in Birmingham!" he said. "It happened on Enon Ridge."

For months I had known that threats had been received by Negroes in Birmingham who had purchased homes in a sparsely settled area adjoining a white neighborhood, because the whites had contended that the vacant area was part of a restricted zone.

From the newspaper report I knew that the bombed homes were less than a mile from our house. The long distance circuits were busy when I tried to put through a telephone call. Friends who knew what this meant to me phoned or came to my apartment and debated the subject pro and con while I waited. As they talked, I wondered if this bombing would touch off the "race riot" which was always threatening to break out in Birmingham.

It was past midnight when my call was completed and I learned that my family was safe. Mama was worried about Bobby, who had worked with me at the Anniston USO. Bobby and his wife and three pretty little girls had just moved into their new home in the disputed area. When Mama said, "I can't stand it any longer. Now that Mama Ida has gone, I'm ready to leave," I knew that years of living in fear of a hanging sword had taken their toll. That night I thought a lot about Bobby and his brother Joe and remembered how they looked that first day years and years before when I saw them serving at the altar at the Church of the Immaculate Conception—the day I heard my first Mass in Birmingham.

Another home, then another, and still others were bombed on "Dynamite Hill." More than a dozen Negro families had suffered this indignity at the "hands of parties unknown" before I came to understand that this was all a prelude to change.

chapter 16

LEGACY FOR TOMORROW

That this time of change was making inroads upon my personal life did not become clear until the day in 1949 when my sister came home from work and announced her intention to fly to Manila and marry a young Negro who had started a business in the Philippines after being discharged from the U.S. Army. Then she called at the midtown offices of one of the airline companies and picked up tickets for a trip around the world, which was a wedding gift. This, I decided, was the *new Negro.*

Mama came on from Alabama and sewed around the clock to prepare a trousseau for her last daughter. There was an announcement party and two weeks from the day my sister made her dramatic decision she boarded a plane.

Thus started a steady stream of letters, pictures, and trinkets from faraway places. Not only were we proud of our broadening horizons, but we were also pleased over the addition of another male member to the immediate family group.

Before the newlyweds returned eight months later, a news item of national interest had given us added cause to be proud. The major syndicates carried the story and pictures of an elderly Negro who was the first of his race to gain admittance to the University of Oklahoma. From the picture legends we learned that he had been forced to sit behind a partition in order to abide by the state laws which forbade Negroes and whites to sit in the same classroom. The man was G. W. McLaurin, father of my new brother-in-law, Dunbar S. McLaurin.

Months later, "Professor McLaurin," as he is called in Mississippi, Arkansas, and Oklahoma, came to New York and we were proud to hear him tell his own story. Elizabeth sat on his knee as he described his fight to gain admittance to the graduate school of the University of Oklahoma and the attendant humiliations.

"I'm an old man," McLaurin concluded in the same even tones he had used throughout the recital. "I didn't have to go through all that for myself. It's for these children." He placed his hand on Elizabeth's head. "It's for them that I did it. We have to open the doors—so they can walk through."

In the latter part of 1951 I was appointed director of community relations for the St. Charles School and Community Center Fund, which was conducting a campaign to erect a parochial school and community center in overcrowded Harlem under the leadership of Monsignor Cornelius J. Drew. Catholic, Protestant, and Jewish leaders, Negroes and whites, combined their efforts to build a new St. Charles, a better Harlem, and a stronger America. There were many times when I closed my eyes and thought back to the predictions of ignominious downfall which my townsmen had made when they learned of my conversion to "that new religion." As skills in public relations developed, I was grateful for the opportunity to work toward the fulfillment of my old dream of a community center.

Many spiritual benefits resulted from my association with St. Charles. It was a privilege to work under the same roof with the Blessed Sacrament and to be able to share my sorrows and joys with Him. The St. Charles school is conducted by the Sisters of the Blessed Sacrament and it was thrilling, day by day, to see these nuns in familiar habits, to know that I was "their child" and that they were pleased with the application of my talents which might never have developed if they had not guided me well during the crucial years of my adolescence. It was good to see Reverend Mother Mary Anselm, now Superior General of the order, when she made a visit to the New York houses and to talk with her about the days at Rock Castle. It was almost like reading an old story to listen to Mother Mary Callista, the tall willowy Sister who used to put the lights out on me at night when I wanted to read my Bible during my first days in the school and hear her repeat for my benefit the things I had said so many many years before. We all knew that my old teacher, Sister Timothy, now principal at St. Francis de Sales, was happy because of this brief sanctuary which St. Charles granted me.

The first week of May, 1952, was proclaimed "St. Charles Week" by the Mayor of the City of New York. More than a hundred women, Negro and white, formed a volunteer corps which conducted a public solicitation for funds. Throughout the city these women could be seen with colorful coin boxes, asking the men and women in the streets to contribute to a Catholic school and community center for the Negro children of Harlem. An activity was scheduled for each day and the observance reached its peak with a Carnegie Hall concert of all-Gershwin music at which Todd Duncan, June McMechin, and Hazel Scott donated their services. His Excellency, Bishop Stephen J. Donahue, in the name of His Eminence Francis Cardinal Spellman, conferred the rank of apostolic prothonotary upon Monsignor Drew.

One of the activities connected with this St. Charles Week observance was a parade and public rally, held in front of Blumstein's department store on 125th Street. Schoolchildren from the parishes of Harlem carried flags and banners. The scouts, both boys and girls, were in their uniforms, and as they gathered in 141st Street I thought about the parades of my childhood. Monsignor Drew, who wanted to march with the children, was persuaded to sit in the open car, leading the parade, with the Honorary Mayor of Harlem, Willie Bryant, and Mrs. Roy Wilkins, chairman of the St. Charles Women's Auxiliary. Riding in one of the cars which followed, I was overwhelmed by the cheers and applause greeting the children and the priests who marched with them as they passed through our predominantly Protestant community. One highly vocal bystander summed up the attitude of the crowd when he yelled to Monsignor Drew:

"Stick with it, Reverend. We know what you're trying to do and we're with you one hundred per cent!"

"We *know* what you're trying to do. . . ." There lay the difference. My loved ones had not *known*.

Still another lesson in patience and understanding was to come to me through St. Charles.

In the fall of 1952 I went on a Book Week Lecture Tour which included stops at Raleigh and Durham in North Carolina, Atlanta, Montgomery, and Birmingham. At Montgomery I talked with a group of children attending the elementary school connected with Alabama State. The campus had grown into a little city with modern brick buildings covering the acres that surrounded the grounds where old State Normal had stood. Ollie Brown took me through the new library building over which she presides, and together we visited the president, Harper Councill Trenholm, who has dedicated his life to building this school. When he smiled I saw glimpses of the young professor I had known so many years ago and recalled my friends who were always eager to accompany me on my visits to Cousin Ellen's house so they might see him. Whatever role Alabama State Teachers College plays in the broader fields of education—and it is eminent—nothing will alter the fact that this school is a monument to the labor and determination of Harper Councill Trenholm.

At City of St. Jude I was not to have the pleasure of talking with my old friend Father Purcell; he had passed away while I was planning the trip and looking forward to seeing him. But I saw the realization of his dream in the new hospital and educational institution which includes a high school. I stood on the steps of the "teaching church" and saw buses coming and going with Negro boys and girls from rural areas who would have had to travel the distance to Montgomery daily if Father Purcell had not dared to dream. Walking through the corridors of the hospital, I was proud to recall the day when the priest had confided to me his hopes for such an institution.

At Birmingham my lecture, given in connection with a book

exhibit, was sponsored by a group of civic-minded women, headed by the sister of Emory Jackson, who is considered one of the South's most courageous editors. Ironically this group, known as The Ladies Limited, was not one of the clubs with which I had been affiliated when I lived in Birmingham. To me, the honor implied was all the greater.

The Ladies Limited made a real "homecoming" out of the trip with enough speeches, visits to schools and libraries, sight-seeing tours, and banquets to fill a month, all crowded into the four days I was in Birmingham. Old friends and associates gathered and I sat at the head of one of the banquet tables and listened to the older guests speak with love of their friend "Bob Tarry," and others repeat incidents to show "what a wonderful woman Eula Tarry is."

On "Dynamite Hill," where vengeful white citizens were said to have sworn that Negroes would never live, I saw flowers grow-ing in the yards once pockmarked by bombs and other death-dealing missiles. Neither fire nor destruction had stopped Negro citizens from buying and building homes in the disputed area. When I listened to a story of the sleepless nights and fearful days from two of my friends who live there I wondered if I could have matched their bravery. As in some other Southern areas, Negroes in Birmingham still live behind a tin curtain, though it is full of tiny holes and will fall apart within a few years. Because the tin curtain has not yet fallen, the friends who told me the story of Dynamite Hill will be John and Jim.

John started building his home during the summer of 1947. While the house was still under construction he received numer-ous warnings. When a Negro woman delivered one of the in-timidating messages from the white people for whom she worked, John suggested that whoever sent it should deliver the message in person. His suggestion was not accepted. When the house was completed, John, his wife and two sons moved in. The fol-lowing December Jim moved into the house he had built, a block from John's.

There was much angry talk, but no written threats were received between December and March. John and Jim felt that it was the lull before the storm. Near the end of March the tension was so great John and Jim went to their Negro neighbors and suggested that they band together for the purpose of asking protection from the city authorities. They pointed to repeated instances when fires of unknown origin had damaged homes under construction and there was hardly a day, they said, when angry-looking whites did not walk through the neighborhood, acting suspiciously. A majority of the Negroes had become complacent during the lull; they felt no action was necessary, since "nothing would happen."

One night, after the two men had tried in vain to get their neighbors to appeal for help, one of the homes they had visited earlier that day was dynamited.

"My wife and I ran to the living room when we heard the explosion," Jim recalled. "We were looking out the window when the second house went up and had reached the front porch by the time they threw the third charge. We saw the dynamiters' cars race away in the dust. It was awful to see the debris as it shot up into the air.

"John joined me in a few moments" he said, "and I gave Mary a gun before we went to see how much damage had been done. Strange to say, when we got to the scene there were police cars, a *Birmingham News* truck, and a city transit bus, some blocks away from an established route, already there.

"You read about how they kept bombing—and how Reverend DeYampert and Reverend Henderson stayed in their homes. Well, when the culprits came to the Henderson and DeYampert homes the second time, there was a 'reception committee' on hand to greet them. Because of this 'hot reception' the first charge of dynamite intended for the DeYampert house fell short of its mark. The second charge was thrown from a car and landed in the gutter at the corner. The car and its occupants were riddled.

"The results of this particular incident were hushed up and to most people it remains a mystery. Rumor has accounted for one

death, however, and two or more serious injuries. One of the injured, it is said, met death by suicide."

Jim bit his lips as the memory angered him. "Many nights,"
he went on, "I sat on the porch with a rifle across my knees and
a pistol on the banister so Mary could sleep until two or three
o'clock in the morning. When I felt sleepy I would think about
the children and what had happened to the other homes. Then
I would find myself wide awake. Mary would relieve me when
she woke up and sit in the living room so I could sleep until
daylight. I told her to take the children and go home to her
mother, but she insisted that this was our home for the rest of
our lives—whether they were long or short—and her place was
beside me. And she was right because, awful though it was, I am
sure Mary and I are closer because we fought it out together.
We learned, too, that you have to fight for what you want."

"But look at what happened to me," John broke in, his face
twisted in an ironical smile. "My wife didn't stay. She said all
this danger made me so mean she couldn't stand it. She took
one of the boys and left me with the other. I guess she was right,
too. But if I was mean, it was because I was half-crazy with fear
most of the time."

I never told John or Jim that the friend who sat with me as
they talked had told me that she met John stumbling down the
hill the night the Negro residents arranged a "reception committee" for the dynamiters and that he was covered with blood
and dust.

The "hot reception" did not end the terror of Dynamite Hill
and two days before Christmas in 1951, another Negro home was
bombed. There, too, the damage was repaired and the family
moved in. I thought of this bombing when I made a radio broadcast from this particular home during the Book Week tour. The
Hendersons and DeYamperts, who bore the brunt of seige,
moved, and the derelict houses stood empty until 1954 when a
Dr. John Nixon had them demolished and built a beautiful
modern home of California redwood and old brick on the historic site. A small fire was started while the Nixon home was

under construction, but it was attributed to "labor troubles" and
the family moved in without further incident.

I will long remember the day my daughter Elizabeth came in
from the playground and shocked Mama and me with the declaration: "I don't want to be brown. I want to be your color!"
We learned, by questioning her and a playmate, that several
of the other children had asked Elizabeth how she happened to
be brown when her mother and grandmother looked white. A
few weeks before, Elizabeth had come home from the Catholic
nursery school she attended and told me about a new teacher
named Sister Michael. Without thinking, I had asked, "Is she
colored or white?" The child replied, "No, Mother, she's green."
At that time I had told myself that skin differences made little
impression on her young mind.

Face to face with the problem, we gave her all the scientific
explanations for skin coloring or a lack of it. We pointed out
people of various races who were beautiful and others who were
not. We told her stories of Negro achievement and after a period
of time I complimented myself on the job which had been done.

Years passed and we gave little thought to this awareness of
color differences in Elizabeth. When the blow came it was like
turning a sharp corner and bumping into someone you had not
expected to meet.

One night I was washing my hands in the bathroom sink as
my daughter stood in the doorway watching.

"You know what I wish?" Elizabeth began.

"No," I laughed, "what is it now? And how much will it
cost me?"

"I wish," she began slowly and deliberately, "I wish I was
your color."

"Why?" I managed to ask.

"So I could go to Florida," she blurted.

"What on earth are you talking about?"

"I want to go to Florida and stay in a hotel," she said.

"Please tell me what being my color has to do with you going to
Florida and staying in a hotel?" I heard myself ask before I

thought it through. "And get it straight," I continued heedlessly, "regardless of my color—or lack of it—I *am* a Negro." "But *they* don't always know it," she shot back. "Don't try to kid me, Mother. You know the hotels in Florida don't accept Negroes."

"You don't know what you're talking about," I began. "Actually, the situation is . . ."

Elizabeth interrupted to remind me of an incident which had been publicized in the Negro press the previous winter.

"But there *are* hotels in Florida that accept Negroes as guests," I persisted. "The Lord Calvert in Miami was built for us."

"The best ones don't take them," she was equally persistent. "And *I* want to stay in the best hotels when I go to Florida."

I knew that Florida was only a symbol to Elizabeth, but the defiance in her manner and the hard lines in her childish face frightened me. The night in Knoxville when she was only eighteen months old came back like an old motion picture. I could see the red-faced clerk with the crewcut looking down at the papers in his hand when he said, "We don't have any hotel accommodations for Negroes in Knoxville."

The picture continued to unfold and I made the flight to Birmingham all over again. I heard the driver at the airport say once more, "Is that a *nigger* baby . . . ?"

That, I reminded myself, had happened in 1946 before aviation and military operations shrank the globe and gave men from one side of the world the opportunity of looking into the windows of homes on the other; before Americans of all races and creeds bled together on the frozen hillsides of Korea; before men realized that the atom which destroys cities also offers a key to an era of enlightened living. My child was standing on the threshold of this cataclysmic awakening with unlimited opportunities spread out before her—if only her vision could be freed from superficial obstacles.

"Listen well," the words tumbled out as I grabbed Elizabeth by both shoulders, "and remember this. If you have enough education and ability, by the time you are grown you can stay anywhere you can afford to pay the bill!"

That night Elizabeth fell asleep hugging her pillow, unaware that I would sit for hours thinking of the implications of what she had said. I was curious about the values she was establishing which made the "best hotel" in Florida seem so important to her.

Later that evening a friend came in and I told him about my daughter's wish. As we talked I happened to glance out of our living room window overlooking the Harlem River. A bright new moon was silvering the rippling waters. I remembered the night when Elizabeth was a baby and I had made a wish for her on the new moon.

"I believe what I told her!" I startled my friend. "I wasn't trying to fool her. I do believe that by the time she is grown she can go anywhere her position in life warrants. By then, Negroes in America will be accepted on their merit and she can rise or fall according to her own efforts."

Long into the night we argued about this new hope, this up-beat of the democratic spirit. My friend charged me with being too optimistic. I pointed to complete integration within the Armed Forces and among civilian personnel on Army posts. I told him about Dynamite Hill in Birmingham and the First Congregational Church, Papa's church, with its shining cross which now stands guard over the beautiful homes in which our people live in the once disputed area. We discussed a letter from a militant Negro editor who had written me that over four hundred Negroes were enrolled at the University of Oklahoma that summer (1953), counting students attending summer sessions and those registered in professional schools. I pointed to the five cases still to be argued before the Supreme Court of the United States which would determine whether or not segregation in public schools was a violation of the Constitution.

For the first time I was secure in the knowledge that my brown child had a chance to live a fruitful, useful, and normal life in the country of my various and varied ancestors.

On May 17, 1954, the Supreme Court ruled unanimously that racial segregation in public schools *is* a violation of the Constitution and must end. Though the ruling was on five specific cases, this decision will ultimately wipe out segregation in seventeen states where it is mandatory and in four where it was permitted. It also spelled the end of segregated schools in the District of Columbia.

When Chief Justice Warren read the twelve-page document hailed by many Negroes as the "Second Emancipation Proclamation" he said: "...We cannot turn the clock back...." The NAACP and men like G. W. McLaurin had, in fact, opened doors for all of the little brown boys and girls of America. Though the final word as to how the decision was to be implemented had yet to be given, this was the beginning.

As relatives and friends came to our apartment to share this day of jubilation, over and over Elizabeth heard phrases like: "Thurgood Marshall and the NAACP have finally won, thank God!" and "It's a new day for the Negro." She became curious.

We told her that the Supreme Court ruling was a reminder to the people of the United States that all men are created equal and entitled to equal educational advantages. Segregation in public schools, we told her, would be against the law.

Segregation is a hard word for a nine-year-old to understand. We went to the dictionary and the definition, "to separate from the main body and collect in one place," helped her to understand the Southern custom of separating Negroes from whites in schools, eating places, theaters, parks, on trains or buses, then collecting them in another place.

"But things will be different now," I assured her. "We may even be able to live in Alabama one day."

Our jubilation lasted until news of adverse reaction in the South seeped through. The white South was girding for a battle, we heard, and some Negroes had misgivings. Not only was the reporter in me aroused, but my thoughts were occupied by the old dream of going home again to find a democratic way of life taking shape. Almost automatically, I began making plans for a trip that would carry me into the South. Although my native Alabama is one of the recognized tension areas, I wanted to know how people in Virginia, Tennessee, North and South Carolina, and Georgia were thinking and acting. Trains would not carry me close enough to the people, I reasoned aloud, and an understanding friend donated the use of an automobile. Another friend offered to drive. By the time we had routed the trip we had another passenger.

"You said things were going to be different in the South," my daughter reminded me. "Why can't I go with you?"

Many times I had wondered how I could explain the seeming inconsistency of my love for Alabama's rich red earth to my Northern-born child, who had learned that in my birth state people like us were separated from the whole and collected in another place. How would she understand my disagreements with race-relations "experts" who often base their conclusions on life in areas above the Mason-Dixon Line, if she never had the firsthand experience of being a Negro in the South? I had told her things would be different; now I had to make good my words. It was a big chance to take, but I gambled and packed her bag in the trunk of the car.

Against the advice of friends who were fearful of the Fourth of July traffic and everything connected with the South, we scheduled this trip so it would begin on the first of this holiday month. It was late evening as we reached the New Jersey Turnpike, which would soon lead us into a short strip of Delaware, then a long Maryland road into Baltimore. The friend who was driving had brought along a nine-year-old nephew to be company for my daughter. The temperature was soaring, there was a thunderstorm, and we laughed to be leaving New York in a blaze of glory when a rainbow appeared ahead of us in the sky.

"It's a good sign," one of the children said, and we all decided we were going to have a wonderful trip.

In Baltimore we stayed with friends who extended genuine hospitality. Our city-bred children, having known only apartments and suburban cottages, were awed by the spaciousness of large homes. After a night's rest we left Baltimore, and each mile of the countryside provided new thrills for the youngsters. Alternate roads in an unfamiliar area often present a problem to the tourist and for a few miles between Maryland and Virginia we thought we were lost. My friend slowed down when we saw a group of men in the distance who appeared to be working on the road.

"Could you tell us if we are on Route 11?" I had already called out when I realized that the Negro workmen were part of a convict gang and the white man to whom I had addressed my question was a guard with a gun on his shoulder.

The man with the gun scowled as he glared at each of us in turn, then said gruffly, "Keep straight," as if it pained him to spare two words.

The convicts dared not look up from their work, but we detected a nodding of heads so that we might have added assurance that we were on the right road.

"Now you know we are in the South," my friend whispered. "Study the map carefully. We will try not to ask questions."

"Mother!" Elizabeth said, "that man was eyeballing us because he thought you were white and he wondered what we were doing in the car with you."

Being accustomed to variegated skin tones, we had forgotten that three brown faces in a car with one pale face on the front seat would attract attention.

"You see," my friend whispered after the children's attention had been diverted, "the man wasn't hostile. He was just confused. Maybe we had better stop and let you buy some brown powder."

The children named the car "Old Toughie" and conferred upon it the female gender. She was a thirsty gal with an unusual appetite for gas and we pulled in to the Old Stone Shop just outside Strausberg, Virginia, to care for her needs. The motor was still running when a young white attendant ran out with a broad smile on his face.

"What can I do for you, ma'am?" he asked my friend at the wheel of the car. "If it's gas you want, maybe you'd like to get a bite while I'm filling her up. There are rest rooms, too, if you care to use them."

Moments later when we drove away he called out: "Thank you, ma'am. Come back again."

"I never heard a Southern white man say ma'm to Negroes

before," I told my friend when we reached the highway. "This must be the new South."

"*That* was the young South," she said. "I was down here six months ago. You had better reserve your conclusions."

For miles, signs warned us that we were approaching one of the wonders of the world. The children's curiosity had grown with each sign by the time we stopped at the Natural Bridge Park to get refreshment which might also counteract the one hundred degree heat. We walked around the concession stand and looked at souvenirs of Natural Bridge after the children had eaten their ice cream. My friend remained in the car and when we rejoined her, the youngsters put on a one-act skit to show how the natives had "eyeballed" and stared at us with open mouths. To them it was a joke and I had to pretend to share their mirth.

The spectacle of the mountains of Virginia behind us and the proud mountains of Tennessee looming ahead drew exclamations of wonder. The old feeling of getting closer and closer to the Creator of the beauty which surrounded us grew stronger as Old Toughie climbed higher and higher.

"Look at that sign!" one of the children yelled when we reached the top of Pulaski Mountain.

"This area reserved for colored," it read. "White area," was printed on a second sign.

The magic of the mountains faded, the sun disappeared and we drove through the twilight in silence. Neon signs blazed the names of the motels along the way and when the children made a game of choosing the prettiest ones for their own we knew they were tired and wanted to stop and rest. We also knew the motels along the way were for whites only.

"Wait until we get to the next town," my friend told them. "You will stay in a house that is much more beautiful than any of these motels."

The children were extremely tired and irritable by the time we drove into Bristol, Tennessee. We were glad that our hostess was not at home because, from the time we opened the door with a key the next-door neighbor gave us, the youngsters were wide-eyed and vocal. They walked around huge rooms, gazing up at the high ceilings. They felt the silky finish of oriental rugs and stared at crystal chandeliers.

"Who's 'eyeballing' now?" I teased.

"This sure is a pretty house," the boy said.

"It's better than those motels we saw," my daughter admitted grudgingly.

Our hostess returned from a church meeting and served a delicious supper. After a bath, my daughter came to the upstairs guest room we were to share. I watched her try out the chaise longue and finger the crisp organdy curtains at the wide windows. Our lone male companion had a room to himself and both of the youngsters went to bed without urging. Satisfied that they were asleep, I joined friends downstairs and we sat around and talked over tall, cooling drinks.

Feeling my way, I casually mentioned the Supreme Court decision and was confounded by the reaction. There was no jubilant enthusiasm; just a quiet acceptance of an accomplished fact. We talked about nearby Nashville, a college town, where one friend's husband is on the faculty of a Negro school.

"The white papers carried angry editorials the first few days after the decision was handed down," I was told. "Then the excitement died down. Now we don't hear much about it."

"What are Negroes saying?" I asked.

There was a pause. Glances were exchanged and shoulders shrugged.

"Well, it's here," someone finally said. "We will have to see how it works before we get excited."

They pointed to the fact that a white girl was graduated from Fisk University in Nashville last year (1954), and that Negroes were enrolled in summer sessions at Peabody and Vanderbilt.

As we drove down State Street the next morning the children were intrigued by the fact that one side of the street was in Tennessee and the other in Virginia. When we reached Knoxville, the South was in the clutches of a pre-Fourth of July heat wave which was later to shatter a fifty-seven-year record. After lunch at the home of a friend, we took to the road again and I swapped seats with the driver. When the good roads ran out and we began meeting interstate trucks on two-lane roads that curved around the sides of tall mountains, I conceded the fact that I made a better navigator than driver.

"I could have told you it would be like this," my friend laughed as she slipped under the wheel once more. "Folk down here are too busy upholding segregation to worry about good roads."

Gadsden, Alabama, was our destination for the day and we crept through a narrow strip of Tennessee and Georgia with the children asking every time we reached a town, "Are we there yet?" From Fort Payne, Alabama, the roads became even more narrow and it was almost midnight when we drove into Gadsden and bedded two weary youngsters.

Our Gadsden hostess was a young woman who had been my classmate in high school. A widow of comfortable means, her home was spacious and furnished with a quiet elegance.

"Mother," my daughter whispered before she went to sleep, "are all the people in the South rich?"

News of arrivals spreads fast in small communities and despite the lateness of the hour old friends gathered. This time I did not have to ask what was happening. I had only to listen to the conversation to hear that Negro homes had been raided by local officers under the guise of keeping Etowah County "bone dry." This and other petty persecutions were alleged to have followed the May 17 decision.

A journalist friend pin-pointed the element I found so baffling.

"You may be fooled by the surface activity," he said, "but there is a subtle, underlying *fear* gripping Negro and white communities in areas affected by the Supreme Court ruling. It's almost a joke, because the whites are afraid Negro children will rush to their schools in droves. Actually, about the only way anybody could get these Negro children in Gadsden to go to a white elementary school would be to take them by the hand and lead them into the building. And I doubt that many parents will dare to lead them."

A week later I was to have an experience which made me more

tolerant of the Negro parent who hesitates to expose a young child to the barriers erected by Southern whites intent upon upholding white supremacy.

On the hottest Fourth of July I can remember, our hostess's lawn was covered with tea guests, some of whom I had known in Birmingham and others as a USO worker at the Anniston Club. Many of the friends I asked for were away in summer school, but there was pleasant talk all around. My ears were cocked and I sifted all conversation, most of which was ordinary and folksy. The guests gradually left until only a handful of us remained by the time the street lamps were lighted.

In the group was my friend the journalist, a Negro officer from a nearby Army installation, and a visitor from a midwestern metropolis who had grown up in Gadsden.

"I understand that Negroes have been completely integrated at Fort McClellan," somebody said.

"Over a year ago," the officer replied.

"What about transportation for the military after they leave the Army reservation and the employment of Negro civilian personnel?" I asked.

Once a soldier leaves the post, my friend admitted, local law and custom obtains. Negro civilian personnel is employed, but he could not point to one professional position held by a Negro that was comparable to the jobs mutual friends had held at McClellan during World War II, when official integration was still a part of the future.

"Perhaps," the journalist said, "that will help you to understand why many Southern Negroes are fearful. They are not sure of their jobs in the integrated community."

When we separated that night, I was more impressed with the importance of the remaining months of 1954 than at any time since May 17.

The Fourth of July, 1954, was officially celebrated on the fifth and the children of the neighborhood held their own barbecue party. A picnic on the banks of the Coosa River was planned for the adults. A friend from Birmingham had telephoned to say he was en route and the procession of cars waited until he joined us before they drove away. We were less than an hour behind schedule, but when we reached the selected site it had been taken by whites. Remembering another good spot, the driver of the lead car proceeded a few feet up the riverbank before he discovered that the second site was also occupied by white picnickers. After some debate we parked the cars in a clearing between the two groups and made ourselves as comfortable as possible. Remembering similar occasions when whites left a location as soon as Negroes arrived on the scene or asked the Negroes to leave, I was impressed by the fact that everybody stayed put and so expressed myself.

As the day wore on the two groups of whites seemed to develop a need to communicate with each other. They walked back and forth, each trip causing them to walk through our spot. Having become accustomed to Southern "eyeballing" I attached no significance to these repeated trips.

My Birmingham friend led me over a footpath which spanned a dam and I sat on a slope of huge rocks set in cement and dipped my feet in the clear cool water which seeped through. I lay back on the rocks and tried to breathe in enough fresh air to last a long time. My friend referred to the construction of the slope on which I lay as "bull work" and told me how Negroes of an earlier generation had dammed rivers, built roads, and tapped the natural resources of our state, usually receiving no more than subsistence wages for their labor.

I was aware of the gaze of the white people who were fishing from the banks of the river but didn't give it much thought. When we rejoined our friends it was time for dinner and the women were preparing Southern barbecue. After we had eaten, one of the men got out his fishing tackle and found a spot near the whites. He had been angling only a short time when he came back laughing and I saw a group gather around him. They, too, were amused by whatever it was he told them, but became quiet when I approached.

"What's so funny?" I asked.

"The people over there." My traveling companion from New

York pointed. "They were excited because they thought you were white."

"The man who spoke to me," the fisherman related, "comes in the shop where I work. I was sitting there fishing when he came over and said, 'Ain't that a white woman you all got down there?' "

"I told him 'Not quite' and kept on fishing. He stood there a minute then said, 'Well, she sure looks like it.' 'Almost,' I laughed, 'but not quite.' He got the hint and left me alone."

Our friend's sense of humor had kept the Fourth of July celebration safe and sane for us and for our white neighbors.

The next day I drove over to Anniston with my daughter. The home in which we stopped was less than two months old and we christened the guest room. That night a friend drove me out to Fort McClellan so that I might get a first peep at the wonder of integration on an army post in the South. A National Guard encampment was under way, and the Officers' Club, which was our first stop, was crowded. For a few moments after we walked in, the "eyeballing" made me wonder if someone had made a mistake about integration. We were the only Negroes in the club and my friend admitted that he was currently the only Negro officer stationed at McClellan. A white major from New Jersey joined us, and as the men talked I thought of all the times I had passed this club with Negro friends and we had wondered how it looked inside and made jokes about going in and getting thrown out.

During the 1943-44 period when I had worked with military personnel from this reservation, the two or three Negro officers stationed here did not have access to the Officers' Club and were forced to use their living quarters for recreation. The Negro noncoms of World War II were given club rooms in an area near a row of latrines. I asked about recreational facilities for enlisted men and was promised a tour of the post for the next day.

Fort McClellan is now a chemical warfare center and the permanent home of the WAC. It was good to see the post by daylight and when we stopped at South Gate to get a pass from a courteous Negro MP, who was one of a mixed unit, I remembered the time I had been insulted at this gate by a white guard.

There was construction all around us but one small group of soldiers attracted my attention. I could not tell whether they were working on a problem or improving the road, but they were digging away and there was only one Negro in the group. During World War II I had never seen white soldiers with shovels and picks on any of the army reservations where I had worked.

An alert young Negro sergeant showed us around the Fort. The building which had housed the Colored Service Club during World War II was now Club Chevron and soldiers of both races were using the facilities. Wherever we went we saw mixed groups, until we stopped at the Officers' Club I had visited the night before. My daughter was attracted by the swimming pool where wives and children of the officers were seeking relief from the heat wave. There were no brown faces there, however.

When we drove along "Brass Row," where ranking officers and their families live, I saw a group of whites working on a lawn.

"I never saw that before," I commented.

"Yes," one of the Negroes in the car answered, "the white folk have shovels, too, now."

We had refreshments in the cafeteria of the PX, where Negroes and whites mingled without any outward signs of self-consciousness.

Later that afternoon we went shopping in the business district of Anniston. The intense heat had created extreme thirst in all of us, but there was no place, no drugstore, no cafeteria where we could get a cooling drink. So far, the townspeople of Anniston show no outward sign of having been influenced by integration at nearby Fort McClellan.

We left the business district and stopped at the site of the old NCCS-USO where I had served as director of women's activities. The building now houses the Carver Community Center and one of my former junior hostesses was in charge of the library. Children were gathering for a story-hour, while small groups walked around the building to a swimming pool at the rear. I heard a familiar sound and discovered it was my daughter putting a coin in the "coke" machine. Only a few of the soldiers come in town, I was told. Most of them prefer to stay on the integrated post. A new lounge was being prepared for the WAC's who were expected to arrive in a few days.

That evening the ladies who had made up the Senior Hostess Committee of the USO called on me. The group had remained intact during the ten years since I had worked with them. They had, I learned, played an important part in organizing the Carver Community Center. We reminisced over old pictures taken at the USO and they brought me up to date on local happenings. After the war was over, many of the soldiers I had served returned and married local girls. It seemed that everybody I asked about who was not present was away in school working toward a degree, building a new house, or organizing a new business.

The next day I talked with a young soldier who had come down from Atlanta with an Army show. Before entering the service he had been an accompanist to an outstanding Negro singer. A native of Brooklyn, he was thrilled to meet someone from "the Big Apple." The young man only had a few months left in the Army and said he hoped to return to Atlanta and go into the real estate business.

"It's going to be real fine down here," he said, "after everything gets straightened out. I know several other fellows who are thinking about coming back after they get out of the Army. Atlanta is the greatest!"

A Negro exodus in reverse was a new idea to me.

The following weekend we were in Tuskegee, where life in the little town revolves around the school Booker T. Washington founded for his people and the immense veterans' hospital. One of my hosts summed up the attitude of the South to the changes which are inevitable when he said: "The patient is still in a state of shock; almost anything can happen."

There was much talk about "Big Jim" Folsom, governor-elect, who was to take office January 17, 1955.

"Things are going to be different when 'Big Jim' gets in," I heard over and over. "He's for all the people—including *us*," they insisted. Folsom's campaign slogan: "Yo'all come" became a pleasant tag for each leave-taking.

A nurse from the hospital reminded me that it was not a Negro institution but a veterans' hospital and that any eligible veteran in need of medical attention would be admitted. When I asked if whites were accepted she reminded me that the area served is predominantly Negroid population and only a few whites have ever applied, though they were accepted when eligible. The medical and surgical staff is all-Negro, but white doctors and surgeons come in on a visiting-consultant basis. Negro nurses, she said, are being integrated in Veterans' Administration hospitals throughout the South.

My daughter returned breathless from a trip to the business district of Tuskegee. She saw two drinking fountains; one marked "white" and the other "colored." She had taken the signs literally and was disappointed to learn that the same transparent water flowed from both.

We returned to Gadsden on our way to Birmingham, but the heat wave was so severe we could not find anybody with enough energy left to drive with us. Even after we decided to take a bus, it was almost impossible to get a colored taxi to carry us to the station. Less than three minutes before the scheduled time of departure we ran into the colored waiting room and seeing the ticket window unattended asked the people sitting around where we could be served. Instead of answering, they stared with open mouths and gave no indication of having heard. From the window I could see my daughter looking at me anxiously as other passengers boarded the big bus. Through the glass partition that separated the two waiting rooms I could see a clerk selling tickets to white passengers. There was no other way to get transportation and I transferred to the line in the white waiting room.

The Negro taxi driver approached me as soon as I walked out with the tickets. "Miss," he said, "you got away with that, but we had a whole lot of trouble down here one time because a woman who looked like you went in the white waiting room."

The bus was ready to pull out and there was no time for explanations. The driver accepted my tickets, motioned me forward, then scowled when I pushed my daughter in front of me and told her to take a seat near the rear of the bus.

"You'll have to get up," I whispered to the child when she stopped one seat too soon and sat beside a white man. The Negroes on the long back seat were looking straight ahead as if they saw nothing.

"Why can't I sit here?" Elizabeth asked. "You told me to go to the rear."

It was easier to help my daughter move than supply the reason she had to move. A Negro soldier offered his seat over the wheels and we managed to squeeze into the space.

"The heat has me perspiring," I told Elizabeth as the bus pulled out and I pretended to wipe my forehead so the hand-kerchief could hide the hurt and anger.

A peal of laughter from the front where the white passengers sat in comfort reminded me that we were not enjoying "separate but equal" accommodations. I had to get to Birmingham by a certain hour and this bus was my only means of transportation. This was not a new experience for me, but it had never happened to my child since she had been old enough to understand.

"I don't like buses in Alabama," she interrupted my thoughts.

I tried to make her more comfortable by putting her hatbox on the floor so she could rest her feet. The bus stopped at Atalla and the occupants of the long seat over the wheels shifted position. I knew the child wanted an explanation and I dreaded what she might say. I did not have to wait long.

"Mother," she asked, "did segregation win or lose?"

"It lost," I answered after a moment of deliberation. "But a few years will pass before it is destroyed."

"I don't like the South any more," she continued and I knew that the beautiful homes she had admired and the warm hospi-tality of my friends had faded when human dignity had been denied.

"Now you understand what separating from the whole and collecting in another place means," I said. "All my adult life I have fought the law which says we have to sit back here because we are colored. Yet you are sitting here today and I am helpless. Promise me that you will always remember this and work toward a better understanding between all people so that your children will never be forced to sit on this seat when others are available."

In Birmingham, as in other places throughout the state, I heard talk of petty retaliation which had followed the Supreme Court decision. Permission for Negroes and whites to compete in professional sports had been revoked, they said. Vulcan Park, operated by the city, had been closed to Negroes again, I was told.

These charges were refuted in part by the local editor, Emory O. Jackson, who is the closest approach to an American Negro martyr I have ever known personally.

"As far as the Locke Recall Partition, which was a pro-segregation amendment preventing Negroes and whites from participating in professional sports, is concerned," he said, "I don't feel the timing was responsbile for it being passed as much as the fact that Negroes and well-intentioned whites did not wage a vigorous campaign against it. Nobody spoke out! Also, the wording on the petition was so confusing many people who thought they had voted against it later found they had cast a vote in its favor. The Supreme Court decision was handed down on May 17 and we voted on the partition on June 1, so there had been a slight cooling off period.

"In regard to Vulcan Park," he continued, "I've heard a rumor that it has been closed to us again, but have seen nothing to confirm it."

Jackson, too, expressed the belief that the new governor, Folsom, would be cognizant of the plight of Alabama's Negro citizens and would use his office to try to raise the living standards of all the people, regardless of race.

Many of my friends, I was told, were already in New York working toward degrees at Columbia and New York Universities.

Others were in Montgomery attending Alabama State Teachers College for Negroes. All of the teachers were determined to be qualified for whatever was coming.

The evening before leaving Birmingham I sat on the lawn of the Negro YWCA and talked with an educator engaged in research for a foundation, a supervisor of Negro schools, and Emory Jackson. These men advanced the theory that not only does segregation affect the Negro child, but that the American white child who is educated in an all-white school learns only to live with people like himself. Thrown with children from different cultures, the average southern white child would be a misfit, they said. With so many official connections involved, a sort of gentleman's agreement kept us from discussing the problems which a change of system will present in the Birmingham public schools.

Plans were made to return to New York by a coastal route and to rely upon commercial accommodations for ourselves and the children. It was early morning when I joined my friend and her nephew in Gadsden and by early afternoon we were in Atlanta.

Altanta was behind us and we had stopped at a filling station outside Greenville, South Carolina, when Elizabeth next saw the "colored" and "white" signs. This time they were used to set rest rooms apart. There was a bright light burning over the door marked "white," but we had to take a flashlight from the car to find our way to the other one. When we paid for the gas, however, the station attendant said, "Thank you, ma'am. Come back again." Since we had only used one brand of gas on the trip, we decided that this particular gas company probably distributed a manual instructing its employees to be polite to cash customers regardless of color.

We reached Charlotte late that night while a rain and wind storm was leveling trees on either side of us and flooding the road ahead.

"I will ask about accommodations," my friend suggested. "They'll know I am a Negro and we'll avoid complications."

A white boy ran out to serve us when we stopped at a filling station.

"Can you tell me where I can find a hotel for colored?" my friend asked.

"Yes, ma'am," he said. He pointed. "You drive right down there to Hotel Barringer and I think they'll take you. If you can't get in, try Hotel Charlotte."

As soon as we reached the main thoroughfare and saw the huge neon signs over the respective hotels, we knew the boy had tricked us and we were leading the children into another embarrassing situation. We saw a lone cop walking his beat in the rain.

"Can you tell me where we can find a colored hotel?" I called out to him.

"Nobody ever asked me that before," he said pleasantly, "but I'll find you one." He went to a nearby telephone, then returned with the information.

It was five minutes past twelve when we checked in the "colored" hotel at a cost I am sure would have paid for more comfortable quarters at Hotel Barringer or Hotel Charlotte.

The next morning we headed north after a short stop at Concord, North Carolina, where I had once found Jim Crow in a Catholic Church. We passed field after field of tobacco and the children enjoyed the warehouses in Raleigh and Richmond, Virginia, where they could see huge piles of the cured plant waiting to be rolled into cigarettes. Darkness overtook us and the youngsters made jokes about Baltimore running away from us because we were behind schedule. It was so late when we reached the Maryland city that we decided not to disturb our friends. We would try to find a motel.

A few miles outside Baltimore the children became restless and cross and we pulled into a gas station with an adjoining motel and told the proprietor our plight.

The man thought a long time before he said: "I'm sorry. I don't know of a motel in the state of Maryland that takes colored."

A half hour later we found a motel we had seen two weeks earlier, with a sign on it which said "colored." There was a bar and dance hall less than a hundred feet away from the ramshackle cabins and we went to the hall in search of the manager.

The boisterous crowd reminded me of pictures I have seen of dance halls on the old Barbary coast. I was ready to turn back, but my friend reminded me that we had to find a place for the children to sleep.

The owner of the cabins and the hall was a young white woman. She apologized for the appearance of the rooms and did what she could to make us comfortable. The night was cool in contrast to the heat of the past weeks. I held Elizabeth in my arms when her teeth chattered and she trembled as the noise from the dance hall grew louder and the merrymakers made more merriment in cars parked outside our door. I thought about an order blank I had received a few days before we left. It was for the *Negro Travelers' Green Book* of which the editors said: "This is the guide which keeps you from running into embarrassing situations."

The sun was rising when we hit the New Jersey Turnpike. It was a grand feeling to be able to turn off the road at the nearest Howard Johnson's and be seated for breakfast without asking for a "colored" dining room. The children talked about getting home in time to go to a swimming pool, and we all agreed that Old Toughie had done her name proud. There had not been a sputter to cut down our traveling time.

"St. Christopher has brought us home." My daughter pointed to the medal over the driver's seat, as we started on the last lap of the trip.

We whizzed past a sign which said: "New York 50 mi." Then there was a deafening noise like the shot from a gun. The car began to wobble.

"That," announced my friend as she guided the car toward a shoulder of the road, "is our first blowout."

I was unlocking the trunk to get out a spare when I called my friend's attention to a car which had stopped farther up the highway.

"They are Negroes," she cried, "and they're coming to help us."

"We saw you didn't have a man in the car," one of them said

when they reached us. "So we came back to see what was wrong."

The two men, we learned, were brothers. They worked fast and in a few minutes had changed the tire and accepted our profuse thanks.

"We have to take care of our womenfolk on the road." The brother who acted as spokesman smiled as they walked away toward their own car. "If we don't, who will?"

"Remember that rainbow we saw as we were starting out?" my friend said as when we drove away. "It was just about here that we saw it."

The journey was ended on a Saturday at high noon. Many times since I have heard my daughter telling her playmates about the beautiful homes in which we stopped, the historic scenes we passed, and the new friends she made. Not once have I heard her mention the ride from Gadsden to Birmingham on a Jim-Crow bus or the night we spent outside Baltimore in a cabin "for colored" which might better have housed livestock. Yet she has learned something few Northerners ever come to know. She knows the South has two faces because she has seen them both.

I know that time must still pass, hearts must be changed, and minds freed of fear, greed, and bigotry before the signs "colored" and "white" will be torn down and relegated to the trash cans of the New South and the history books written about the Old South. Southerners are slow to act but the ultimate change must come from within.

The New South will welcome the talents of gifted Negro citizens, and prophets will be received with honor in their own land. As the yoke of ignorance and oppression is cast aside, a new era of prosperity will begin and the South will no longer be a poor relation. Her towns and cities, her parishes and villages will once more become a symbol for "gracious living," but this time "with dignity for all."

Each time another Negro is signed by a major-league ball team I think of Papa, who, in my memory, remains the most ardently energetic baseball fan I have ever known. Next in line for this title is George E. Wood, Jr., eccentric proprietor of

Harlem's "Red Rooster," who has become nationally famous as
a Giant fan. More than a dozen Negro ballplayers are employed
by major-league teams, and there is reason to believe that their
number will increase.

The owners of the Birmingham Barons must have made mental
calculations regarding the cash customers Willie Mays might
have attracted if the "Say, hey," boy had been hired by his hometown team before the Giants signed him.

When Marian Anderson became the first Negro to sign with
the Metropolitan Opera Company, Mama and I also thought of
Papa and recalled the zeal with which he took me to concerts
during my childhood. Sometimes we went to the Baptist church
where the auditorium was filled to capacity. Other times, at the
Congregational Church, Papa and I were two of an audience of
ten or twenty who came to hear some fledgling sing or play the
piano. Always, though, there was a bouquet for me to present
to the lady artist and a word of encouragement and appreciation
for the man. We smiled over the remark that Papa, if he had
lived, would have been among the first patrons to arrive at the
Metropolitan Opera House the night Miss Anderson made her
initial appearance as Ulrica in Verdi's *Masked Ball*. He would
have sent red roses, too.

These early memories dominated a recent reunion with my
friend Alice, who had gone through Slater and into high school
with me. Alice is the director of a community center in one of
the Northwest's largest cities, and we compared present-day living
with that of our childhood.

"Those were good days," she said. "Probably they were good
because we were so protected and so unaware of what we did not
have."

When we talked of the dreams we had or had not seen come
true, she, too, marveled that the pendulum has swung so far
over a period of forty years.

Birmingham remains one of the spotty areas in the nation's
pattern of human relations. Yet I am convinced that both sides
know they will have to give a little and take a little. Years may

pass before Negroes who have fled the tyranny of white sepremacy can go home again—in the fuller sense—but we refuse to relinquish the dream.

In my adopted home, New York City, I have seen changes, too. On 125th Street where a dark face was seldom seen behind a counter or over a desk twenty-five years ago, Negroes now form the greater part of the army of workers who man the stores and offices in Harlem's shopping district. Negroes are also employed in department stores and other businesses throughout the city.

Harlem is no longer the gay, boisterous ghetto my friend Claude McKay wrote about in the 1920's, because Harlem is no longer forced to sing or dance for a living. In the classroom, on the production line, and in the laboratory, the Negro of today is seriously preparing for the status of "first-class citizen." He has at long last learned to save his gaiety for his own entertainment or until such a time as it can be presented professionally on a competitive basis.

Harlem is justly proud that one of her residents, Hulan E. Jack, was chosen to become Borough President of Manhattan, the highest elective office to be held by any American Negro in municipal government. All of the Harlems of America are proud, too, when mention is made of Ralph J. Bunche, Nobel Prize winner who also holds the highest office of any American in the United Nations.

In the field of medicine, Negro surgeons and physicians have overcome the obstacles of limited medical schools and segregated hospital facilities to contribute to the world of science. Harlem has ample cause to point with pride to the fact that her own Peter Marshal Murray, as president of the New York County Medical Society, became the first Negro ever to head a component society of the American Medical Association. Dr. Murray was also the first Negro elected to the AMA's House of Delegates, the policy-making body of that august organization. And our crown prince of the early thirties, Adam Clayton Powell, is today one of America's three Negro congressmen.

As we rejoice in these triumphs, Negro America has not for-

gotten the trials which those three oddly mated standard bearers
—Joe Louis, Marian Anderson, and Jackie Robinson—faced during the years between 1937 and 1947. We know they carried the
destiny of their race on their shoulders while white America and
the world watched and waited.

The eyes of the world have once more been focused on America, watching and waiting for her compliance with the ruling of
her highest court by which segregation in public schools is out-
lawed.

My heart sang a few weeks ago when a letter was received from
a young friend who is studying in Paris on a Whitney Fellow-
ship:

"... The world still walks up to me daily (in the person of an
African, a Turk, a Korean, or what not) and says; 'Aren't you
relieved to be over here where you're treated like a human being?
Aren't you grateful? Aren't you happy?'
"They are quite disappointed when I say, 'No.'"

In the realm of personal interests there have been many
gratifying gains. A quarter of a century ago, when I criticized
Claude McKay's *Home to Harlem*, there were few published
books in which a Negro protagonist was depicted as a man or
woman with whom the American reading public could identify,
or whom they could love or respect. A few courageous editors and
publishers have changed this. In our present literature, the Negro
protagonist is usually an American with a brown face whose
special problems, achievements, or romances make good reading.

In the juvenile field, when I started my teaching career, there
were almost no books for young readers which showed the Negro
as other than Uncle Remus or Little Black Sambo. Though
Uncle Remus must be reckoned as an outstanding contribution
to the folklore of the world and Sambo is universal, as a steady,
exclusive reading diet such books would have given children a
stereotyped idea of the Negro. Today, there are many beautifully illustrated juvenile books on library shelves which show
Negroes in all walks of life. To have had a small part in adding

to this list has been a privilege. Of such intangibles are the riches of an eventful life.

In Catherine de Hueck's little 138th Street apartment, and at Friendship House on 135th Street we talked of a Catholic Community Center for Harlem. Ten years ago while working for NCCS-USO I dreamed of a community center and a residence club. Last spring, His Eminence, Francis Cardinal Spellman dedicated the Lt. Joseph P. Kennedy, Jr., Community Center, which is located one block from the site where the first Friendship House stood. Before too long there will be another center connected with the projected St. Charles School. My friends, the Handmaids of Mary, are already working toward the realization of a residence for working girls.

It has been high adventure, during this past quarter century when wars, inventions, and daring achievements have wrought revolutionary changes throughout the world, to watch the pendulum swing across the dial of American history. It has been rewarding, if at times difficult, to hold on to the belief that "things will be different someday." Though that day is only dawning, tomorrow will come! Descended from slaves, rebels, and a vanquished people, I have lived to write boldly "American" beside my name; to know that my child is, in fact, free. I salute my ancestors, my parents, and my friends who worked and prayed for this day. I rejoice for those who helped me to hold my head high, then joined our Creator before their faith was justified. As I walk forth to meet the new freedom for which they prayed, I carry in my heart the image and memory of Papa, Mama Ida, my rebel grandfather, Nannie, Father Hyland, and the Trappist monk I had known as Father Vincent Smith. I salute them *in absentia*. This is their victory, too!

One day soon all who are concerned with a legacy for our children will join hands. If hostile forces contrive to separate us we will find ways to reach out to each other, regardless of race, just as my ancestors of another century found ways to "steal away to Jesus." The old North Star, which once led countless Negroes to freedom, still shines in God's Heaven. Then, when we are united, there will be no door in America marked "colored" and no door marked "white." Instead there will be the third door—free from racial designations—through which all Americans, all of God's children, will walk in peace and dignity. So ends my song of hope for tomorrow. *Deo Gratias!*